Assessment of Personal Injury Damages

Assessment of Personal Injury Damages

Second Edition

by

CHRISTOPHER J. BRUCE, Ph.D.

Professor
Department of Economics
University of Calgary

Butterworths
TORONTO   VANCOUVER

Assessment of Personal Injury Damages

© Butterworths Canada Ltd. 1992

The Butterworth Group of Companies

Canada	Butterworths Canada Ltd., 75 Clegg Road, MARKHAM, Ontario, L6G 1A1 and 409 Granville St., Ste. 1455, VANCOUVER, B.C., V6C 1T2
Australia	Butterworths Pty Ltd., SYDNEY, MELBOURNE, BRISBANE, ADELAIDE, PERTH, CANBERRA and HOBART
Ireland	Butterworths (Ireland) Ltd., DUBLIN
New Zealand	Butterworths of New Zealand Ltd., WELLINGTON and AUCKLAND
Puerto Rico	Equity de Puerto Rico, Inc., HATO REY
Singapore	Malayan Law Journal Pte. Ltd., SINGAPORE
United Kingdom	Butterworth & Co. (Publishers) Ltd., LONDON and EDINBURGH
United States	Butterworth Legal Publishers, AUSTIN, Texas; BOSTON, Massachusetts; CLEARWATER, Florida (D & S Publishers); ORFORD, New Hampshire (Equity Publishing); ST. PAUL, Minnesota; and SEATTLE, Washington

Canadian Cataloguing in Publication Data

Bruce, C. J.
  Assessment of personal injury damages

2nd ed.
ISBN 0-409-89768-X

1. Damages - Canada. 2. Personal injuries - Canada.
3. Death by wrongful act - Canada. I. Title.

KE1237.B78 1992   346.7103″23   C92-093059-X
KF1257.B78 1992

Sponsoring Editor — Fran Cudlipp
Editor — Lisa Krueger
Cover Design — Patrick Ng
Production — Kevin Skinner

**Printed and bound in Canada by
John Deyell Company Limited.**

For Julia and Andrew

ACKNOWLEDGEMENTS

Throughout the preparation of this book, I was fortunate to have the assistance of Annemarije van der Wal, who conducted much of the bibliographic research, undertook many of the mathematical calculations, prepared many of the tables, and wrote parts of two chapters. My thanks go to her for her uncomplaining enthusiasm; without it, I would not have been able to complete this book on time.

I have also received research assistance from Cara Brown and Denise Froese; and I have benefitted from conversations with Ken Cooper-Stephenson, Doug Kalesnikoff, and Bob McGlynn. I would also like to thank the Canadian Institute and the Saskatchewan Trial Lawyers Association for inviting me to speak to them during the last year. Their audiences provided unwitting sounding boards for much of the material which appears in the first three chapters of this book. Finally, I would like to thank Paul Kubicek who provided me with considerable assistance in writing the computer program which was used to create the tables in Chapters 1, 2, and 3.

TABLE OF CONTENTS

TABLES AND FIGURES

HOW TO USE THIS BOOK

In order to best understand how it is intended that this book is to be used, it is first necessary to recognize that the book is divided into three distinct sections:

I. The Calculation of Damages — This section (Chapters 1-3) discusses the techniques which are used to evaluate losses in personal injury and fatal accident actions. It describes the various components of each claim, identifies the most common sources of information concerning these components, summarizes the statistical information which is available concerning each component, and demonstrates how the lump-sum award is calculated.

II. Statistical Information — Whereas the purpose of Section I is to provide a broad-based introduction to the method by which damages are calculated, the purpose of Section II (Chapters 4-13) is to provide detailed information concerning many of the components of this calculation. In particular, as each concept is introduced in Section I, the reader is directed to the relevant pages in Section II where this additional information may be found. For example, under the discussion of fringe benefits in Chapter 1, the reader is told both: that fringe benefits among white collar workers typically equal approximately 10-20 percent of "straight-time" earnings and that Chapter 6 provides additional, detailed information concerning this factor.

III. Additional Issues — Chapter 14 deals with the selection, examination, and cross-examination of expert witnesses; while Chapter 15 deals with various issues arising from the use of structured setlementments.

My suggestion is that, each time that the practitioner opens a new file, the relevant chapter in Section I be reviewed quickly in order to accomplish two goals. First, even among those of us who calculate damages in hundreds of cases every year, it is possible to forget about the complexities and pitfalls of specific types of injuries. A brief review of the relevant chapter in Section I will act as a reminder of these problems and, therefore, help the practitioner to avoid them. Second, a review of Section I will point the user to those chapters in Section II which contain information which may be of value to the prosecution of the particular action in question. For example, the introduction to fringe benefits in Chapter 1 will act both as a reminder that fringe benefits are to be included in damage assessment and as a pointer to information (in Chapter 6) concerning the values of fringe benefits which are paid in various Canadian industries.

In short, whereas the first edition of this book may be considered to have been a *textbook*, this version has been written as a *handbook*. It is not intended to be read once, in order to obtain general background information concerning damage assessment, but to be referenced each time that a new case arises, in order to provide hints and reminders concerning the best procedures to follow.

1

PERSONAL INJURY — EXCLUDING COST OF CARE

This Chapter discusses all of the heads of damages which are normally associated with personal injury actions *except* the future "costs of care". The latter head, which includes ongoing, *future* costs of items such as medicine, wheelchairs, housing and automotive adaptations, nursing care, and prostheses, will be discussed in Chapter 2.

The Chapter is divided into six sections. The first three of these deal, respectively, with the calculation of the streams of losses associated with: loss of earnings capacity, loss of pension, and impairment of the ability to perform such "household activities" as lawn-mowing and automobile repairs. The fourth section describes the techniques which are employed to obtain lump-sum values of these streams. In particular, it explains the role of the "discount rate" and describes how life expectancy is incorporated into the present value calculation. The possibility of raising a claim for loss of marital prospects, in cases of serious disability, is canvassed in Section V. Finally, Section VI reviews a number of factors which are important to the determination of damages for "pain and suffering". An Appendix is also provided, in which the determination and use of the "multiplier" is discussed.

I. LOSS OF EARNINGS CAPACITY

In broad outline, the calculation of the loss of earnings capacity is undertaken in four stages. In the first, the stream of income which the plaintiff would have earned, from the date of the trial to the date of retirement, had he/she not been injured is calculated. Second, a similar calculation is made for the stream of income which the plaintiff is expected to earn now that the injury has occurred. Third, the stream of losses is calculated by taking the difference between the first two streams and adjusting for life expectancy. Finally, a calculation is made of the amount which would have to be invested at the date of the trial in order to replace the stream of losses (and leave nothing at the end of the period of loss). It is the first two of these stages which will be discussed in this section. The third and fourth stages will be analysed in Section IV of this chapter. Also, it is only in Section IV that a formal distinction will be made between the pre- and post-trial periods of loss.

1. Earnings Stream — If Accident Had not Occurred

Five major factors enter into the determination of the stream of income which the plaintiff would have earned had the accident not occurred: the annual income which would have been earned in the first year following the accident, the "base year income", the growth rate of that income over time, the positive and negative contingencies to be applied to the potential earnings, and the retirement age. Each of these factors will be considered in a separate subsection. In addition, a sixth section will consider two additional factors which often arise in personal injury actions — the effect of absences from the labour force (for example, to attend university or look after young children) and the difficulty of forecasting the incomes of plaintiffs who were minors at the time that their injuries were incurred. A seventh section considers the special case of an individual who was self-employed. Finally, a sample calculation is presented.

(a) Base year income

The simplest method for calculating the future stream of earnings is to begin with an estimate of the first year's earnings and then increase (or decrease) that income by some annual rate of growth until retirement. Thus, the first step is to estimate the income which the plaintiff would have earned (*before taxes*) in the first year following the accident had the accident not occurred. To my knowledge, there is no official source, such as Statistics Canada or the provincial departments of labour, which publish annual information concerning incomes by occupation. Instead, I find the following sources to be the most useful:

Employers — if the plaintiff had been working at the time of the accident, most employers will be able to identify what his/her income would have been in the first year following the accident; and many will also be able to estimate the income which would have been earned in each year between the date of the accident and the date of the trial or settlement negotiation — for example by identifying the income stream of the individual who replaced the plaintiff.

Unions — union agreements, where applicable, generally set out in considerable detail the earnings for which their members are eligible.

Employer/trade organizations — a surprising number of employer organizations conduct wage and salary surveys of their members. Sometimes, these surveys are conducted informally by the organization itself;

other times it will be conducted by an external organization such as
a management consulting firm.

Colleges, trade schools, and universities — post-secondary educational institutions — particularly those which specialize in training for
specific labour market openings, such as trade schools, junior colleges,
and university schools of business — often undertake surveys to determine the incomes of their recent graduates.

Telephone surveys — if no reliable information can be obtained from
an existing source, I recommend that a telephone survey of employers
be conducted. With the assistance of a copy of the Yellow Pages, this
can usually be done fairly easily by a clerk, articling student, or legal
assistant. This approach has the added attraction that it often identifies individuals who would make desirable witnesses. (For example,
recently, while telephoning employers to determine whether an individual
who had lost a leg could work as a bench welder, I was fortunate enough
to speak to an individual who had lost a leg and was working in that
occupation.) If a more formal approach is deemed desirable, it is always
possible to employ a management consulting firm to conduct the survey on your behalf.

> Additional information concerning base year incomes may be found in
> Chapter 4. That Chapter also discusses the special cases of self-employed
> individuals and of minors and young adults who have not yet established
> clear lifetime earnings patterns. (Minors and young adults are also dis-
> cussed in subsection (f), below, and self-employed individuals are discussed
> in subsection (g).)

(b) Growth rate of income

There are four sources of earnings growth. These are (i) annual increases
due to factors specific to the individual, such as merit increases, job
changes, and changes in hours worked; (ii) annual increases due to inflation; (iii) annual increases due to advances in the economy as a whole
(usually called "productivity" increases); and (iv) irregular increases due
to promotions.

In the pre-trial period, information concerning the inflationary and
productivity-based increases can generally be obtained from two sources.
First, the individual's employer or union will often be able to identify
the increases which the plaintiff would have received, or the increases
which a similar employee has actually received. Second, actual percentage increases in average weekly earnings, by industry, are available from
the Statistics Canada publication *Employment, Earnings, and Hours*,
(Cat. No. 72-002). For example, if the individual had been working

as a construction labourer in Ontario, earning \$12 per hour in 1988, it might be possible to estimate his 1989 and 1990 potential earnings by increasing that \$12 per hour figure by the average rate of increase experienced by workers in Ontario construction between 1988, 1989 and 1990.

With respect to the remaining two sources of earnings growth and with respect to all future increases in earnings, however, less precise sources must be relied upon.

(i) Factors specific to the individual:

In order to calculate average rates of increase of earnings due to merit increases, promotions, etc., I recommend that information be obtained concerning average earnings by age. Some professional organizations, such as engineers and chartered accountants, publish this type of information. For most occupations, however, the primary source is Census data, published by Statistics Canada. The general finding from this source is that the earnings of individuals without post-secondary education grow at approximately 2.0 percent per year from age 25-35, 0.50 percent per year from 35-50, and − 1.0 percent per year from 50 until retirement. In general, the equivalent growth rates for individuals with post-secondary education are 4.0 percent (25-35), 2.0 percent (35-50), and − 0.75 percent (50-retirement). (Note: these rates *exclude* the effects of inflation and economy-wide productivity increases.)

(ii) Inflation:

In addition to those increases which arise from personal advancement, most wages increase from year to year in line with the increase in the consumer price index. Inflation is currently expected to average approximately 2-4 percent per year over the future.

(iii) Productivity:

Even when the individual job or occupation does not become more productive over time, the earnings paid in that job increase over time in line with the overall increase in economy-wide productivity — otherwise workers would leave that job for those jobs whose earnings were increasing. Thus, for example, even though the productivity of sales clerks or janitors or waiters has changed only very little over the last 40 years, their incomes have risen in line with changes in the economy. Current expectations are that economy wide changes in productivity will average 0.5-1.5 percent per year over the future. (See, however, the discussion of the paper by Carter and Palmer in Chapter 11.)

(Note: it is my understanding that the British Columbia regulations require that the "productivity factor" be set equal to zero.)

(iv) Promotions:

Occasionally, sufficient information is available to predict that the individual would have been promoted at a particular age. Such information is usually only available from the individual's employer or union.

Additional information concerning the growth rates of earnings may be found in Chapter 5.

(c) Positive contingencies

In addition to their "base salaries," most individuals receive income in the form of fringe benefits and overtime payments. These sources are often referred to as "positive contingencies" and it is common to enter them, not as dollar amounts, but as percentage additions to the base year salary. For example, if an individual has been receiving fringe benefits, bonuses, and overtime payments equal to approximately $2,500 per year on a base salary of $25,000, those payments would be taken into consideration by adding 10 percent to the annual salary.

Most studies report that workers, other than the least skilled or the self-employed, earn fringe benefits and overtime valued at between 10 and 20 percent of their base salaries. Therefore, I generally recommend that a figure between 13 and 17 percent be applied for this factor. For the unskilled, statutory requirements often imply that fringe benefits amount to 4-6 percent, and some allowance for overtime may also be made. Only the self-employed receive no fringe benefits, as these are included in their employment income.

When developing a plaintiff's claim, or reviewing the claim which has been made by the plaintiff, it is important to keep the following factors in mind:

(i) Pension benefits:

Often 50 percent or more of the fringe benefit payments made by the employer represent contributions to the employee's pension plan. It would be double-counting to add these payments to the employee's annual loss of earnings *and* to compensate the employee for a loss of pension benefits subsequent to retirement.

Most pension plans are "actuarially fair"; that is, the total contributions made by employers and employees are exactly sufficient to provide a fund from which the post-retirement benefits can be paid. As a result, under most circumstances if the employee is compensated for the loss of the contributions which his/her employer would have made to the pension plan, he/she will receive exactly the same amount of money as if he/she had been compensated for that portion of *post-*retirement benefits which would have been financed by the employer's pre-retirement contributions. *The plaintiff is eligible to claim for only one of these amounts — not both.*

In general, I would recommend that the loss of pension benefits be evaluated by compensating the plaintiff for the loss of the employer's contributions to the pension fund, while the plaintiff was working, rather than for the loss of post-retirement benefits. The reason for this is that, whereas it is generally a fairly straightforward matter to measure the employer's pension contributions, it is often more difficult to determine what portion of the pension benefits would have been derived from the employer's contributions (as opposed to the employee's contributions).

The primary exception to this recommendation occurs when the plaintiff would have been nearing retirement and the pension is of the *defined benefit* type. (Defined benefit pensions typically determine the post-retirement pension benefits by multiplying the number of years of pensionable service by some percentage, such as 2 percent, times the employee's average salary in the years immediately prior to retirement.) In these cases, the increase in the value of the stream of post-retirement benefits which results from working from the current age until retirement usually far exceeds the value of the contributions which the employer will make to the pension fund over that time period. Hence, in such cases, an attempt should be made to estimate the value of the benefits lost, rather than the value of the contributions lost.

(ii) Employee contributions to fringe benefit plans:

In the calculation of positive contingencies, no allowance need to be made for the employee's own contributions to fringe benefit plans. For example, assume that the employer had been deducting $20 per month from the employee's cheque to pay for life insurance. Because that $20 is included in the calculation of the base salary, discussed in section (a) above, there is no need to include it also in the fringe benefit package. The plaintiff will be compensated for the loss of base salary and will, therefore, still have that $20 with which he/she may still purchase life insurance.

(iii) Holiday and vacation pay:

In their calculation of the value of their fringe benefit packages, many employers will include the earnings payable during holidays and vacations. In most circumstances, these amounts must not be included in the value of the fringe benefit package for the purposes of the calculation of lost earning capacity. The reason for this is that the estimation of the base salary, discussed above, assumed that the individual would have worked 52 weeks per year. (Negative contingencies for unemployment, labour force absences, etc. will be discussed in Section (c) below.) That is, the base salary already includes payments for holidays and vacations.

The exception occurs when the individual would not have worked sufficiently steadily to have been entitled to either holiday or vacation pay. In that case, most provinces require that the employer pay an amount equal to 4 percent of earned income in lieu of holiday and vacation pay. This percentage does represent a legitimate positive contingency.

(iv) Overtime:

It has been my experience that plaintiff's counsel often neglect to make allowance for possible overtime pay for which their clients might have been eligible. Hence, it is worth emphasising here that positive contingencies include overtime as well as fringe benefits.

> **Additional information concerning positive contingencies may be found in Chapter 6.**

(d) Negative contingencies

There are various reasons why an individual might not work a full week or full year. For example, he/she might be injured, ill, or unemployed; or might work only part-time during certain years. As with the fringe benefits and overtime payments, these "negative contingencies" are usually entered as percentage adjustments to the annual salary.

It is common to allow for two types of negative contingencies: unemployment and long-term disability. Most forecasts of unemployment suggest that the rate of unemployment in Canada will average approximately 7 percent, with most occupations falling in the range of 3 to 10 percent. It should be remembered, however, that most individuals are eligible for unemployment insurance, which will pay for as much as 60 percent of the individual's lost earnings. Accordingly, the negative contingency for unemployment should equal approximately 50 percent of the unemployment rate.

Unemployment rates vary both by occupation and by age, with rates being highest for young workers and for labourers and construction workers. That unemployment rates tend to be high among young workers proves to be extremely important for the calculation of loss of earnings capacity. Many plaintiffs are under the age of 25 — individuals in this age group have an unfortunate propensity for being injured in automobile accidents — and their work histories show high unemployment rates. It is tempting to conclude from this observation that they would have continued to experience high unemployment rates had they not been injured. But this is rarely this case. Most individuals begin to "settle down" in their mid- to late-twenties and their unemployment rates fall accordingly. I recommend that statistical evidence from the Census and from Statistics Canada's Labour Force Survey be employed to identify the extent to which unemployment rates vary with age.

The average Canadian also has a probability of becoming severely disabled of approximately 5 percent, although this may be slightly higher for particularly dangerous occupations and slightly lower for sedentary occupations.

> Additional information concerning negative contingencies may be found in Chapter 7.

(e) Retirement

With respect to all but the self-employed and farmers, the evidence is that Canadians tend to retire between ages 60 and 65. Hence, for most individuals I recommend use of a retirement age of 62 or 63. For farmers or the self-employed, however, I would suggest use of a later age — perhaps 65 to 70, depending upon information about the individual.

> Additional information concerning retirement patterns may be found in Chapter 9.

(f) Other factors

In addition to the factors identified above, it is also important to remember that many individuals would have been absent from the labour force at some time even had the accident not occurred. Also, special calculations have to be made if the plaintiff was a minor at the time of the accident.

(i) Absences:

Three common "absences" are:

(a) the plaintiff is currently a child and has not yet begun work. In this case, the absence will run from the current time period until the child is expected to start work;

(b) the plaintiff is currently at school or is expected to return to school during some future time period;

(c) the plaintiff is expected to leave the labour force to bear and raise children and then return at some later date.

For example, assume that the plaintiff is a young woman who was in school at the time of the accident and who was expected to enter the labour force after graduation before taking an absence from work to bear and raise children. Her employment income would have been zero in those years in which she was at school and in those years in which she was at home. Based upon the most recent statistical evidence, I would suggest that four to six years be allowed for absences due to childbearing for the average woman, as most Canadian women have two to three children and leave the labour force for approximately two years per child. Only if information specific to the plaintiff indicated otherwise would it be justifiable to use absences which differed significantly from these.

Additional information concerning female absences for childbearing may be found in Section I of Chapter 7.

(ii) Minors and young adults:

The younger the plaintiff is at the time of the injury, the less certain can one be concerning his or her pre-injury earning potential. Nevertheless, the studies cited in Sections II and III of Chapter 4 suggest that family and individual characteristics of the plaintiff can be used to predict the educational level which the plaintiff would have reached. Census data for individuals with that educational level can then be used to forecast the plaintiff's lifetime earnings stream. The family characteristics which I believe to be of greatest predictive importance are: parents' occupation, education, income, and motivation; siblings education, occupation, and school records; and the plaintiff's pre-accident school records. The latter often include intelligence tests, which will be invaluable if the plaintiff has been brain-injured.

Also, if the plaintiff was a teenager or in his/her early twenties at the time of the accident, there is some statistical support for the suggestion that the individual's expressed interests, before the accident, are predictive of the occupation ultimately chosen.

(Note: the statistical correlation between family characteristics and a child's educational/occupational choice is sufficiently weak that I believe that it would *never* be justifiable to argue that the child would follow the same occupational stream as his/her parents. It is my view, for example, that the assumption in *Teno v. Arnold*[1] that the infant daughter would have become a teacher, like her mother, is not supportable from the statistical evidence. Rather, in such a case, I believe that the strongest argument which can be based upon statistical sources

---

[1] *Arnold v. Teno*, [1978] 2 S.C.R. 287, 83 D.L.R. (3d) 609, 19 N.R. 1, 3 C.C.L.T. 272.

is that the daughter would have received a university or other post-secondary education — an argument which, by the way, would have produced a predicted income stream very similar to that which would be predicted for teachers alone.)

> Additional information concerning the earnings potential of minors and young adults may be found in Sections II and III of Chapter 4.

(g) Self-employed individuals

The determination of the foregone income of self-employed individuals is an extremely complicated problem, fraught with possible traps for the unwary. This complex issue is discussed in some detail in Section IV of Chapter 4, but for the moment, allow me to set out some of the more common problems of which the practitioner should be aware. Most of these problems arise from the fact that the benefit which the self-employed individual obtains from his or her business often far exceeds the value of the wages which he or she is paid by that business. Some of the sources of this difference include:

(i) Expense allowances:

Self-employed individuals are often able to claim personal consumption expenditures as business expenses. Portions of mortgage and car payments, for example, may be paid for by the business, owners of food stores may provide part of their family's food expenditures out of the business, etc. Not only would these benefits not have appeared in the individual's income statements, but they would have been received tax free.

(ii) Investment in the company:

Many owners of small businesses reinvest a significant portion of their income in the company. To the extent that this is done, the income paid to the owner will understate — sometimes dramatically — the amount of income earned. There are a number of ways in which income can be generated which will not be paid to the owner in the current period. One obvious way of reinvesting income in the company is to use the owner's profits to purchase additional capital equipment or to pay down mortgages. In this case, the growth of the value of the assets owned by the company represents a gain to the owner. An injury which prevented that individual from operating the company would reduce his or her ability to generate these types of gains as surely as it would reduce his/her ability to generate a salary from the company.

In addition, there are a number of less obvious ways in which the continued operation of a company may create benefits to its owner. A company which owns real assets, such as land and buildings, can expect to obtain capital gains from increases in the market value of those assets. And, similarly, a company which is operating successfully may accumulate "good will" which will have a surrender value at the time the owner decides to sell the company (perhaps upon retirement). The loss of the ability to accumulate these asset values will also represent a loss of income to the plaintiff.

(iii) Income splitting:

It has been my experience that many small businesses are actually one-person operations, founded almost exclusively upon the skills of the proprietor. Simple examples include welders, accountants, and building contractors. Often these individuals incorporate in order to "split" their incomes with their spouses or children, even though the spouse or children make only a minor contribution to the operation of the company. In such cases, I recommend that the individuals be interviewed in order to determine the actual number of hours contributed by the spouse or children to the company. Then estimate the value of those hours based upon wages for comparable workers in the local labour market. Finally, estimate the total income generated by the company and deduct from that the imputed value of the spouse and children's contributions in order to estimate the true value of the plaintiff's contributions.

(iv) Dividends:

Finally, it is important to remember that self-employed individuals receive dividends as well as salaries.

> Additional information concerning the earnings potential of the self-employed may be found in Section IV of Chapter 4.

(h) Sample calculation

Assume that the plaintiff was a 50-year-old engineer whose base year salary was $44,923 per year and whose projected retirement age was 62. Assume also, that this individual's salary would have increased at the rate of inflation, 5 percent, plus the economy-wide productivity rate, 0.5 percent, (i.e., at approximately 5.5 percent in total[2]); that

---

[2] Technically, if the inflation rate is 5 percent and the "real" growth rate is 0.5 percent, the joint growth rate is found by multiplying (1 + inflation rate) times (1 + growth rate) and then subtracting 1. In this case, the growth rate would be found to be:

the positive contingencies amounted to 15 percent; and that negative contingencies were 10 percent. The first column in the Table 1, below, identifies how the base year salary would have increased over time (before allowance for positive and negative contingencies is made). The second column adds positive contingencies to the figures from the first column; while the third column deducts negative contingencies from the figures in the second column, to arrive at the stream of foregone earnings. (Note: the figure in the last column is obtained by multiplying the figure in the positive contingencies column by 0.90 (= 1.00 − 0.10).)

TABLE 1

NET EARNINGS STREAM IF ACCIDENT HAD NOT OCCURRED

Age	Base Earnings	Earnings Plus Positive Contingencies	Earnings Inclusive of both Positive and Negative Contingencies
50	$44,923	$51,661	$46,495
51	47,394	54,503	49,053
52	50,000	57,500	51,750
53	52,750	60,663	54,597
54	55,651	63,999	57,599
55	58,712	67,519	60,767
56	61,941	71,232	64,109
57	65,348	75,150	67,635
58	68,942	79,283	71,355
59	72,734	83,643	75,279
60	76,734	88,245	79,420
61	80,954	93,098	83,788

[*Note:* The figures in the last column of Table 1 could have been obtained by first adjusting the base year salary for positive and negative contingencies, to produce the $46,495 figure reported in the last column of the first row, and then increasing that figure by 5.5 percent per year.]

joint growth rate $= (1 + 5\%) \times (1 + 0.5\%) - 1$
$= (1.05 \times 1.005) - 1$
$= .05525$
$= 5.525\%$

not 5.5 percent. 5.5 percent has been used in the text for ease of calculation.

2. Earnings Stream — After Accident Has Occurred

Again, five major factors enter into the determination of the stream of income which the plaintiff will earn now that the accident has occurred (presuming that it has been determined that the plaintiff is capable of earning an income): the annual income which will be earned in the first year following the accident i.e., the "base year income", the growth rate of that income over time, the positive contingencies to be applied to the potential earnings, the negative contingencies to be applied, and the retirement age. Each of these factors will be considered in a separate subsection. Finally, a sample calculation is presented.

(a) Base year income

All of the sources which I listed with respect to the "no-accident" scenario — employers, trade associations, unions, etc. — can also be employed to identify the base income of the injured plaintiff. Nevertheless, the injured plaintiff presents a number of special problems. The first of these involves the identification of the set of occupations which the plaintiff is now capable of undertaking; and the second involves the identification of the effects which the disability will have upon annual earnings in those occupations.

(i) Identification of occupation:

The best advice which can be given here is that a vocational psychologist should be hired to test the plaintiff. Furthermore, the psychologist should test both aptitude *and* interest/attitude. I have seen a number of cases in which a psychologist has determined that the plaintiff was physically and mentally *capable* of performing some function in which it was clear that he/she was not at all interested. For example, in my experience, most cases of paraplegia involve young males who have dropped out of high school after grade 10 to engage in manual labour of some sort. Aptitude tests may well indicate that such individuals are capable of becoming, say, sales clerks or computer programmers; but to the extent that these occupations require that the individual sit behind a desk in an office all day, such plaintiffs may simply not be psychologically prepared to perform these tasks day in and day out for the rest of their lives. They need physically oriented jobs, not mentally oriented ones in order to function at their best.

(ii) Effect of disability on base earnings:

Statistics concerning the disabled show that even when they are able to obtain employment, they tend to earn less than non-disabled individuals in the same employment. *Even the individual who has returned to the job which he or she was performing before the injury may suffer a reduction in earnings.* Wherever possible, it is desirable to identify this effect by examining the actual experience of the plaintiff. But, of course, most seriously disabled individuals have not returned to work by the time that settlement negotiations, or even a trial, takes place. Accordingly, it is often necessary to rely upon statistical data concerning the effects of disability upon earnings.

With respect to this matter, Canada now has some of the best information available anywhere in the world concerning the earnings of the disabled. These data are drawn from a survey conducted in conjunction with the 1985 Census — the Health and Activity Limitation Survey (HALS). For a small fee, usually between $300 and $800, Statistics Canada will provide users with information concerning the effect on earnings of virtually any kind, or combination, of disability which might arise. Contact Statistics Canada, either in your local region or in Ottawa.

> Additional information concerning the base year earnings of the disabled may be found in Section I of Chapter 8.

(b) Growth rate of income

Again, the same factors which were discussed with respect to the "no-accident" scenario, above, apply with respect to the "post-accident" scenario. The primary difference is that the incomes of the seriously injured may grow more slowly than those of the non-disabled. Information concerning income by age of the disabled may be obtained from the Health and Activity Limitation Survey.

(c) Positive contingencies

To my knowledge, there is no specific information concerning the effect of disability upon fringe benefits. However, it is important to remember that a disabled individual who has returned to the job at which he or she was employed before the accident may suffer a reduction in overtime pay, which is one of the components of the positive contingency figure. Indeed, in one recent case, I calculated that the loss of the future opportunity to earn overtime would cost the plaintiff over $100,000, even though the individual had returned to the "same" job as before the accident.

Also, if the individual's injuries are such that he/she is forced to work part-time after the accident, whereas he/she would have worked full-time had the accident not occurred, fringe benefits may be reduced substantially — simply because part-time workers receive substantially fewer fringe benefits than do full-time workers.

(d) Negative contingencies

Among those suffering major injuries, the most important negative contingency arising from disability is that of *non* labour force participation[3]; whereas among those suffering from minor injuries, negative contingencies tend to derive from both increased unemployment and increased part-time, as opposed to full-time, work. The Health and Activity Limitation Survey indicates, that among those disabled who are in the labour force, the unemployment rate is only slightly higher than that experienced by the non-disabled. The non-participation rate, however, is much higher among the disabled than the non-disabled — often as much as 20 percent higher. Thus, *in addition* to the fact that those who are disabled earn less than the non-disabled if they are employed, they are much less likely to be employed. This reduction in probability of employment, we enter as a negative contingency.

(Note: it is important to note here that the statistics appear to indicate that even if the disabled individual has changed occupations, in order to mitigate the effects of the injury, he or she can still expect to suffer a higher rate of unemployment than will be experienced by the average non-disabled employee in the new occupation. It is not, as one judge recently suggested to me, double-counting to assume that the disabled plaintiff's earnings will fall both because of a reduction in wages per hour and because of a reduction in numbers of hours worked.)

Also, even if the disabled individual is not less likely to be employed because of the disability, it sometimes seems likely that the disability will increase the probability that the individual will *become* seriously disabled in the future. For example, a labourer with back problems may be more prone to being involved in a workplace accident than he or she would have been had she not suffered those problems. In these cases, I would recommend increasing the negative contingency for disability.

Additional information concerning negative contingencies incurred by the disabled may be found in Chapter 8.

---

[3] Statisticians distinguish between those individuals who are either working or looking for work and those who are not looking for work. Individuals who are not working but are looking for work are considered to be members of the labour force, along with the employed, and are called *unemployed*. Those who are not working and are not looking for work, or have given up looking for work, are considered to be outside of the labour force — they are not *participating* in the labour force.

(e) Retirement

Numerous studies have shown that the most consistent determinant of early retirement is poor health. To the extent, therefore, that a serious personal injury may be considered to have created a situation of poor health, such an injury may be expected to shorten the plaintiff's working lifespan. Depending upon the nature of the injury, it might be argued that a disabled individual can be expected to retire 3 to 5 years earlier than an otherwise equivalent non-disabled individual.

Additional information concerning retirement may be found in Chapter 9.

(f) Sample calculation

Assume that the 50-year-old engineer discussed in Section 1 (g), above, has suffered serious back injuries which will keep him from work until he is 54 and will cause him to retire 3 years early, at age 59. Assume also that his "base salary" will not be affected but that his positive contingencies will be reduced by 5 percent (to 10 percent) because of reduced opportunity for overtime and that his negative contingencies will be increased by 20 percent (to 30 percent) to allow for the possibility that he may become unemployed or be forced to leave the labour market. In this case, his stream of earnings may be represented by the figures in the last column of Table 2.

TABLE 2

NET EARNINGS STREAM AFTER ACCIDENT HAS OCCURRED

Age	Base Earnings	Earnings Plus Positive Contingencies	Earnings Inclusive of both Positive and Negative Contingencies
50	$ 0	$ 0	$ 0
51	0	0	0
52	0	0	0
53	0	0	0
54	55,651	61,216	42,851
55	58,712	64,583	45,208
56	61,941	68,135	47,695
57	65,348	71,883	50,318
58	68,942	75,836	53,085
59	0	0	0
60	0	0	0
61	0	0	0

II. LOSS OF PENSION INCOME

If the loss of the employer's contributions to the plaintiff's pension plan(s) has not been incorporated into the loss of earning capacity, through the expedient of including it as a positive contingency (see Section I.1 (c) above) the loss of pension income may be included as a separate head in personal injury cases. The general approach to be employed is identical to that described in Section I regarding the evaluation of the loss of earnings capacity. One determines the stream of pension payments which the employer's contributions would have generated for the plaintiff had the accident not occurred and then deducts from that the stream of pension benefits which the employer's contributions are expected to generate for the plaintiff now that the accident has occurred. (A simple method for determining the portion of the plaintiff's pension benefits which can be attributed to the employer would be to estimate the percentage of the annual contributions to the pension plan which are made by the employer and then to multiply that figure by the annual, total value of the pension benefits for which the plaintiff will be eligible. For example, if the employer had been contributing an amount equal to 7.5 percent of the employee's annual salary to the pension plan, while the employee had been contributing an amount equal to 5 percent of his/her salary, approximately 60 percent (7.5/12.5) of the pension benefits could be attributed to the employer.)

In these calculations it is important to include both the value of the benefits which the individual would have received from the employer's private pension plan and the value which would have been received from the Canada/Quebec Pension Plan.

III. REPLACEMENT OF HOUSEHOLD SERVICES

A personal injury will often leave the plaintiff with a reduced ability to complete household chores such as cooking, cleaning, and yardwork. In cases involving a severe injury, compensation for this loss will usually be included under the head of "cost of care" (see Chapter 2). In cases involving minor injuries, however, this head of damages is often overlooked.

Normally, the hourly cost of replacing household services can be obtained simply by telephoning companies which provide maid, lawn care, and household repair services; while the number of hours which the plaintiff is unable to work because of the injury can be obtained from the plaintiff's own testimony. If corroborating information is desired, however, various agencies, particularly Statistics Canada, provide statistics concerning the average numbers of hours which individuals spend on various types of activities. This issue is considered in greater detail in Section I.3 of Chapter 3, as loss of household services is generally of greatest interest in fatal accident cases.

> Additional information concerning the valuation of household services may be found in Chapter 10.

IV. CALCULATION OF LUMP-SUM DAMAGES

The first step in the calculation of the lump-sum damages is to divide the stream of losses into two: the stream of losses incurred before the date of trial or settlement and the stream of losses which will be incurred after that date. The reason for this is that different techniques are used for calculating the lump-sum value of damages in the two cases.

1. Calculation of the Pre-Trial Loss

With respect to pre-trial losses, most provinces have stipulated that simple interest is to be added to each time period's loss, from the time of the loss to the date of trial or settlement. The most straightforward method of calculating simple interest is to divide the pre-trial loss into different periods. With respect to each period, add together the interest rates which have been stipulated from that period until the date of settlement; add those figures to 1; then multiply the resulting sum by the loss in question. Repeat this process for each pre-trial period and then add all the resulting figures together.

For example, assume in the example of the engineer who was injured on his 48th birthday, developed in Section I, above, that the date of settlement is the engineer's 50th birthday. (That is, his 50th birthday separates the pre- and post-trial periods.) It is seen from Table 1 that if he had not been injured, he would have earned $46,495 in his 48th year and $49,053 in his 49th year. As it was also assumed that his injuries left him unable to work during those years, these are also his losses during those years.

Assume now that the legislature has stipulated that the pre-trial, or judgement, interest rate two years ago was to be 10 percent and that one year ago it was to be 12 percent. To calculate the present value of the loss during the engineer's 48th year, multiply his loss in that year by 1 plus the sum of the judgement interest rates, i.e., 22 percent (= 10 + 12). That is, the present value of that loss is to be $46,495 x (1 + 0.10 + 0.12) = $56,723.90. Similarly, the present value of the loss during the engineer's 49th year is found by multiplying $49,053 by (1 + 0.12) for a figure of $54,939.36. Thus, the total, pre-trial loss, inclusive of judgment interest proves to be \$111,663.26 (= \$56,723.90 + \$54,939.36).

2. Calculation of the Lump-Sum Value of the Future (Post-Trial) Loss

The calculation of the lump-sum value of the future loss is conducted in two steps. First, the stream of future losses is adjusted for the probability that the plaintiff might die. Second, an estimate is made of the amount of money which would have to be paid to the plaintiff such that, if that amount were invested, sufficient funds would be available to replace the plaintiff's "mortality-adjusted" stream of lost income.

(a) Mortality adjustment

The final column of Table 1 indicates the stream of income which it is predicted a hypothetical plaintiff would have earned had he not been injured; while the final column of Table 2 indicates the stream of earnings which it is predicted he will now earn. The difference between these two streams is his loss of earnings in each year *if he lives to that year*. To take account of the possibility that the plaintiff may not live to any particular year, the approach which is generally taken is to multiply the loss in that year by the probability that the individual will still be alive in that year. That is, in each year the loss is reduced by the probability that the individual would *not* have lived to that year — the probability of mortality is treated like any other negative contingency.

In Table 3, the net loss of *future* earnings (i.e., from age 52 onwards) is calculated. The first column repeats the last column from Table 1; the second column repeats the last column from Table 2; and the third column reports the difference between these two sets of figures. The fourth column provides the probabilities that a 52-year-old Canadian male will live to each year beyond his 52nd birthday[4]. For example, the entry in the row against age 61 indicates that there is a 0.9036 probability that he will live from his 52nd birthday until his 61st year. Finally, the amounts to be compensated are found by multiplying the

---

[4] Because the individual in question could have been expected to receive his income monthly, the technically correct procedure would have been to calculate the probability of survival to each possible month in the future. However, as this would have required that Table 3 have 120 lines, 12 for each of 10 years, I have simplified the exposition by employing the probabilities that a 52-year-old Canadian male would live to the mid-point of each future year. For example, the 0.9967 probability which appears in the first row indicates that there is a 99.67 percent probability that a 52-year-old male will live to age 52.50.

third column by the fourth. These amounts, here referred to as "compensation", are reported in the fifth column.

TABLE 3

CALCULATION OF THE FUTURE STREAM OF LOSSES

AGE	PRE-INJURY INCOME	POST-INJURY INCOME	LOSS OF INCOME	PROBABILITY OF SURVIVAL	COMPEN-SATION
52	$51,750	$ 0	$51,750	0.9967	$51,579
53	54,597	0	54,597	0.9897	54,035
54	57,599	42,851	14,748	0.9820	14,483
55	60,767	45,208	15,559	0.9735	15,147
56	64,109	47,695	16,414	0.9642	15,826
57	67,635	50,318	17,317	0.9540	16,520
58	71,355	53,085	18,270	0.9429	17,227
59	75,279	0	75,279	0.9308	70,070
60	79,420	0	79,420	0.9177	72,884
61	83,788	0	83,788	0.9036	75,711

Note: In the calculation of the figures in this Table, I have assumed that the plaintiff had a normal life expectancy. Often, however, the accident reduces the plaintiff's life expectancy — particularly if the plaintiff has become a paraplegic or quadriplegic. In these cases, each of the pre- and post-accident income streams must be multiplied by the life expectancy probabilities appropriate to that stream. The "compensation" figures are then determined by subtracting the life expectancy-adjusted post-injury stream from the life expectancy-adjusted pre-injury stream.

Additional information concerning life expectancy may be found in Chapter 7.

(b) Calculation of the lump-sum loss

The goal of the court, in the case described above, is to pay the plaintiff an amount of money today, such that if he invests that amount and withdraws from his investment a stream of dividends equal to the figures indicated in the last row of Table 3, he will have nothing left after he makes the last withdrawal. Only two factors need to be known before the calculation of this lump-sum can be made. The first of these is the "compensation" stream, which was identified in Table 3. The second is the interest rate, or *discount rate*, at which the plaintiff can be expected to invest his or her award.

As it usually proves easier to predict what the interest rate *net* of the rate of inflation will be than to predict what the actual interest rate will be, most calculations of the lump-sum damage award begin by predicting the interest rate net of inflation — which is usually called the discount rate.

Six provinces have set specific values for the discount rate by regulation. At the time of the writing of this book (May 1991), these mandated values were:

British Columbia: for calculations of loss of income: 2.5 percent
                  for calculations of costs of care: 3.5 percent
Ontario, New Brunswick, and Nova Scotia: 2.5 percent
Saskatchewan and Manitoba: 3.0 percent

In the remaining four provinces, including Alberta, no mandated rate exists. The discount rate is set by the court following the evidence of experts. It has become my view that the long-run discount rate will average 3-3.5 percent; but that over the short-run the rate will be much higher than this because of government attempts to bring down the rate of inflation. Accordingly, I generally recommend that a discount rate of 5 percent be used for the next four or five years (until 1996), followed by a rate of 3-3.5 percent for all remaining years.

Additional information concerning the discount rate may be found in Chapter 13.

If the investment of the plaintiff's award is to be managed for him/her by a third party, such as a trust company, that party will normally charge a management fee which can be calculated as a percentage of the amount invested. For example, if $100,000 is to be managed a trust company might charge 0.5 percent of $100,000 per year. If the investment was earning 10 percent per year, the charge of 0.5 percent per year as management fee will have the effect of reducing the effective interest rate to 9.5 percent. Thus, in calculating the discount rate, it is sometimes argued that a management fee — usually a small percentage, such as 0.5 percent — should be deducted from the mandated rate.

I believe that it is unnecessary to make such a deduction. The reason for this is that the discount rate specified in most jurisdictions implicitly includes a management fee. That is, the interest rates which are used to obtain the discount rate are derived from easily-purchased investments such as Government of Canada bonds and trust company term certificates. Most plaintiffs are capable of purchasing such investments without the assistance of financial experts. Experts are only required if the plaintiff wishes to invest in a mixed "portfolio" of slightly more risky financial instruments. But if the plaintiff does choose to pursue this course, he or she can expect to obtain a higher rate of return than could be expected from investment in government bonds or trust company certificates. It is from this higher return that the management fee will be deducted, leaving the plaintiff (at least) no worse off than if he/she had invested the funds in "safe" instruments.

Indeed, the argument made here suggests, not that a management fee should be deducted from the discount rate to be used when the plaintiff is financially unsophisticated, but that a higher than normal discount rate should be used when the plaintiff is financially sophisticated. That is, if the plaintiff is able to earn a rate of return which is as high as that which would be earned by a professional portfolio manager, the plaintiff will earn a higher rate of return than is mandated by the rules of court in most provinces.

> Additional information concerning the management fee may be found in Chapter 13.

Once the discount rate has been determined, the interest rate can be obtained using the following formula:

interest rate = [(1 + discount rate) x (1 + inflation rate)] − 1

For example, if the inflation rate is predicted to be 5.0 percent and the discount rate 3.0 percent, the interest rate which is implied is 8.15 percent:

$$
\begin{aligned}
\text{interest rate} &= [(1 + .03) \times (1 + .05)] - 1 \\
&= [1.03 \times 1.05] - 1 \\
&= 1.0815 - 1 \\
&= 0.0815 \\
&= 8.15\%
\end{aligned}
$$

If it is assumed that 8.15 percent is the interest rate which is to be used in the numerical example developed in Tables 1, 2, and 3, it is now possible to determine the award necessary to compensate that individual. This figure proves to be $276,234. Before explaining how this figure was obtained, it will be useful to show how the award will be invested and spent, to leave nothing at the end of the plaintiff's period of loss, (i.e., on his 62nd birthday, which would have been his age of retirement). This I do using Table 4.

This Table has a very straightforward interpretation. Assume that the plaintiff receives $276,234 on his 52nd birthday. From Table 3 it was seen, that in order to compensate him for the income he will lose during the forthcoming year, he will need to be paid compensation of $51,579. Accordingly, in the first row of Table 4, I show that the plaintiff begins with $276,234, from which he takes $51,579. This leaves him with $224,655 which he can invest. Assume that this amount is invested for one year at the assumed rate of interest, 8.15 percent. One year from now, on his 53rd birthday, he will have $224,655 *plus* 8.15 percent of $224,655; that is, he will have $242,965 (= 1.0815 x $224,655). If he now removes $54,035 from this amount, to compensate himself for his loss of earnings during his 53rd year, he will have $188,930 remaining in his investment account. If he again invests this amount at 8.15 percent, he will increase the value of his investment to $204,328 within one year, (i.e., by his 54th birthday). If the plaintiff continues to remove compensation from his investment in this manner, reinvesting what remains each year at 8.15 percent, he will find that on his 61st birthday he has exactly $75,711 remaining, which is what he needs to replace his lost income in that year.

TABLE 4

INVESTMENT AND EXPENDITURE OF THE LUMP-SUM AWARD

AGE	AMOUNT IN INVESTMENT ACCOUNT AT BEGINNING OF THE YEAR	COMPEN-SATION	AMOUNT IN INVESTMENT ACCOUNT AFTER DEDUCTION OF COMPENSATION
52	$276,234	$51,579	$224,655
53	242,965	54,035	188,930
54	204,328	14,483	189,845
55	205,317	15,147	190,170
56	205,669	15,826	189,843
57	205,315	16,520	188,795
58	204,182	17,227	186,955
59	202,192	70,070	132,122
60	142,890	72,884	70,006
61	75,711	75,711	0

Given this interpretation of Table 4, it proves to be a very simple matter to understand how it was constructed. In order to assist in this process, it is useful to construct a table like Table 4a, which displays all of the information which is available before the calculation is to be done, as well as all of the blanks which are to be filled. As can be seen, information is available concerning two factors: (i) the amount of compensation which is to be paid to the plaintiff in each year (from Table 3) and (ii) the "Amount in Investment Account After Deduction of Compensation" in the last year of the plaintiff's loss — which is to be $0. The only other information which is available is that the interest rate is to be 8.15 percent, (i.e., the discount rate is 3 percent and the rate of inflation is 5 percent). These pieces of information prove to be sufficient.

The first step is to recognize that if $0 was to remain after the plaintiff had removed $75,711 from the investment account in year 61, there must have been $75,711 in that account at the beginning of year 61. Thus, the blank appearing in the first column of row 61 can be filled in: it is $75,711.

<u>TABLE 4a</u>

INVESTMENT AND EXPENDITURE OF THE LUMP-SUM AWARD

AGE	AMOUNT IN INVESTMENT ACCOUNT AT BEGINNING OF THE YEAR	COMPEN-SATION	AMOUNT IN INVESTMENT ACCOUNT AFTER DEDUCTIONS OF COMPENSATION
52	$ _____	$51,579	$ _____
53	_____	54,035	_____
54	_____	14,483	_____
55	_____	15,147	_____
56	_____	15,826	_____
57	_____	16,520	_____
58	_____	17,227	_____
59	_____	70,070	_____
60	_____	72,884	_____
61	_____	75,711	0

In the second step, it is recognized that the $75,711 available at the beginning of year 61 was obtained by investing some amount, Z, at interest rate 8.15 percent the year before. That is,

$$\$75,711 \ = \ 1.0815 \text{ x } Z$$

which implies that

$$Z \ = \ \$75,711/1.0815$$
$$= \ \$70,006$$

That is, once you know how much was available after investing the previous year's amount at 8.15 percent, it is possible to determine what the previous year's amount must have been. This amount is entered in the blank in the right-hand column of row 60.

Now we can add the payment which was made in year 60, $72,884, to the amount which remains after deduction of that amount, $70,006, to determine the amount which must have been available at the beginning of year 60. This amount is $142,890. All other blanks in Table 4a can now be filled in following the same procedure. (The Table which is obtained following this procedure should exactly reproduce Table 4.)

The calculation which was performed in deriving Table 4 is usually called the "actuarial calculation" by the courts. As you have just seen, this name did not arise because it is a calculation which requires the special expertise of actuaries. Indeed, with sufficient patience, a pocket calculator, and enough paper, any of you could follow the procedure set out here and calculate your own lump-sum awards. Alternatively, a Calgary-based economic consulting firm, Economica Ltd., markets a computer program — *TortEx/Injury* — which will perform these calculations for you in a matter of minutes. (It will generate the equivalent of Tables 1, 2, 3, and 4 in less than 2 minutes; and can generate a selection of alternative scenarios, for settlement purposes, in less than one minute per scenario.) A demonstration version of *TortEx/Injury*, called *Injury Demo*, is available for free from:

Economica Ltd.
750 Canada Place
407 — 2 St. S.W.
Calgary, Alberta
T2P 2Y3
(403) 297-0012

(You will need to specify whether you wish a Macintosh-compatible or IBM-compatible version and whether you prefer 3 1/2 inch or 5 1/4 inch disk.)

V. IMPAIRMENT OF MARITAL PROSPECTS

At any one time, approximately 75 percent of Canadians aged 20-65 are married.[5] Furthermore, over the duration of a lifetime, approximately 86 percent of Canadians can be expected to become married at least once.[6] Among the seriously disabled, however, this percentage may be reduced significantly. Guttman found, for example, that of 1,505 spinal cord injured of marriageable age, only 61 percent (919) were

---

[5] Canada. Statistics Canada, *Population: Demographic Characteristics Marital Status by Age Groups*, Cat. No. 92-825, (Ottawa: Statistics Canada, 1978).

[6] O. B. Adams and D. N. Nagnur, *Marriage, Divorce, and Mortality: A Life Table Analysis for Canada and the Provinces* (Ottawa: Statistics Canada, September 1988). Cat. No. 84-536.

married at the time he surveyed them.[7] (Of these, 639, or 70 percent of those married, had been married before their admission to hospital.) Similarly, an American survey of 437 individuals who had been spinal cord injured for 4 years found that only 54 percent were married.[8] And the National Census of the Deaf Population, conducted in the United States in 1972, found that 60 percent of the deaf were married at a time when the comparable rate in the general population was 74.3 percent.[9] Thus, a serious disablement may have much the same effect on a young, single individual as would the death of a spouse. By removing or reducing the opportunity for the plaintiff to marry, the disability has also removed the opportunity to obtain support from a spouse. It should be possible, under *restitutio in integrum*, to press a claim for the loss of this support.

The type of case in which such a claim would appear to be most compelling is that in which the plaintiff: (i) is a young woman who could have been expected to have married and spent a significant amount of her life out of the labour force had she not been injured and (ii) has now suffered a disability of sufficient severity that she cannot be expected either to marry or to obtain gainful employment. It is clear that the plaintiff would not be fully compensated in such a case if damages were to be based solely on the plaintiff's loss of earnings and cost of care. Full compensation, in my view, would also have to include an assessment of the expected value of her dependency upon her husband. As the evidence indicates that individuals tend to marry within their own socio-economic class,[10] estimates of the value of this dependency could be based upon the same type of information which had been employed to predict the future earnings of the plaintiff.

The type of situation which I describe here arose in British Columbia in a case which was tried in May of 1989, *Reekie v. Messervey*.[11] In this case, the trial judge, Locke, J., concluded:

> . . . I am convinced that the general proposition [that the plaintiff had suffered a monetary loss due to her reduced opportunity to marry] is right, and that, just as the prospects of marriage are taken account of in Canada in deciding damages under the Fatal Accidents Act — as are the prospects of divorce — this is a real head of damage.[12]

---

[7] Sir Ludwig Guttman, *Spinal Cord Injury*, 2nd ed. (Oxford: Blackwell, 1976) at pp. 499-501.

[8] John Young *et al.*, *Spinal Cord Injury Statistics* (Phoenix, Arizona: Good Samaritan Medical Center, 1982) at p. 56.

[9] J. D. Schein and M. T. Delk, Jr., *The Deaf Population of the United States* (Silver Spring, Md.: National Association of the Deaf, 1974) at p. 39.

[10] G. Becker, E. Landes and R. Michael, "An Economic Analysis of Marital Instability" 1977, 85 *Journal of Political Economy*, at pp. 1141-87.

[11] *Reekie v. Messervey* (1986), 4 B.C.L.R. (2d) 194 (S.C.), additional reasons at 10 B.C.L.R. (2d) 231 (S.C.).

[12] *Ibid.*, at pp. 223-24.

Justice Locke's decision was later affirmed by the British Columbia Court of Appeal.[13]

VI. NON-PECUNIARY DAMAGES "PAIN AND SUFFERING"

The Canadian courts have ordered that one head of damages in personal injury cases is to be:

> Compensation for physical and mental pain and suffering endured and to be endured, loss of amenities and enjoyment of life, loss of expectation of life.[14]

Further, the Supreme Court of Canada has established that there is to be a ceiling on these "non-pecuniary" damages of $100,000[15] measured in "January 1978 dollars".[16] That is, any injury for which the $100,000 ceiling would have been paid had settlement been reached in January 1978 — such as quadriplegia — will be eligible for $100,000 increased by the rate of consumer price inflation between January 1978 and the date of payment of the damages for that injury. For example, as the rate of inflation in Canada between January 1978 and January 1991 was approximately 136.8 percent, the damages payable for quadriplegia would have been approximately $236,800 (= $100,000 x (1.0 + 136.8%) = $100,000 x (1.0 + 1.368)) in the latter month.

More importantly, perhaps, the Court's ruling in this matter has been interpreted to suggest that the value of an award with respect to any personal injury can be updated to the present by increasing that award by the rate of consumer price inflation between the date of the award and the present. For example, assume that in July 1984 an individual was awarded non-pecuniary damages of $60,000 for loss of a leg. The comparable figure in June of 1991 could be found by increasing $60,000 by the rate of inflation between July 1984 and June 1991. Using the all-Canada index, for example, the rate of inflation between those two months was approximately 36.5 percent. Hence, the June 1991

---

[13] *Reekie v. Messervey* (1989), 36 B.C.L.R. (2d) 316, 59 D.L.R. (4th) 481, 48 C.C.L.T. 217, 17 M.V.R. (2d) 94 (C.A.), rev'd in part, [1990] 1 S.C.R. 219, 43 B.C.L.R. (2d) 145, [1990] 3 W.W.R. 673, 39 C.P.C. (2d) 1).

[14] Kirby J., in *Andrews v. Grand & Toy Alberta Ltd.*, [1974] 5 W.W.R. 675, at p. 683, 54 D.L.R. (3d) 85 (Alta. Q.B.).

[15] Decided in the "trilogy" cases: *Andrews v. Grand & Toy Alberta Ltd.*, [1978] 2 S.C.R. 229, 8 A.R. 182, [1978] 1 W.W.R. 577, 83 D.L.R. (3d) 452, 19 N.R. 50, 3 C.C.L.T. 225; *Arnold v. Teno*, [1978] 2 S.C.R. 287, 83 D.L.R. (3d) 609, 19 N.R. 1, 3 C.C.L.T. 272; and *Thornton v. S. Dist. No. 57 Board of S. Trustees*, [1978] 2 S.C.R. 267, [1978] 1 W.W.R. 607, 83 D.L.R. (3d) 480, (*sub nom. Thornton v. Prince George (Board of Education)*) 19 N.R. 552, 3 C.C.L.T. 257.

[16] *Lindal v. Lindal*, [1981] 2 S.C.R. 629, 34 B.C.L.R. 273, [1982] 1 W.W.R. 443, 129 D.L.R. (3d) 263, 39 N.R. 361, 19 C.C.L.T. 1.

figure which was comparable to the July 1984 figure of $60,000 would be $81,900 (= $60,000 x (1 + 36.5%) = $60,000 x 1.365).

The following Table provides a simple means of updating the value of any award to June 1991, using the annual average consumer price index for Canada. As an example of the use of this Table, assume that an award of $30,000 had been made in 1980. The comparable value in 1990 would be found by multiplying $30,000 by 1.885, (i.e., $56,550).

TABLE 5

INFLATIONARY ADJUSTMENT BETWEEN VARIOUS DATES AND JUNE 1991, CANADA

DATE	CONSUMER PRICE INDEX (1986 = 100)	INFLATIONARY ADJUSTMENT
January 1978	53.5	2.368
1978 (average)	55.9	2.267
1979 (average)	61.0	2.077
1980 (average)	67.2	1.885
1981 (average)	75.5	1.678
1982 (average)	83.7	1.514
1983 (average)	88.5	1.432
1984 (average)	92.4	1.371
1985 (average)	96.0	1.320
1986 (average)	100.0	1.267
1987 (average)	104.4	1.214
1988 (average)	108.6	1.167
1989 (average)	114.0	1.111
1990 (average)	119.5	1.060
June 1991	126.7	1.000

Source: Canada. Statistics Canada, The Consumer Price Index, Cat. No. 62-001, (Ottawa: Statistics Canada) published monthly.

The figures in the second column of Table 5 were obtained by dividing the consumer price index for June 1991, the most recent index available at the time this book was written, by the relevant figures in the first column. For example, the inflationary adjustment for 1985 was derived by dividing 126.7 by 96.0, (1.320 = 126.7/96.0). Thus, the inflationary adjustment at any future time can be obtained by telephoning Statistics Canada, asking for the most recent consumer price index for Canada, and dividing that figure by the relevant figure obtained from Table 5. For example, if the consumer price index provides to be 133.7 in November 1992, the inflationary adjustment between 1985 and November 1992 will be 1.393 (= 133.7/96.0). Similar adjustments can be obtained for individual, major cities; but, as the figures listed in Table 5 are for the Canada-wide index consumer price index, it will be necessary to have Statistics Canada provide the city index for *both* the current year and the relevant year in the past.

APPENDIX: THE "MULTIPLIER"

If two future streams of earnings incorporate identical: discount rates, rates of growth of earnings, mortality assumptions, and initial and retirement ages, their present discounted values will differ in exact proportion to the ratio of their base year losses. For example, assume that the first year's loss is $10,000, the discount rate is 8.15 percent, the growth rate of the loss is 5.5 percent per year, and that the plaintiff is a 52-year-old male who plans to retire on his 57th birthday. Table 6a, below, reveals that the lump-sum value of his loss is $46,309.

TABLE 6a

CALCULATION OF THE MULTIPLIER:
BASE YEAR EARNINGS OF $10,000

AGE	INVESTMENT: BEGINNING OF YEAR	LOSS OF EARNINGS	PROBABILITY OF SURVIVAL	COMPEN-SATION	BALANCE
52	$46,309	$10,000	0.9967	$ 9,967	$36,342
53	39,303	10,500	0.9897	10,392	28,911
54	31,267	11,025	0.9820	10,827	20,440
55	22,106	11,576	0.9735	11,269	10,837
56	11,720	12,155	0.9642	11,720	0

Now, assume that the assumptions concerning the rate of growth of the loss, the duration of the loss, and the probability of survival are left unchanged but the base year loss is reduced by 20 percent, to $8,000. Table 6b indicates that the lump-sum value will also be reduced by 20 percent, to $37,047. ($46,309 x 0.80 = $37,047) It is easily seen from Tables 6a and 6b why this proportionality is obtained. When the loss incurred at age 52 is reduced by 20 percent, each subsequent year's loss, which is only a multiple of the first year's loss, is also reduced by 20 percent. Therefore, the annual amounts required for compensation are reduced by 20 percent and the lump-sum value required to replace the entire stream is reduced accordingly.

This finding allows the following calculation to be made: divide the lump-sum award by the base year loss, (i.e., the loss in the first year). In the case described in Table 6a, for example, divide $46,309 by

$10,000, to obtain 4.63. This figure, which is called the *multiplier*, can now be used to obtain the lump-sum award associated with *any* base year loss, provided that the assumptions concerning the discount rate, growth rates, mortality rates, and age of retirement are left unchanged. This is done simply by multiplying the base year loss by the multiplier. For example, the lump-sum award when the initial year's cost is $8,000 could have been found by multiplying $8,000 by 4.63. The result, $37,040, differs from the result displayed in Table 6b, $37,047, only because the multiplier was "rounded off" from 4.6309.

TABLE 6b

CALCULATION OF THE MULTIPLIER:
BASE YEAR EARNINGS OF $8,000

AGE	INVESTMENT: BEGINNING OF YEAR	LOSS OF EARNINGS	PROBABILITY OF SURVIVAL	COMPEN-SATION	BALANCE
52	$37,047	$8,000	0.9967	$7,974	$29,073
53	31,442	8,400	0.9897	8,313	23,129
54	25,014	8,820	0.9820	8,661	16,353
55	17,686	9,261	0.9735	9,016	8,670
56	9,376	9,724	0.9642	9,376	0

The multiplier is a useful concept because it often happens that the parties do not disagree over the elements which go into the construction of the multiplier — growth rates, life expectancy, period of the loss, and the discount rate — as much as they do over the annual value of the loss. In the determination of the loss of earning capacity, for example, they may agree that the loss is to continue until the plaintiff's 62nd birthday and that the annual earnings loss will grow at 5 percent per year, but disagree as to whether the annual loss is to be $5,000 or $6,000 — perhaps because they disagree as to the allowance which is to be made for negative contingencies. In this case, if the court is given a multiplier, then no matter what annual loss is chosen, the judge will find it easy to calculate the lump-sum value of the award.

2

PERSONAL INJURY — COST OF CARE

Many personal injuries disable the victim in such a way that medical and personal care expenses will be required well into the future. Litigators generally refer to these expenses as *costs of care*. This chapter will be concerned with the valuation of these costs.

The calculation of the lump-sum award for the costs of care is undertaken in a manner which is very similar to that which is used to calculate loss of future earnings. First, the base year annual cost is calculated. Next, a growth rate is applied to this figure in order to determine the manner in which costs will change over the future; and a time period is specified during which the loss is to be incurred. Finally, these factors are combined with assumptions concerning the discount rate and life expectancy to obtain a lump-sum value of the award.

The most important difference between the calculation of loss of earnings capacity and that of costs of care concerns the treatment of the taxes which are levied on investment income. Whereas the courts have ruled that no allowance is to be made for the taxes which are charged on the income which derives from investment of a lump-sum award for loss of earnings; they have ruled that such allowance *is* to be made when the income derives from investment of an award for costs of care. When this allowance is made, the award is said to be "grossed up" for income taxes. The manner in which this "gross up" is calculated will be discussed in Section III of this Chapter.

I. BASE YEAR COSTS

It will be convenient to divide costs of care into three categories, which I will call non-disabled consumption expenditures, disabled consumption expenditures, and medical expenditures. Within each category, further sub-categories will be distinguished.

1. Non-Disabled Consumption Expenditures

This category of costs includes all expenditures which the plaintiff would have made whether or not he or she had been injured. On the basis of the assumption that most individuals will devote all (or most) of their incomes to such expenditures, these expenditures are usually accounted for by compensating the plaintiff for the loss of his or her earnings stream. For example, if a plaintiff was dividing her $20,000 income into $8,000 on food, $2,000 on clothing, $6,000 on shelter, and $4,000 on transportation, she will be just as well compensated if she receives $20,000 to replace her income as if she receives $8,000 for food, $2,000 for clothing, $6,000 for shelter, and $4,000 for transportation. The advantage of using the income-replacement approach instead of the consumption-replacement approach is that it is very much simpler. Whereas it is often a relatively straightforward matter to identify the plaintiff's potential earning stream, it is generally extremely difficult to forecast his or her future expenditure pattern, particularly if one has not first forecast the plaintiff's income stream.

My experience has been that in most cases in which the consumption-replacement approach has been applied, the plaintiff has been undercompensated, for three reasons: (i) because it is easy to leave out some items inadvertently; (ii) because there is a tendency to compensate the plaintiff only for "necessities;" and (iii) because the implicit assumption is made that the costs of consumption expenditures rise only with the increase in the consumer price index, whereas such expenditures normally rise also with increases in the plaintiff's income. Generally, therefore, it is best to divide the plaintiff's pecuniary losses into two distinct categories: loss of earnings capacity and costs of care.

A minor exception occurs when the plaintiff's injuries are so severe that he/she has to be placed in a long-care institution which provides all of the plaintiff's consumption necessities. In such cases, it may be desirable to estimate the portion of the institution's annual fee which represents expenditures on the plaintiff's various consumption needs — food, clothing, personal care, housing, etc. These estimates may then be compared with estimates of the amounts which the plaintiff would have devoted to these categories had he or she not been injured. If the institution's expenditures are less than the expenditures which would have been made by the plaintiff, a claim may be made for the shortfall.

2. Disabled Consumption Expenditures

Many of the normal activities of daily living will be more expensive for the disabled individual than for the non-disabled. For example, an individual whose arm has been amputated may require special kitchen utensils; a paraplegic may wear out certain types of clothes more quickly than a non-disabled individual; the deaf will require special attachments to their telephones, replacements for their door bells, and special home security systems; plaintiffs whose disabilities require that they use a wheelchair will need architectural alterations to their homes and adjustments to their automobiles; and most disabled persons will require assistance with physically demanding household chores, such as gardening and home repairwork.

In each such case, the courts have ruled that the amount which is to be compensated is the difference between the expenditure which the plaintiff would have incurred had the injury not occurred and the expenditure which is now deemed necessary. For example, in the case of the paraplegic who requires a van equipped with hand controls and an entry lift, it is not the total cost of such a van which is to be included in the cost of care, but the difference between the cost of such a van and the cost of the automobile (or other means of transportation) which the plaintiff would have purchased had he/she not been injured.

It is also important to note that, although there remains some uncertainty in the law, it appears that the plaintiff's damages are not to be reduced if a relative or other individual offers to provide assistance at no charge to the plaintiff.[1] For example, if a wife agrees to care for her paraplegic husband, or a parent for her disabled child, compensation may be claimed for the value of that individual's services. In general, I would recommend that these services be valued at the cost of obtaining similar services in the competitive market. To pay less than this amount, on the argument that the individual providing the voluntary service would have earned less in her alternative employment, would place an onus on that individual to continue providing the service indefinitely. On the other hand, to pay more than this amount, on the argument that the individual providing the voluntary service would have earned more in her alternative employment, would lead to the overcompensation of the plaintiff if that individual was later to be replaced by an assistant hired from the competitive market.

The following is a non-exhaustive list of items which might be included under the general heading of "disabled consumption expenditures:"

Category	Examples of Expenditures
Food	— It is not common for the victims of tort actions to require special expenditures on food. However, certain types of ailments may require special diets and individuals such as quadriplegics may be unable to chew or swallow normally.

---

[1] For an excellent discussion of this issue, see K. Cooper-Stephenson and I. Saunders, *Personal Injury Damages in Canada* (Toronto: Carswell, 1981), at 317-20.

Shelter	— Individuals in wheelchairs require widened corridors, lowered counters, handrail access to baths and showers, etc.
	— Individuals with restricted hand, leg, or arm movement, such as those with arthritis or amputation, may require adjustments to their kitchens and stairs.
	— Gardeners, maid services, day care services, painters, repair workers, and other individuals needed to perform those household services which the plaintiff would have undertaken had it not been for the accident.
Furnishings	— Special kitchen appliances may have to be provided for those with restricted hand and arm movement; and for the blind.
	— Computers may be required for those who have difficulty writing, such as amputees and quadriplegics.
	— Cordless telephones are recommended for those with mobility restrictions.
Clothing	— Special clothing for those with amputations.
	— Supplementary clothing allowance for those whose injuries cause clothing to wear out quickly.
Mobility/transportation	— Alterations to vans/automobiles, such as hand controls, entry lifts, and car telephones.
	— Taxis, buses, etc. for those whose disabilities prevent them from driving.
	— Canes, wheelchairs, etc.
Recreation	— Membership in a health club/spa, if it is to replace the activities in which the plaintiff would normally have engaged in order to obtain exercise.
	— Special equipment to allow the plaintiff to engage in their normal recreational acitivities, such as modified skis, golf clubs, boating equipment, etc.
	— Attendants to accompany the disabled person on holiday.
	— Home gym system.

Additional information concerning the cost of "household services" may be found in Chapter 10.

3. Medical Expenditures

In addition to the expenditures listed above, the plaintiff may require certain expenditures simply to maintain his or her health. This category includes expenditures on: medicines, prosthetics, (e.g., artificial limbs), doctors, chiropractors, nurses, orderlies, and any form of hospital or institutional care associated with the plaintiff's injuries.

II. GROWTH OF COSTS

In the application of a rate of growth of expenses, the annual costs of care are often divided into two categories: goods and services on the one hand and costs of personal care workers on the other. The reason for this is that whereas the costs of goods and services can be expected, on average, to increase at the rate of consumer price inflation, the costs of such workers as nurses, orderlies, gardeners, and housekeepers may be expected to increase at the same rate as the economy-wide growth rate of productivity. The latter rate, as suggested in Chapter 1, is currently expected to lie between 0.5 and 1.5 percent per annum over the long-term.

The primary situation in which this distinction between the costs of goods and the costs of workers may not be relevant occurs when the productivity of the care workers can be expected to increase over time. In such a case, the cost per unit of service provided by the worker may remain unchanged even when the cost per hour of such a worker is increasing. For example, assume that allowance has been made for the plaintiff to receive 10 hours of dental work per year at a projected cost of $200 per hour. If a 10 percent increase in fees is matched by a 10 percent reduction in the amount of time required to perform the desired work, the total cost of the dental work will not increase over time. If the set of personal care workers recommended for the plaintiff includes occupations whose fee increases can be expected to be offset by increases in productivity, it would not be appropriate to include "productivity" increases in the estimates of the growth rate of costs of care.

However, it should be noted that many, if not most, care workers recommended in personal injury cases are required for specific periods of time. For example, a severely disabled individual who requires that an orderly be present 24 hours per day cannot "make do" with care for only 20 hours per day when the orderly's productivity increases. Thus, the cost of such individuals increases at the same rate as the rate of increase of wages, *not* at the rate of price inflation.

> Additional information concerning the rate of price inflation may be found in Section I of Chapter 5; and concerning the rate of growth of earnings in Section II of Chapter 5.

III. CALCULATION OF LUMP-SUM DAMAGES

1. Evaluation of Annual Costs of Care

Evaluation of the expenses for costs of care is usually best done by a support agency, such as the Canadian National Institute for the Blind or the Canadian Paraplegic Association, or by a private firm specializing in the provision of home nursing care to the disabled. Also, if extensive renovations are to be made to the plaintiff's residence, it may be worthwhile to contact an architectural firm which specializes in this type of work.

My experience has been that the agencies which are qualified to estimate these costs often are not familiar with the manner in which such costs are to be categorized for legal purposes. For this reason, I would suggest that the following points be clarified when the initial request for a cost estimate is made: first, as both loss of earnings and cost of care are components of the claim for tort damages, the cost of care element need identify only those increases in costs which have resulted from the plaintiff's disability. Therefore, costs which would have been incurred had the plaintiff not been injured must be excluded. For example, if it is felt that a paraplegic will need a van equipped with a wheelchair lift and hand controls, only the lift and controls should be considered to be costs of care if the plaintiff would have purchased a van had she not been injured. Furthermore, when the disability requires, not an additional item of expense, but a more expensive item than would otherwise have been purchased, some effort must be made to separate these two costs. For example, if the plaintiff now requires a hospital bed and mattress costing $2,500 instead of the $1,000 bed that would have been bought if it had not been for the injury, it is only the $1,500 difference between the two which should be identified as a cost of care.

Second, a clear distinction must be drawn between those expenditures which can be expected to be incurred on a recurring basis and those which constitute capital outlays. The latter category will include such items as renovations to the plaintiff's residence, alterations to a motor vehicle, and the purchase of prostheses. Recurring expenses will include purchases of medicine, employment of nursing aides and homemakers, and incremental expenses on clothing and laundry. Also, in order to ensure that capital goods can be replaced as they wear out, it is common to set aside an amount each year as a replacement reserve.

Finally, those who are not financial experts may require some assistance in selecting an appropriate method for calculating the annual allowances for the replacement reserve. For example, assume that the plaintiff requires a $4,500 electric wheelchair which is to be replaced every 5 years. It may be tempting to divide $4,500 by 5 to obtain a replacement allowance of $900 per year. But this approach ignores three factors: (i) between the time of purchase of the wheelchair and the time of its replacement 5 years later, inflation will have increased the cost of the chair substantially. (ii) The procedure which is generally employed to calculate the present value of future costs assumes that payments from the invested sum increase at the rate of inflation. That is, implicitly, it is assumed that if $900 is allocated to the replacement reserve in the first year, $900 increased by the rate of inflation will be allocated in the second year, etc. (iii) The plaintiff will be able to earn interest on the amounts allocated to the replacement reserve.

The formula for calculating the annual replacement reserve allowance under these circumstances is:

$$R = \frac{C(1 + P)^n \left(1 - \dfrac{1 + p}{1 + i}\right)}{(1 + i)^n - (1 + p)^n}$$

where R: annual replacement allowance
C: current cost of the capital expense
P: rate of price inflation
i: nominal rate of interest
n: number of years until replacement is to take place.

For example, if C is $4,500, P is 10 percent, i is 13 percent, and n is 5 years, R is found to be:

$$R = \frac{4,500 \, (1 + .10)^5 \left(1 - \dfrac{1 + .10}{1 + .13}\right)}{(1 + .13)^5 - (1 + .10)^5}$$

$$= \frac{7,247.30 \, (1 - 0.97345)}{1.84244 - 1.61051}$$

$$= 7,247.30 \left(\frac{0.02655}{0.23193}\right)$$

$$= 7,247.30 \, (0.11447)$$

$$= \$829.63$$

That is, 5 years hence, the plaintiff will need to spend $7,247.60 to replace the wheelchair which initially cost $4,500. In order to accumulate that amount, the plaintiff will have to set aside $829.63 at the beginning of the first year, $829.63 increased by 10 percent, or $912.60, at the beginning of the second year, etc., investing each of those amounts at a rate of interest of 13 percent.[2]

2. Duration of Expenditure/Life Expectancy

Occasionally, the costs of care are expected to be incurred over a limited time period. For example, it might be expected that the plaintiff will recover from his/her injuries within five years. Clearly, in these cases, damages are to be calculated over only that specific period.

More commonly, however, it is presumed that the plaintiff will continue to require the same annual costs of care until he or she dies. In this case, the method for allowing for life expectancy is the same as that which was employed in constructing Table 3, Chapter 1; that is, each annual cost is multiplied by the probability that the plaintiff will live to that age in order to obtain the annual amount required for compensation. When this approach is employed, it is incorrect to "cut off" the period of loss at any arbitrary age. Rather, allowance is made for the probability that the plaintiff will die before, say, age 100, by the fact that the probabilities of survival begin to approach zero as age 100 is approached. Thus, in calculating the present value of an ongoing stream of costs, it is appropriate to continue that stream to the oldest age allowed for in the life tables. In general, this is approximately age 100.

If the plaintiff's injuries have reduced his or her life expectancy, it is the reduced probability of survival figures which are to be used in the calculation of the future costs of care.

> Additional information concerning life expectancy may be found in Chapter 7.

3. Sample Calculation — Without Income Tax "Gross Up"

Assume that the 52-year-old engineer, whose loss of income was discussed in Chapter 1, will require $2,000 worth of medicine for each of the next 5 years. (An example of a situation in which the loss continues until death will not be given, simply because such an example would require too much space.) In Table 7a it is shown that if the discount rate is 8.15 percent and the rate of growth of the costs of care is 5 percent, the present value of this stream of costs is $9,260.

---

[2] The $829.63 figure is 92 percent as large as the $900 figure which would have been obtained by the "rule of thumb" method of dividing $4,500 by 5 (years). This result would not have been altered significantly had the interest rate been raised to 15 per cent. In that case, the ratio of the "correct" value to the "rule of thumb" value would be (786.11 ÷ 800 = 0.87). Similarly, if n is raised to 10 there is only a small reduction in this ratio — to (386.94 ÷ 450 =) 0.86 when i is 13 percent and to (349.54 ÷ 450 =) 0.78 when i is 15 percent.

TABLE 7a

CALCULATION OF THE COST OF FUTURE CARE AWARD

AGE	INVESTMENT: BEGINNING OF YEAR	COST OF CARE	PROBABILITY OF SURVIVAL	COMPEN-SATION	BALANCE
52	$9,260	$2,000	0.9967	$1,993	$7,268
53	7,860	2,100	0.9897	2,078	5,782
54	6,253	2,205	0.9820	2,165	4,088
55	4,421	2,315	0.9735	2,254	2,167
56	2,344	2,431	0.9642	2,344	0

4. The Income Tax "Gross Up"

(a) Method of calculation

Income taxes affect the lump-sum value of an award by reducing the after-tax value of the interest which is earned when the award is invested. For example, assume that one wished to provide $11,000 to the plaintiff one year from today. If the interest rate was 10 percent and there were no taxes on interest income, this would require that $10,000 be invested today. ($10,000 + (0.10 x $10,000) = $11,000.) Assume, however, that the plaintiff was earning sufficient income from other sources and that any interest income he/she earned would be taxed at 40 percent. The effect of this tax would be to reduce the net (after-tax) interest rate to 6 percent. That is, if $10,000 were invested at 10 percent, $400 of the $1,000 interest which that investment would generate would be taxed away and the plaintiff would be left with a net return of only $600. Thus, to estimate the amount of money which would have to be invested today in order to produce $11,000 one year from now, one would employ an effective interest rate of 6 percent. When this is done, it is found that it would be necessary to invest $10,377.36 today in order to generate $11,000, after taxes, one year from now. ($10,377.36 + (0.06 x $10,377.36) = $11,000.) *The $377.36 difference between the case in which taxes were ignored and that in which they were included is what is often called the "income tax gross up."* (I have highlighted this sentence as I know that most practitioners are under the mistaken impression that the calculation of the income tax gross up is conceptually so complex that lawyers could not be expected to understand it!)

To check that this method finds the correct answer, imagine that $10,377.36 was invested at 10 percent and that 40 percent of the resulting interest was removed as taxes. The investment would generate interest of $1,037.736, (i.e., 10 percent of $10,377.36). Of this, 40 percent, or $415.09, would be taxed away, leaving the investor with a net interest income of $622.64 (= 0.6 x $1,037.736). Adding this income to the initial amount invested, $10,377.36, it is found that the investor's capital amount will have grown to $11,000 (= $10,377.36 + $622.64).

It is seen, therefore, that the so-called "income tax gross-up" is simply the difference between the value of the lump-sum award which is required when no taxes are deducted from investment income and the lump-sum award which is required when investment income is taxed. Thus, the value of the "grossed up" award can be *estimated*[3] simply by employing an estimate of the after-tax interest rate instead of the pre-tax interest rate. For example, assume that one wished to determine the value of the award which would be necessary to provide the stream of costs of care described in Table 7a, above, inclusive of an allowance for the effects of income taxes. This could be done by reproducing Table 7a exactly, but substituting an estimate of the relevant after-tax interest rate for the one which was used there. For example, if the plaintiff described there was in the 30 percent tax bracket, the effective, after-tax rate of interest would be $(100 - 30 =)$ 70 percent of the before-tax rate of 8.15 percent. That is, the relevant discount rate would become $(0.70 \times 8.15 =)$ 5.705 percent. If this interest rate is used instead of 8.15 percent, Table 7a becomes Table 7b, below.

It will be noticed that, when an income tax rate of 30 percent was taken into account, it was necessary to increase the award in this case from $9,260 to $9,682, an increase of 4.56 percent. This percentage increase is normally referred to as the income tax "gross up." This gross up will be higher, the greater is the number of years over which the costs are to be incurred and the greater is the average income tax rate.

---

[3] For two reasons, the technique which is employed to derive Table 7b *cannot* be used to obtain a precise calculation of the income tax "gross up." First, because the amount of interest which is earned on the invested sum varies from year to year, the income tax rate will also vary from year to year. Hence, in a complete calculation, it is necessary to allow for this variation. The assumption of a single, average rate suffices only to generate *estimates* of the gross up.

Second, because the percentage value of the "gross up" varies depending upon the number of years into the future that the loss is forecast to continue, it is not technically correct to weight each year's loss by the probability that the plaintiff would have lived to that year and then to discount the resulting series back to the present. Rather, the correct procedure calculates the present value of the stream of costs of care for each possible number of years that the plaintiff might live and then weights each of those possible present values by the probability that the plaintiff will live exactly that number of years. It should be noted that most "experts" do not recognize that this adjustment has to be made and, hence, produce estimates of the gross up which are in error. (The technique used to obtain Table 7b overstates the gross up.)

TABLE 7b

CALCULATION OF THE COST OF CARE AWARD
INCLUSIVE OF TAX "GROSS UP"

AGE	INVESTMENT: BEGINNING OF YEAR	COST OF CARE	PROBABILITY OF SURVIVAL	COMPEN- SATION	BALANCE
52	$9,682	$2,000	0.9967	$1,993	$7,689
53	8,128	2,100	0.9897	2,078	6,050
54	6,395	2,205	0.9820	2,165	4,230
55	4,471	2,315	0.9735	2,254	2,217
56	2,344	2,431	0.9642	2,344	0

(b) Determination of the income tax rate

The tax "gross up" will be higher the higher is the assumed rate of taxes upon investment income. Careful attention must be paid to the assumptions which are made concerning the following two factors:

(i) The rate of increase of tax credits:

Under current rules, the values of the tax credits which taxpayers are allowed to claim are increased each year by the rate of consumer price inflation since the previous year *minus* three percent. For example, if the tax credit in question had been $1,000 in the first year and if inflation between year 1 and year 2 had been 7 percent, the tax credit in year 2 would be calculated by adding 4 percent (7 percent minus 3 percent) to $1,000; that is, it would become $1,040. In calculating changes in the tax system over the future, most financial experts assume that tax credits will continue to grow at inflation minus 3 percent over the long run. Although this assumption is plausible, it should be noted that it is subject to question. In particular, if tax credits continue to grow at a rate which is 3 percent less than the rate of inflation, over the lifetimes of most taxpayers the "real" (purchasing power) value of tax credits will be reduced by approximately 75 percent.[4] Thus, if it is felt that taxpayers will not accept such an erosion of the value of their tax credits, it may be argued that, for long-term forecasts, a different assumption

---

[4] If the rate of inflation averages 7 percent in the long run, then the purchasing power of a tax credit will be reduced to 27.8 percent of its initial value by the time that a 20-year-old reaches age 65.

should be made concerning the adjustment of these credits. One might, for example, assume that credits would be adjusted by the rate of inflation minus *two* percent.

(ii) Base income:

The tax rate which the plaintiff will have to pay on income derived from investment of the lump-sum award for cost of care will be higher, the greater is the income which the plaintiff derives from other sources. Some obvious such sources are employment income, welfare and disability payments, and pension income. A less obvious source, and one which many financial experts fail to take into account when calculating the income tax gross up, is the income which the plaintiff will receive from investment of the award for loss of earning capacity. Accordingly, when evaluating the reports of financial experts, it is important to check to determine whether this factor has been considered. In serious injury cases, its omission will reduce the tax gross up dramatically.

3

FATAL ACCIDENT CLAIMS

The calculation of damages in a fatal accident action is similar to that in a personal injury action in the sense that the first step in both is to calculate the streams of income and household services which the injured party (in this case, the deceased) would have generated had it not been for the accident. Also, in both, the stream of losses suffered by the plaintiff (in this case, the deceased's dependants) is discounted back to the present.

The two cases differ in a number of significant ways, however. First, whereas the injured party is compensated for his or her loss of *pre-tax* earnings, the plaintiffs in a fatal accident action are compensated only for their dependency upon the deceased's *after-tax* earnings. Second, the dependants may not claim for the full value of the deceased's after-tax earnings, but only for that percentage — the *dependency rate* — which will be necessary to allow them to enjoy the same standard of living which they would have enjoyed had the deceased lived. Third, whereas no allowance is made for the income tax gross up in the calculation of loss of earnings capacity, such an allowance *is* made for loss of dependency upon the deceased's earnings. Fourth, in addition to the claims which may be made in a personal injury case, the dependants in a fatal accident action may also claim for loss of "care and guidance" and for "loss of estate". Finally, a number of recent decisions have indicated that the dependency of the deceased's spouse is to be reduced both by the probability that the survivor and the deceased would have divorced had the deceased not been killed and by the probability that the survivor will now remarry someone whose income will equal or exceed that of the deceased, thereby bringing the dependency to an end.

The chapter is organized as follows: Section I discusses the calculation of the deceased's stream of earnings, household services, and pension income. Section II identifies a method for determining the survivors' dependency rates. Section III discusses the manner in which the lump-sum value of the damages are to be calculated. This Section includes discussions of the income tax "gross up" and the remarriage and divorce contingencies. Section IV introduces the claims for loss of estate and loss of care and guidance. Section V considers the special case in which both of a minor's parents are killed. Finally, Section VI reviews the arguments that a claim can be made under *Lord Campbell's Act* for loss of a child.

I. EARNINGS, PENSIONS, AND HOUSEHOLD SERVICES

1. Earnings Stream

The method for projecting the stream of income which the deceased would have earned is virtually identical to that which is employed when projecting the stream of income which a plaintiff would have earned in a personal injury action. Hence, rather than repeating that discussion here, the reader is referred to Section I.1 of Chapter 1.

The only difference between the two cases arises from the treatment of income taxes. Whereas the injured plaintiff is compensated for loss of income *before* deduction of income taxes, the dependants in a fatal accident action are compensated for loss of dependency upon the deceased's *after-tax* income. Hence, once the deceased's stream of gross earnings has been calculated, a deduction for income taxes must be made.

Additional information concerning foregone income may be found in Chapters 4, 5, 6, and 7.

2. Pensions

In addition to the issues concerning pension evaluation which were discussed in Sections I.1(c) and II of Chapter 1, an additional issue arises in fatal accident actions. When the dependants have made a claim for loss of support out of a pension which was to be paid to the deceased, the question arises as to whether any payments which that pension makes to the survivors should be deducted from their claim, or whether those payments should be treated as a collateral benefit.

For example, assume that the deceased would have received a monthly pension of $2,000 from his employer's pension fund. If it is found that the wife would have benefitted from 70 percent of this pension, i.e., that her "dependency rate" — see Section III, below — was 70 percent, she would have a claim for a loss of $1,400 per month. Assume, however, that the employer's pension fund has agreed to pay the widow a survivor's pension of $1,200 per month. Should the widow's claim be reduced by that $1,200 — to $200 — or should she be allowed to claim for the full $1,400? To my knowledge, no defintive answer to this question has yet been provided by the Canadian courts. Nevertheless, it may be useful to present two arguments for treating the survivor's pension as a collateral benefit. The first of these arguments relates primarily to private pension plans, whereas the second relates specifically to the Canada/Quebec Pension Plan.

(a) Private pensions

Most private pensions provide a lower monthly benefit to beneficiaries who choose a joint survivor scheme than to those who select a single life option. That is, when the survivor is eligible for a payment from the spouse's pension plan — the joint survivor scheme — the amount payable to the spouse while he or she is alive is normally less than the amount which would have been payable had a plan been selected which paid pension benefits only as long as he or she lived — the single life scheme. For example, in the situation described above, the widow was eligible for 60 percent of her husband's $2,000 pension if he died. Had her husband opted instead for a plan in which he received pension benefits only as long as he was alive, he would have been eligible for a larger pension while he was alive, say $2,300 per month. It can be argued that the difference between the amount receivable under the single life scheme and that receivable under the joint survivor scheme — in this case, $300 per month — is analogous to a premium paid under a life insurance policy. The primary beneficiary of the pension plan "pays" $300 per month — in the form of reduced pension benefits — in order to obtain an agreement by the pension fund to pay his or her survivor an annuity should the primary beneficiary die. In this light, the pension which is received by the survivor may be considered to be a life annuity which has been purchased by the deceased. As such, it should be treated as a collateral benefit.

(b) Canada/Quebec Pension Plan

Because the C/QPP has not been self-financing, it is difficult to argue that the payments made to widows and widowers come at the expense of the payments made to the primary beneficiaries. On the other hand, because there has been little or no correlation between payments into the scheme and disbursements — particularly disbursements to survivors — it may be argued that widow and widower benefits under the C/QPP have been nothing more than social security payments, like welfare or old age security. In this sense, these payments are, again, correctly treated as collateral benefits.

3. Household Services

(a) Valuation of services

The most convincing method for determining the number of hours that the deceased would have spent helping around the household is to have the surviving spouse prepare a time budget in which he or she keeps a day-by-day record of the situations in which the deceased would have provided such assistance. An alternative approach is to rely on statistical studies which have been conducted to determine these values for the "average" family. What these studies show is that the average male spends 7-11 hours per week performing household chores. Among employed women, this number of hours averages approximately 18-20 if they have no young children and 30 if they do have young children. Finally, among women who are not employed in the labour market, the average number of hours spent in housework is 35-40 if they have no young children and 40-50 if they do have young children.

The average cost of each hour of cleaning and cooking can generally be determined by obtaining the rates charged by commercial housekeeping services. The costs of childcare can be obtained from daycare centres or from nanny services. The costs of general repairs can be obtained from firms which provide general maintenance and repair services.

(b) Some legal issues

Two important legal issues which arise with respect to claims for loss of household services are: (i) Will the claim fail if the survivors do not intend to hire third parties to replace the deceased's services? (ii) Does the actual expenditure pattern of the survivors offer compelling evidence concerning the level of services which they wish to replace? The answers to both questions appear to be "no." With respect to the first question, it is generally held that the plaintiffs have suffered a loss if they are required to perform services which had previously been performed by a third party. For example, even though a widow may mow the lawn herself, rather than hire someone to replace her husband in that job, she can still claim to have suffered a loss, a loss upon which a pecuniary value can be placed.

With respect to the second question, it must be recognized that, with the death of a family member, family income will be reduced. Hence, that the survivors have not replaced a service which (they claim) was previously performed by the deceased does not necessarily provide any information concerning the value of that individual's services. It could well be that the survivors simply do not have enough income to replace these services. Indeed, it has been my experience that the actual expenditure by the survivors provides so little information concerning the value of the deceased's services that it is rarely worth collecting.

Additional information concerning household services may be found in Chapter 10.

II. THE DEPENDENCY

Once the values of the deceased's income and household services have been calculated, it becomes necessary to estimate the portions of those values which would have benefitted the dependants — and, therefore, which may be claimed by them as damages. The determination of these portions normally proceeds in two steps. In the first, an estimate is made of the percentage of the family's income which the survivors will require in order to leave them as well off as if the deceased had lived. In the second, it must be determined whether this percentage is to be applied to the deceased's after-tax income or whether it is to be applied to the family's total income. In this section, these questions will be discussed, first, with respect to wage and pension income and, second, with respect to household services.

1. Dependency on Wage and Pension Income

(a) Dependency rate

It is tempting to presume that in a family of two individuals, 50 percent of family income is spent on each individual; that in a family of three individuals, 33 percent of family income is spent on each; etc. Furthermore, following from this presumption, it would be logical to conclude that if one member of a two-person household was killed, the survivor would require 50 percent of family income in order to maintain his or her standard of living; that in a three member family, the survivors would each require 33 percent of family income; etc. A moment's reflection indicates, however, that these simple presumptions are wrong. The reasons for this are (i) that many expenditures benefit all members of the family equally and (ii) that some items are less expensive per person, the greater is the number of individuals who are consuming those items.

A simple example of the former category is housing. Generally speaking, the survivors will require the same stock of housing as would have been required had the deceased been alive. In order for her standard of living to be maintained, a widow will have to live in the same house, with the same furniture, as she had lived in with her husband. In this case, the dependency rate upon housing expenditures is 100 percent. To see how this factor might affect the survivor's total dependency upon the deceased's income, consider the following simple example. Assume that a married couple had been spending 30 percent of their disposable income on housing and 70 percent on other items. Assume also that the widow's dependency upon housing is 100 percent and on the other items is 50 percent. Her total dependency upon her husband's income will be 65 percent — (0.50 x 70%) + (1.0 x 30%) — and not 50 percent as the naive approach might suggest.

The second reason why the dependency rate on income might be greater than is suggested by the naive approach is that there are "economies of scale" in consumption — costs per person are lower, the greater is the number of individuals. A simple example of this category of goods is food. It is commonly found, for example, that if one person is removed from a two person family, food expenditures per person will rise by 10 to 15 percent. Thus, if food expenditures had previously been divided evenly between the spouses, in order to maintain his/her standard of living, the survivor will need between 55 and 57.5 percent as much as the couple required together.

In Chapter 11 of this book, a number of calculations of dependency rates are presented, using average data for Canadian families. What these data indicate is that, for most income classes, the dependency of one spouse, regardless of whether it was the wife or the husband, on the other is within 1 percent of 70 percent. That is, in most cases, one can be confident that the survivor's dependency upon the deceased's after-tax income will approximate 70 percent. Furthermore, the data also suggest that each child, up to four children, adds approximately 4 percent to the survivors' total dependency rate. For example, a family of one adult and two children will have a dependency rate of 78 percent (= 70 + 4 + 4).[1]

The two most important exceptions to these findings come (i) when the deceased had been able to supply the family with perquisites from

---

[1] It is important to recognize that when it is said that each spouse's dependency is 70 percent, that implies that each spouse was spending 30 percent of his or her income on him or herself, 30 percent on his or her spouse, and 40 percent on items which benefited both spouses equally. This further implies that the sum of the benefits to the two spouses exceeds the sum of their (after-tax) incomes. For example, assume that the wife and husband each earned $30,000 after taxes. If the dependency rate was 70 percent, then each spouse spent $9,000 on him or herself, $9,000 on the other spouse, and $12,000 on items which benefited both of them equally. Thus, the wife, for example, benefitted from the $9,000 she spent on herself, the $9,000 her husband spent on her, the $12,000 she spent on joint purchases, *and* the $12,000 her husband spent on joint purchases, for a total of $42,000. Similarly, her husband also benefited by $42,000. As stated above, there are two reasons that this multiplication of benefits was possible. First, many of the purchases made by one spouse, such as those on housing, benefit the other equally; and, second, there are often "economies of scale" from living together, such as in the purchase of food.

In my view, the court in *McNichol v. Mardell* (1984), 32 Alta. L.R. (2d) 82, [1984] 5 W.W.R. 177 (C.A.), leave to appeal to S.C.C. dismissed (S.C.C.), did not recognize the latter point as, once they had determined the surviving husband's loss of dependency upon his wife's income, they then added a further allowance for loss of opportunity to purchase jointly consumed commodities (particularly housing) and to obtain economies of scale (particularly in vacations). (See page 92 of the Court of Appeal decision.)

his or her employment; and (ii) when the death of one spouse had increased the childcare costs of the surviving spouse.

(i) Perquisites:

If the family's costs of living had been reduced because the deceased had been receiving goods and services for free, or at a reduced price from his or her employer, the family's cost of living will increase with the death of that individual. In such circumstances, the dependency may be much higher than indicated above. (In a recent case in which I provided evidence, the family of a baker had a dependency of almost 100 percent because their cost of food had risen so dramatically.)

(ii) Childcare:

If the family had been purchasing daycare before the accident, and will still require daycare after the accident, the dependency will be higher than if the family did not require daycare. The reason for this is that daycare expenses often constitute a significant percentage of family expenditures. If these expenditures do not change with the death of one spouse, the percentage of pre-accident income which will be required to maintain the standard of living will be much higher than if these expenditures had not been required. (Note: if the children had previously been cared for by the deceased spouse, the surviving spouse's claim for the cost of replacing the deceased's childcare services will be included in the claim for loss of household services, not in the claim for loss of dependency upon the deceased's income. Hence, the dependency rate upon lost income will not be affected in such a case.)

> Additional information concerning the dependency rate may be found in Chapter 11.

(b) Cross-Dependency vs. Sole Dependency

The goal of the preceding section was to determine the dependency rate as a percentage of *family* income. Thus, when the deceased was the family's sole source of income, the dependancies calculated there can be applied directly to the deceased's income with no alterations. However, an additional complication is introduced if the deceased was not the only contributor to family income. For example, assume that in a two-person family the husband was earning $30,000 per year, after taxes, and the wife $20,000 per year. Assume also that the wife's dependency on family income is found to be 70 percent. The court must decide whether the loss to the wife, if her husband should die, is to be based upon the *sole dependency* method, in which she receives 70 percent of *his* income

$$0.70 \times \$30,000 = \$21,000,$$

or whether it is to be calculated on the *cross-dependency* method, in which she would receive 70 percent of the *family's* income *net* of her earnings

$$0.70 \times (\$50,000) - \$20,000 = \$15,000.$$

It is important that we be extremely clear as to the differences between these two approaches. A simple way of identifying this difference is to rewrite the cross-dependency equation in a form which makes it equivalent to that used in the sole dependency method. In doing this, it is first necessary to recognize that the family income figure, here $50,000, can be decomposed into the sum of the wife's and husband's incomes, that is, into ($30,000 + $20,000). Thus, the equation for the wife's dependency in the cross-dependency approach may be written

$$0.70 \times (\$30,000 + \$20,000) - \$20,000 = \$15,000$$

Furthermore, we now see that, with rearrangement, this can be represented as

$$(0.70 \times \$30,000) + (0.70 \times \$20,000 - \$20,000) = \$15,000$$

or as

$$(0.70 \times \$30,000) - (0.30 \times \$20,000) = \$15,000$$

That is, with this rearrangement, it is now seen that the difference between the sole dependency approach and the cross-dependency approach is that in the latter, the element (0.30 x $20,000), which is the portion of the wife's income which had previously been devoted to the husband, is deducted from the survivor's loss of dependency. In short, whereas the sole dependency approach "ignores" that portion of the wife's income which would otherwise have been spent on her husband, the cross-dependency approach effectively assumes that the survivor has been made "better off" because funds which she previously spent on her husband can now be spent on herself. What I wish to consider are the circumstances in which it could be argued that one of these approaches is superior to the other.

First, the argument for use of the cross-dependency approach proceeds as follows: Assume that, while the husband was alive, those expenditures which would continue after his death derived in equal proportion from his income and his wife's. That is, as these expenditures constitute the dependency, assume that 70 percent of the husband's $30,000 and 70 percent of the wife's $20,000 were spent on items which benefitted either the family as a whole or the wife alone. Conversely, this implies that 30 percent of each spouse's income would have been devoted to expenditures which arose only because of the presence of the husband.

Under this assumption, the argument that the damages to the widow are equal to her dependency on family income *net* of her own earnings is made as follows: when her husband was alive, the wife received benefits of (0.70 x $20,000 =) $14,000 from her own income plus (0.70 x $30,000 =) $21,000 from that of her husband. In addition, she contributed (0.30 x $20,000 =) $6,000 to her husband's upkeep. Now that her husband has died, however, she no longer has to give up the latter amount. In short, she is "better off" by $6,000. Therefore, although she has lost the $21,000 her husband had contributed to her and to the general family upkeep before his death, that loss is partially offset by her $6,000 gain and her net loss amounts to only $15,000.

On the other hand, the argument that the sole survivor approach — in which the widow receives an award equal to her dependency on her husband's income — should be applied proceeds as follows: first, from his income, the husband had been providing (0.70 x $30,000 =) $21,000 worth of benefits to the wife, and these are now lost. Second, although the wife had previously been providing (0.30 x $20,000 =) $6,000 worth of benefits to her husband, it is not correct to say that she is "better off" by $6,000 when she is prevented (by his death) from spending that money on him. If it is assumed that the wife was rational and that she was not under some external constraint to remain in the marriage, then it must be assumed that she had decided that marriage provided her with greater pleasure than any other option. From this it may further be concluded that her "gift" of $6,000 to her husband also was voluntary and that that use of her money gave her greater pleasure than any other use available to her. Thus, when the death of her husband "freed" her to spend the $6,000 on herself, she was not made better off. She had previously chosen to spend that money on her husband rather than herself. Therefore, she must have obtained greater pleasure from the former course than the latter. The "freeing" of the $6,000 forces her to purchase something — goods and services for herself — which she values less than the items she was purchasing before — goods and services for her husband.

A less emotion-laden example might help to explain this point. Assume that individual A was about to spend $10,000 on a new car. The tortious intervention of individual B, however, has acted to block this purchase. Can B now claim that his intervention has left A better off by $10,000 because A now has $10,000 she would not have had otherwise? The answer is "no." Although A now has the $10,000; she has been deprived of a car on which she had placed a value of at least $10,000. Instead of being better off, she is actually worse off by the difference between the value of the car and the value of the "next best" set of goods and services which she can now purchase. Similarly, the wife who was previously devoting some of her income to her husband, is not better off when she is prevented from spending that money by the tortious action of some third party — rather, like the individual deprived of her car, she is worse off.

Unfortunately, it is not possible to provide an unequivocal answer to the question of whether the dependency should be calculated according to the sole dependency or the cross-dependency approach. Nevertheless, what I propose to do is, first, to consider the arguments for and against each approach and, then, to conclude by pointing out the situations in which one might be preferred to the other.

Sole dependency:

There are two arguments for using the sole dependency approach. The first of these is simply the observation that most couples marry for love; that is, that it is not unreasonable to assume that each spouse devotes part of his or her income to expenditures which benefit the other spouse because he or she obtains pleasure from such expenditures — as the sole dependency method assumes. As an extreme example, imagine a family in which the husband is the sole income earner and in which 30 percent of family income is devoted to expenditures which benefit the wife alone. According to the sole dependency approach, the husband makes these expenditures because he is concerned for his wife's welfare — *not* because he is somehow "forced" to. Therefore, if his wife was to die, he would not consider himself to be better off by the saving in those expenditures.

Second, use of the sole dependency approach avoids a *reductio ad absurdum* which would otherwise follow from a slavish use of the cross-dependency approach; namely, that when the deceased's income is lower than is the survivor's, the cross-dependency approach often produces the result that the survivor is "better off" now that his or her spouse is dead. For example, assume that the dependency rate is 70 percent and that, after taxes, the wife had been earning $20,000 per year and the husband $50,000. According to the cross-dependency approach, if the wife has died, the husband has lost the $(0.70 \times \$20,000 =)$ $14,000 contribution which his wife was making to joint living expenditures but has gained the $(0.30 \times \$50,000 =)$ $15,000 contribution which he had been making to her personal expenditures. Thus, he is "better off" by $1,000 now that she is dead. (That is, $(\$50,000 - (0.70 \times (\$20,000 + \$50,000)) = \$1,000$.) The sole survivor approach, on the other hand, would have found that the husband had lost $(0.70 \times \$20,000) = \$14,000$.

Cross-dependency:

Consider a case in which husband and wife had each contributed $25,000 to family income. Assuming a dependency of 70 percent, the wife may be considered to have devoted $17,500 of her earnings to joint, family expenditures and to herself, and $7,500 of her earnings to her husband. According to the sole dependency approach, the wife made this $7,500 expenditure strictly in return for "love and affection". Therefore, if her husband dies, she has not gained $7,500 worth of goods, she has merely substituted those goods for the love of her husband, when she would have preferred the latter. The theoretical weakness of this argument is that the couple may not have married for reasons of love, but for reasons of financial gain. From a purely financial perspective, the marriage described here has cost the wife $7,500. In return, however, she will have received the benefit of the expenditures her husband will have made on her — plausibly, $7,500 in this example — and will have benefitted from the cost reductions which are obtained when two people live together.

If the latter view of marriage is accepted by the courts, the appropriate method of calculating the plaintiff's loss will be to use the cross-dependency approach — i.e., to deduct her after-tax income from her dependency out of total family income, after taxes. At the other extreme, if the courts accept that people marry primarily for love, the appropriate technique for calculating the plaintiff's loss will be to employ the sole dependency approach — i.e., to evaluate her dependency out of her husband's after-tax income alone. That is, her own income should be ignored. Selection of an intermediate value of the plaintiff's loss would imply that the courts had accepted the view that couples married for both love and money.[2]

---

[2] In order to maintain an objective stance, I have given equal weight to the hypotheses that couples marry for reasons of love and affection and that they marry for financial reasons. My subjective view is that most couples marry for reasons of "love" (as I have used the latter term). I do not believe that, when they take their spouses out to dinner, most individuals do so because they expect their spouses to take them out to dinner, or to purchase some other set of goods or services, in return. Nor do they think to themselves, when they see that their spouses have spent $100 on clothes: "if he/she had not spent that money, I could have spent it on something for myself". Rather, they spend money on their spouses because they derive pleasure from making their spouses happy. Indeed, I would go so far as to argue that most happily married individuals derive as much pleasure from money spent on their spouses as they do from money spent on themselves. Thus, to divert those expenditures from their spouses to themselves, by "removing" their spouses, does not make them better off.

2. Dependency on Household Services

(a) Dependency rate

It is generally assumed that the survivors will require 100 percent of the value of the deceased's household services. The reason for this is that the consumption of household services by one member of the family does not diminish the consumption by any other member. All members benefit equally from each such service. Thus, when one member of the family is removed, the amount of services required by the remaining members is not diminished. For example, the amount of benefit which any member of the family derives from having the lawn mowed or the living room painted is not affected by the number of other family members living in the house. When one family member is removed from the household, the number of household services which are required in order to maintain the standard of living of the remaining family members is not reduced. If the deceased had mowed the lawn once a week, the survivors' standard of living will only be maintained if the lawn continues to be mowed once a week.

Only when some service performed by the deceased benefitted the deceased alone, will the survivors' dependency be less than 100 percent. An example of such a service might be repairs which the deceased made to his or her own car; or ironing of his or her own clothes. Where instances such as these — which prove to be relatively uncommon — occur, the dependency rate will have to be reduced by the amount of time devoted to activities which benefitted the deceased alone.

(b) "Income" base

Assume that the survivor had been providing some service specifically for the deceased such as ironing clothes or repairing vehicles. It may be argued that the survivor has been made "better off" because he or she will not have to continue to perform these services. This argument is analogous to the argument made above, that the survivor is "better off" by that portion of his or her income which had previously been devoted to expenditures benefitting the deceased, and are now available to the survivor.

> Additional information concerning household services may be found in Chapter 10.

III. CALCULATION OF LUMP-SUM DAMAGES

Once the survivors' stream of losses has been estimated, the procedure for calculating the present discounted value, or lump-sum value, of that stream is very similar to that which was described in Section IV of Chapter 1; and the procedure for calculating the income tax gross up is very similar to that which was described in Section III.3 of Chapter 2. Hence, these analyses will not be repeated here. Rather, this Section will concentrate upon those areas in which the calculation of lump-sum damages in fatal accident actions differ from those in personal injury actions. Three such areas will be considered: the influence of joint life expectancy, divorce, and remarriage; duration of the childrens' periods of dependency; and the effect on the income tax gross up of the division of the award among the dependants.

1. Life Expectancy, Divorce, and Remarriage

The surviving spouse's dependency upon the deceased may come to an end for any one of four reasons. First, as in a personal injury action, the plaintiff/survivor may die. Second, had the accident not occurred, the deceased might yet have died before the plaintiff. Third, had the accident not occurred, the deceased and the plaintiff might have divorced. Finally, now that the accident has occurred, it is possible that the plaintiff might marry someone who will be able to provide the same economic advantages as had the deceased.

Each of these probabilities is taken into account in a manner which is similar to that which was employed to take mortality into account with respect to personal injury actions (see Section IV. 2.a in Chapter 1). That is, the probability that the dependency would have continued (will continue) to each time period is calculated and that probability is multiplied by the loss in that period in order to obtain the amount which will be required for compensation. Of the four factors which might bring a dependency to an end, the one which will usually have the greatest effect upon the projected loss is the probability of remarriage, especially if the surviving spouse is a young male.

Table 8 is offered here as an example of the relative effects of the four probabilities. In this Table, it is assumed that the deceased and her husband were each 30-years-old and that they would have experienced the average probabilities of Canadians of their age of dying, divorcing, and, for the survivor, remarrying. The first column reports the probability of survival of the deceased alone, had the accident not happened, from age 30 to each of ages 30 to 40. Also, at the bottom of that column, the average life expectancy of a 30-year-old woman — 50.88 years — is reported. The figure of 50.88 indicates that she would, on average, have lived to age 80.88, i.e., 50.88 years beyond age 30. The second column reports the *joint* probability of the husband and wife living to each year. It is seen in this column that the average number of years that they could have both expected to live is 40.47,

10 less than the wife's life expectancy alone. The third column reports the probabilities that both spouses would have been alive *and* still married to one another; while the final column reports the probabilities that both spouses would have been alive and married to one another *and* that the survivor, the husband, will *not* have remarried. Although the inclusion of divorce probabilities reduces the average duration of the dependency by 9 years (relative to the joint life expectancy), this is relatively minor compared to the effect of including the probability of remarriage, which reduces the period of dependency by 24 years.

TABLE 8

THE EFFECTS OF LIFE EXPECTANCY, DIVORCE, AND REMARRIAGE ON THE AVERAGE DURATION OF DEPENDENCY[3]

AGE	SINGLE LIFE	JOINT LIFE	JOINT LIFE AND DIVORCE	JOINT LIFE, DIVORCE, AND REMARRIAGE
30	0.9997	0.9991	0.9899	0.9240
31	0.9992	0.9973	0.9697	0.7733
32	0.9987	0.9954	0.9498	0.6416
33	0.9981	0.9934	0.9302	0.5420
34	0.9974	0.9914	0.9115	0.4583
35	0.9968	0.9893	0.8936	0.3917
36	0.9961	0.9871	0.8764	0.3418
37	0.9953	0.9848	0.8597	0.2973
38	0.9944	0.9824	0.8440	0.2619
39	0.9935	0.9797	0.8286	0.2305
40	0.9924	0.9768	0.8131	0.2007
Expected duration of dependency (years)	50.88	40.47	31.09	7.04

When using divorce and remarriage probabilities to reduce the survivor's award, it is usually assumed that if the couple had divorced, the survivor would have received no matrimonial support from the deceased;

---

[3] The divorce and remarriage probabilities used to construct this Table were drawn from Statistics Canada's publication: *Marriage, Divorce, and Mortality: 1984-1986.* The values shown are approximations only.

and that if the couple had remarried, the survivor's new spouse will contribute as much to the family as had the deceased. If either of these assumptions can be shown to be incorrect, it may be inappropriate to apply average divorce and remarriage rates to the couple in question. Equally, if it can be shown that the couple was more, or less, likely to divorce than the average, or that the survivor is more, or less, likely to remarry than the average, allowance should be made for these possibilities. It should be noted, however, that most objective information concerning the individuals in question — such as information concerning education, income, and number of children — tends to be a poor predictor of variations in divorce and remarriage rates. Other than age, the most important variables tend to be subjective, that is, dependant upon the testimony of the surviving spouse. Hence, the most important determinant of the divorce and remarriage probabilities is the the survivor's credibility as a witness.

> Additional information concerning life expectancy, divorce and remarriage may be found in Chapter 12.

2. Duration of the Children's Dependency

It is often assumed that each child's dependency will end at the time that he or she reaches age 18. There are two major exceptions to this assumption. First, many parents continue to support their children well after age 18 if they attend post-secondary educational institutions. If it can be shown that the children in question are likely to continue their educations beyond high school and that their parents would have supported them, the dependency period can be extended to the predicted age of graduation. Second, even when children are no longer dependent upon their parent's incomes, they often receive valuable services from their parents. It is possible, for example, to claim for loss of parents' babysitting services of grandchildren; advice concerning the establishment or operation of a business; or assistance in building or renovating a house. Each such claim may extend well beyond the child's normal age of dependency.

3. Division of Income Among Family Members

The income tax to be paid on any amount of investment income will be lower, the greater is the number of individuals among whom that income is distributed and the more evenly is that sum divided among them. As a result, the manner in which the damages are to be distributed among the plaintiffs will influence the calculation of the income tax gross up. The gross up on an award which would otherwise be, say, $400,000 will be much lower if that award is to be distributed among four survivors than if it is to be invested by one survivor alone; and it will be lower again if $100,000 is to be awarded to each of four survivors than if one survivor is to receive $250,000 and the remaining three $50,000 each. Thus, it is important to question carefully the assumptions which are made concerning this division.

In the determination of this division it is important to distinguish between the *total* percentage of family income devoted to a particular survivor and the *increase* in the percentage of family income required to maintain the total number of survivors when that number is increased by one. For example, in Section II.1 of this Chapter it was suggested that the surviving spouse normally requires 70 percent of the deceased's income in order to maintain his or her standard of living; and that a surviving spouse plus one child require 74 percent. This does not mean, however, that the family devoted only 4 percent of its income to the child. Rather, in the presence of the child, the parents reduced their expenditure on themselves. Most studies find, for example, that approximately 15 to 20 percent of family income is devoted to the first child. Hence, it might reasonably be concluded that of the 74 percent dependency attributed to the surviving spouse and child together, approximately 59 percent is required for the spouse and 15 percent for the child — until the child's dependency ends, at which point the surviving spouse's dependency becomes 70 percent. If the required award is divided 59 percent to the surviving parent and 15 percent to the child, the income tax gross up may be significantly lower than if the award had been divided 70/4.

IV. LOSSES OF ESTATE AND OF CARE, GUIDANCE, AND COMPANIONSHIP

Two claims which are often made in addition to loss of dependency concern loss of estate and loss of care, guidance, and companionship. These claims will be considered in this Section.

1. Loss of Estate

Two types of claims are often forwarded with respect to the estate of the deceased. The first of these is that, as the survivors have received that estate earlier than they would have had the deceased lived out his or her normal life expectancy, they have enjoyed a benefit from "acceleration of the estate". On the other hand, it may also be argued that, had the deceased lived longer, he or she would have built up a larger estate than is now available and, therefore, the survivors have been deprived of the benefit of that "increment in the estate". My experience suggests (i) that in most cases these two factors offset one another, leaving no net benefit or loss from early death; and (ii) that the factors which determine whether one of these factors will outweigh the other tend to be specific to the family in question. Accordingly, in this section, I offer only a list of factors which should be taken into account when deciding whether or not to launch a claim for either acceleration of estate or loss of increment in estate.

Stocks, bonds, RRSPs, and other financial investments — If the estate consists of investments which could be duplicated by the survivors, there is no loss or gain arising from the early death. For example, assume that the deceased had invested $100,000 at an average annual rate of return of 10 percent. Had this individual lived one more year, the dependants would have benefitted from an estate of $110,000 instead of the $100,000 which will now be left to them. The acceleration of the estate neither benefits nor costs them as long as the investments which were available to the deceased are also available to the survivors. For example, if the deceased had invested the entire amount in trust company guaranteed certificates, the survivors will be able to leave the money in those certificates or reinvest them in the certificates of another trust company at the same, or a similar, rate of return. By doing so, they will be able to provide themselves with the same $110,000 one year from now which they would have obtained from the estate of the deceased had he or she lived one more year. Indeed, as long as they can reinvest the proceeds from the estate in financial instruments which pay the same rate of return which the deceased had been able to earn, the acceleration of the estate will have left them neither better off nor worse off.

This finding suggests that the acceleration of an estate which is composed of financial instruments will only have a net effect upon the claim when either the deceased or the survivors have available to them investments which pay a higher rate of return than is available to the other. If the deceased, for example, had been able to invest in RRSPs at a favourable tax rate, whereas the survivors cannot, it might be claimed that the survivors have been disadvantaged by the acceleration of the estate. Conversely, if the survivors are more sophisticated investors than was the deceased, it might be claimed that they have benefitted from the early death. However, I suspect that either claim would be difficult to make.

Investments in a business — If the deceased had owned and operated a business whose growth was contingent upon application of knowledge and skills unique to the deceased, then the business will be worth less to the heirs, the earlier they inherit it. For example, assume that upon the deceased's death the business can be sold for $100,000; whereas had the deceased lived, the business would have appreciated by 20 percent per year. If the best return which the heirs can obtain by investing their $100,000 inheritance is 10 percent, within one year they will have $110,000; whereas, had the deceased lived for one more year before dying, they would have received an estate of $120,000.

Consumption by the deceased — If an individual had intended to consume a portion of his or her investments, for example, to use the interest from those investments to travel or to pay for day-to-day consumption; that individual's estate will have a greater value, the sooner it is that that individual dies. In such a case, therefore, the suvivors in a fatal accident action could be said to have benefitted from an acceleration of the estate.

Housing and other physical assets — If the deceased would have used some of his or her employment or pension income to pay for such major physical assets as housing, automobiles, furniture, or artwork, and if those assets would have been left to the survivors had the deceased enjoyed a normal life span, the loss of the value of those assets may be considered to be a loss of estate. However, such a reduction in the value of the estate must be considered a loss to the heirs *only* if they were not dependant upon the deceased's income. The reason for this is that in the calculation of the dependency rate, considered in Section II, above, allowance was made for the survivors' dependency upon these items. For example, in the calculation of the widow or widower's dependency upon the income of the deceased, it is normally assumed that the survivor requires almost 100 percent of the amount which the deceased would have spent on housing. For the spouse and the children living at home, the dependency upon the deceased's income already includes an allowance for payments made for physical assets. It is only those survivors who do not live at home, such as adult children, for whom the early death produces a loss of estate.

2. Loss of Care, Guidance, and Companionship

Most provinces now allow for a claim of non-pecuniary damages in fatal accident actions, under the heading of loss of "care, guidance, and companionship". As the Supreme Court of Canada has not established a national guideline concerning the values to be awarded under this heading, it is necessary to refer to the recent decisions of the provincial court in which the action is being brought in order to identify the "normal" value of such awards.[4] The only objective evidence which can be presented in this matter is the rate of inflation between the time at which any particular award was made in the past and the date of the trial in question. Approximate values of the rates of inflation between various times in the past and July 1991 have been provided in Table 5 of Chapter 1.

V. BOTH PARENTS HAVE BEEN KILLED

When both of a child's parents have been killed, it is usually the case that the child is sent to live with its grandparents or its aunt and uncle. In such cases, it may be possible to claim for two types of damages: those for loss of dependency and for cost of child care.

Loss of dependency — The guardians will now have to provide the child with the food, clothing, shelter, transportation, etc., which would previously have been provided by the parents. Thus, a claim which is closely analogous to the dependency claim discussed in Sections I and II may be made. The purpose of this claim will be to estimate the percentage of the parents' income which would have been spent on the child's upbringing and apply that percentage to the parents' after-tax incomes to obtain an estimate of the child's lost dependency. Most studies find that this percentage is approximately 20-30 percent for one child and 35-40 percent for two children.

> Additional information concerning the costs of raising children may be found in Chapter 11.

Cost of child care — In addition to purchasing goods and services for their children, parents also perform many services for them, such as cooking, babysitting, and washing. These services will now have to be provided by the guardians. By analogy with the claim for loss of household services in most fatal accident actions, the child may be able to claim an allowance for these costs of care. As parents normally devote 20-30 hours per week to the care of children, it may be possible to obtain compensation for the guardians for these numbers of hours, valued at the rate normally charged by housekeepers, nannies, and/or day care centres.

> Additional information concerning the numbers of hours (per week) spent caring for children may be found in Chapter 10.

---

[4] Further information concerning recent awards for loss of care, guidance, and companionship is found in W.H.R. Charles, *Handbook on Assessment of Damages in Personal Injury Cases, 2nd Edition*, (Toronto: Carswell, 1990) pp. 67-72.

VI. DEATH OF A MINOR

Although it is difficult for parents to make a claim for damages in the case of the death of a child, particularly a minor, some heads of damage are recognized, and others *may* be argued. In this Section, I consider, in descending order of likelihood of success, seven heads of damages which might be raised in cases of the death of a minor.

Loss of valuable services — If the child was performing some valuable service for his or her parents, a claim for loss of these services may be made. Common examples of claims under this head include those for loss of: household services, farm work, and employment in a family business.

Loss of dependency — If the child was providing financial support to his or her parents, or could have been expected to provide such support, the parents may make a claim for loss of such support. In the case of minors, this claim is extremely difficult to support as statistical evidence suggests that very few Canadians provide significant amounts of support to their parents. The most important exceptions occur when the children are adults who had already begun to provide financial assistance; and when the family comes from an ethnic-cultural group in which there is a strong presumption that children will support their aged parents.

Loss of care, guidance, and support — See Section IV.2, above. Alberta also allows $3,000 for grief.

Negligent infliction of nervous shock — If a parent suffers some physical symptom or recognizable psychiatric illness upon having heard of or seen their child's death, they may raise a claim for "negligent infliction of nervous shock." As such certifiable symptoms are uncommon, or difficult to verify, however, this cause of action is rarely successful.

Negligent infliction of mental suffering — Although the tort of "negligent infliction of mental suffering" does not exist in Canada, it is *possible* that under favourable conditions such a tort could be recognized. In the state of Montana, for example, the Appeal Court heard two cases involving wrongful death on the same docket. In the first,[5] a wife had been a witness to the accident in which her husband was killed and was awarded damages for mental distress from having *witnessed* the accident. In the second,[6] a mother and father claimed for mental anguish resulting from the death of their 17-year-old son, although they had not been present at the accident. It is clear, particularly in the dissenting opinion, that the Court had difficulty justifying refusal of the second claim once it had accepted the first. Accordingly, the second was allowed, "creating" a new tort.

Loss of pecuniary benefit — It is clear that the court will entertain a claim based upon a loss of *pecuniary* benefit. Thus, if it was possible to place a pecuniary estimate upon the value of a child, the court might be willing to hear a claim for loss of that pecuniary value. One approach might be to argue that the *minimum* value which parents place upon their children is the amount of money which they spend raising them. If parents voluntarily spend $X raising a child, they must consider that child to be worth at least $X. Thus, if the child is killed after $X has been spent but before the parents have obtained all of the benefits from that expenditure, it may be argued that a loss, to which a pecuniary value *can* be applied, has been incurred.

For example, assume that an 18-year-old child who was about to leave home has been killed. Assume also that it can be determined that the cost of raising that child to age 18 had been approximately $200,000. If the "heroic", but not unreasonable, assumption is made that only 60 percent of the benefits from a child are enjoyed before the child's 18th birthday and that, therefore, the parents had received the benefit of only 60 percent of their $200,000 expenditure by the time of the child's death, then the "pecuniary" value of the claim in this case would be $80,000, (the 40 percent of the $200,000 "value of the child" which had not yet been received).[7]

Hedonic damages — When deciding how much to spend on projects which are designed to save lives, such as improvements to highways and purchases of hospital equipment, government administrators have been faced with the task of placing a value on human life. Numerous techniques, which usually estimate this value to be between approximately $500,000 and $3,000,000 have been developed. Recently, it has been argued in American courts that these techniques can be used to identify the value of non-pecuniary losses arising from wrongful death. This general approach, which has come to be known as the "hedonic damages" technique, has been widely discussed in the American legal literature.

---

[5] *Versland v. Caron Transport*, 671 P.2d 583 (Mont. 1983).
[6] *Dawson v. Hill & Hill Truck Lines*, 671 P.2d 589 (Mont. 1983).
[7] The argument in this section is made in greater detail in Christopher J. Bruce, "Measure of Damages for the Wrongful Death of a Child" (1987), 66 Can. Bar Rev. 344.

Those who would like to obtain a sample of the available books and articles, may be interested in the following listing:

Brady, J. "Hedonic Damages" (1989), 59 Miss. L. J. 495.

Blount, C.D. "Hedonic Damages: Compensation for the Lost Pleasure of Living: *Sherrod v. Berry*, 827 F. 2d 195 (7th Circ 1987)" (1988), 5 Cooley L. Rev., 861.

"Expert Testimony is Admissible to Enable the Jury to Consider the 'Hedonic' Value of Life in a Wrongful Death Case" (1987), 30 Atla. L. Rep. 408.

"Economists Can Assist with Proof", Nat'l L.J. (September 5, 1988) 15.

"Economists Put a Price on Life", Nat'l L.J. (October 16, 1989) 15.

Fearon, S.J. "Hedonic Damages: A Separate Element in Tort Recoveries?" (October, 1989), Def. Couns. J. 436.

King, E.M. and J.P. Smith, *Computing Economic Loss in Cases of Wrongful Death*, (Stanford, Ca.: The RAND Corp., 1988).

Karns, J.E., "Economics, Ethics, and Tort Remedies: The Emerging Concept of Hedonic Value", 9 *Journal of Business Ethics* 707.

Moore, T.A., "Loss of Enjoyment of Life" (September 1989), Trial 58.

Palfin, R.A. and B.B. Danninger, *Hedonic Damages: Proving Damages for Lost Enjoyment of Living* (Charlottesville, Va.: Mitchie Co., 1990).

Staller, J. M., "Testimony from Oz: 'Hedonic' Damages in Personal Injury" (August 1990), For the Def., 30.

4

BASE YEAR EARNINGS

It is convenient to initiate the calculation of the plaintiff's future stream of earnings by estimating the income which that individual could be expected to earn in the year following the trial if he or she had been able to work full time. That figure can then be adjusted to make allowance for positive contingencies, such as fringe benefits, and negative contingencies, such as unemployment. Finally, assumptions can be made concerning the rate at which this adjusted figure can be expected to grow from the date of trial until the plaintiff's anticipated age of retirement. The purpose of this chapter will be to provide information concerning the initial year's potential income, or *base year earnings*. Chapters 5-9 will then consider the factors which determine the growth of earnings, positive and negative contingencies, and retirement age.

This Chapter has been divided into four sections. In the first, I consider the case in which the plaintiff's potential occupation has been identified and, therefore, the only matter to be determined is the plaintiff's expected annual salary. The second and third sections then consider situations in which the plaintiff is sufficiently young that his or her work history provides little indication concerning the occupation into which he/she could have been expected to enter. Finally, the fourth section considers some of the problems which are encountered when trying to assess the potential earnings of individuals who had been self-employed.

I. EMPLOYED ADULTS

Intuition and economic theory, buttressed by decades of empirical support, indicate that the main determinants of individuals' earnings are age, experience, sex, and education. Thus, as very few individuals make significant investments in education after age 30, the plaintiff's employment record prior to the date of disability generally provides an excellent indication of the employment course he or she would have continued to follow in the absence of disability. That is, as age and years of experience move in predictable ways and as sex and education are assumed not to change, the prediction of base year earnings can be made with a high degree of certainty. In the absence of any evidence to the contrary, this prediction is simply that the individual would have remained in the same earnings stream as he or she was in at the time of the accident. Thus, if it is anticipated that the victim would have remained with the same employer had he/she not been injured (killed), the necessary information will normally be available from that employer. If, however, it is anticipated that the victim would have moved (will move) to a different employer — either because evidence to that effect has been led or because the plaintiff's injuries require such a move — resort will have to be made to statistics concerning average wage rates within the relevant occupation. Some of these sources include:

Employers — if the plaintiff had been working at the time of the accident, most employers will be able to identify what his/her income would have been in the first year following the accident; and many will also be able to estimate the income which would have been earned in each year between the date of the accident and the date of the trial (or settlement negotiation) — for example by identifying the income stream of the individual who replaced the plaintiff.

Unions — union agreements, where applicable, generally set out in considerable detail the earnings for which their members are eligible.

Employer/trade organizations — a surprising number of employer organizations conduct wage and salary surveys of their members. Sometimes, these surveys are conducted informally by the organization itself; other times it will be conducted by an external organization such as a management consulting firm. If you are uncertain whether such an organization exists in the industry which is of concern to you, I would recommend that you consult the following listing of Canadian associations:

Brian Land, ed., *Directory of Associations in Canada* (Toronto: Micromedia, Ltd., 1990).

Colleges, trade schools, and universities — post-secondary educational institutions — particularly those which specialize in training for specific labour market openings, such as trade schools, junior colleges, and university schools of business — often undertake surveys to determine the incomes of their recent graduates.

Telephone surveys — if no reliable information can be obtained from an existing source, I recommend that a telephone survey of employers be conducted. With the assistance of a copy of the Yellow Pages, this can usually be done fairly easily by a clerk, articling student, or legal assistant. This approach has the added attraction that it often identifies individuals who would make desirable witnesses. (For example, recently, while telephoning employers to determine whether an individual who had lost a leg could work as a bench welder, I was fortunate enough to speak to an individual who had lost a leg and was working in that occupation.) If a more formal approach is deemed desirable, it is always possible to employ a management consulting firm to conduct the survey on your behalf.

Statistical sources — some of the most important sources of statistics concerning Canadian earnings are listed in the following bibliography:

BIBLIOGRAPHY OF WAGE STATISTICS

1. Reference Works

Bruce, C., *Economics of Employment and Earnings* (Toronto: Nelson, 1989). (Chapter 14).

Canada. Labour Canada, *Collective Bargaining Information Sources*, Occasional. (Detailed, annotated bibliography of sources of labour market data in Canada.)

Gunderson, M., and C. Riddell, *Labour Market Economics*, 2nd Ed. (Toronto: McGraw-Hill Ryerson, 1988). (Chapters 19, 20, and 21 offer an excellent review of trends in Canadian wage developments.)

Ostry, S. and M. Zaidi, *Labour Economics in Canada*, 3rd Ed. (Toronto: Macmillan, 1979). (Chapters 11, 12, and 13 offer an historical overview of Canadian wage trends.)

Queens University, Industrial Relations Centre, *The Current Industrial Relations Scene in Canada*, Annual. (An indispensable sourcebook of current information concerning wages, fringe benefits, collective bargaining developments, working conditions, and labour legislation in Canada. In 1989, this publication was divided into a number of smaller publications, the most important of which is *Wages, Productivity and Labour Costs Reference Tables.)*

Queens University, Industrial Relations Centre, *Canadian Industrial Relations Information*, May 1979. (Explanations of the methods employed to collect such commonly used series as the consumer price index and the unemployment rate; bibliographies of sources of information concerning all aspects of the labour market; and a glossary of industrial relations terms.)

2. General Sources of Wage Data

Canada. Labour Canada, Surveys Division, *Wage Rates, Salaries, and Hours of Labour*, Annual (discontinued). (Wage rates, salaries, and hours of labour by industry for a wide variety of occupations. Separate reports were available for each of the following urban areas: St. John's, Charlottetown, Halifax-Dartmouth, St. John, Montreal, Quebec, Trois Rivieres, Ottawa-Hull, Hamilton, Kitchener-Waterloo, London-St. Thomas, St. Catharines-Niagara, Thunder Bay, Toronto, Windsor, Winnipeg, Regina, Saskatoon, Calgary, Edmonton, Vancouver, Victoria.)

Canada. Revenue Canada, Taxation, *Taxation Statistics*, Annual. (Summarizes information from T1 individual tax returns. Usually 3 to 4 years out of date.)

Canada. Statistics Canada, *Employment Income by Occupation*, Cat. No. 93-116 (Detailed, Census information concerning average annual incomes by occupation, age, sex, and province for 1985. The equivalent figures for 1990, from the 1991 Census, may be available by early 1993.)

Nova Scotia. Department of Labour and Manpower, *Wage Rates, Salaries and Hours of Labour in Nova Scotia*, Annual. (Occupational wages and salaries by industry and region.)

New Brunswick. Department of Labour and Manpower, *Wages, Salaries, and Hours of Labour*, Annual. (Occupational wages and salaries by industry and region.)

The Montreal Board of Trade, *Survey of Wages and Working Conditions of Hourly-Paid Employees*, Annual. (Detailed information concerning 35 hourly-rated jobs.)

The Montreal Board of Trade, *Executive Compensation Survey*, Annual. (Minimum, maximum, and average salaries for various executive positions.)

Saskatchewan. Department of Labour, *Salaries, Wages, Working Conditions and Fringe Benefits in Saskatchewan*, Annual. (Wage and salary rates, working conditions, and employee benefits in Saskatchewan, by occupation, industry, etc.)

Alberta. Bureau of Statistics, *Alberta Pay and Benefits*, Annual (discontinued). (Wages, salaries, and benefits for over 400 occupations, by region.)

3. Collective Bargaining Statistics

By Region

Canada. Labour Canada, Collective Bargaining Division, *Collective Bargaining Review,* Monthly. (Provisions of individual, major collective agreements.)

Nova Scotia. Department of Labour and Manpower, *Collective Agreement Settlements in Nova Scotia,* Monthly. (Major provisions of recent contract agreements.)

Nova Scotia. Department of Labour and Manpower, *Trends in Collective Agreement Settlements—Base and Skilled Rate Changes,* Annual. (Summarizes changes in collective agreement settlements and reviews base and skilled wage rates on an annual basis.)

Quebec. Ministry of Labour and Manpower, *Conditions de Travail,* Annual. (Summary of collective agreement provisions.)

Ontario. Ministry of Labour, *Collective Bargaining Settlements and Negotiations in Ontario,* Monthly. (Provisions of recent collective agreement settlements in Ontario.)

Manitoba. Department of Labour and Manpower, *Major Provisions and Negotiated Working Conditions in Manitoba Collective Agreements,* Annual. (Provisions found in collective agreements coming under provincial jurisdiction.)

By Industry

Ontario. Ministry of Labour, *Hours, Wages and Related Payments in the Ontario Construction Industry,* Annual. (Wage rates and fringe benefits established by collective agreements in construction.)

Education Relations Commission, Research Services, *Teacher/Board Collective Agreements.—A Provincial Overview,* Approximately every 2 months. (Address: Suite 400, 111 Avenue Road, Toronto, Ont., M5R 3J8)

Education Relations Commission, Research Services, *Teacher/Board Collective Agreements—Individual Summaries,* Annual. (Address: Suite 400, 111 Avenue Road, Toronto, Ont., M5R 3J8)

Alberta. Department of Labour, Planning and Research Branch, *Alberta Construction Industry—Union Wage and Benefit Report,* Annual. (Wage rates and benefits paid to Alberta construction workers.)

British Columbia Teachers' Federation, *Summary and Analysis of Teachers' Salary Agreements,* Annual. (Address: 2235 Burrard Street, Vancouver, B.C., V6J 3H9.) (Salaries, benefits and other contract provisions by school district.)

United Steelworkers of America, *Summary of Collective Agreements* Annual. (Address: United Steelworkers of America, 55 Eglinton E., Toronto, Ont., M4P 1B5.)

4. Wages by Occupational Group

Farm Wages

Canada. Statistics Canada, *Farm Wages in Canada*, Cat. No. 21-002, Quarterly. (Average wage rates by the hour, day, and month, with and without board.)

Clerical and Sales

The Montreal Board of Trade, *Survey of Salaries and Working Conditions of Clerical Employees*, Annual. (Surveys 57 clerical jobs.)
The Montreal Board of Trade, *Salesmen's Compensation Survey*, Annual.
Vancouver Board of Trade, *Clerical Salary Survey*, Annual. (Detailed survey of average monthly salaries and salary ranges for a wide variety of clerical positions.)

Education

Canada. Statistics Canada, *Salaries and Qualifications of Teachers in Public Elementary and Secondary Schools*, Cat. No. 81-202, Annual. (Salaries of teachers by teaching level and sex.)
Canada. Statistics Canada, *Teachers in Universities*, Cat. No. 81-241, Annual. (Salaries of university teachers by rank, region, sex, field, country of degree, citizenship, age qualifications, and years since appointments.)
Canada. Statistics Canada, *Salaries and Salary Scales of Full-Time Teaching Staff at Canadian Universities*, Cat. No. 81-258, Annual. (Salaries of university teachers by rank and by institution.)
Canada. Statistics Canada, *Educational Staff of Community Colleges and Vocational Schools*, Annual. (Includes data on salaries.)

Professional Occupations

Association of Professional Engineers, Geologists and Geophysicists of Alberta, *The Value of Professional Services*, Annual. (Engineers' salaries and fringe benefits in Alberta. Comparisons with engineers in B.C., Quebec, and Ontario, and with non-engineers in Alberta.)

Association of Professional Engineers of British Columbia, *Salary Schedule for Professional Engineers*, Annual. (Recommended salary schedule for current year as well as recommended and actual salaries for previous years.)

Association of Professional Engineers of Ontario, *Report on Engineers' Salaries*, Annual.

Association of Professional Engineers of Ontario, *Report on Membership Salary Survey of Canadian Professional Engineers*, Annual. (Annual salary data by province and year of graduation for professional engineers.)

Canadian Association for Business Economics, *Membership Directory and Salary Survey*, Annual.

Quebec. Conseil du Tresor, *Remuneration des Cadres*, Annual. (Information concerning managerial salaries.)

5. Other

Canada. Labour Canada, *Women in the Labour Force, Part II: Earnings of Women and Men*, Annual. (Comparisons of wages earned by women and men in various occupations and industries.)

II. MINORS

This Section will be divided into four subsections. In the first of these, I survey that literature which presents statistical correlations between various characteristics of individuals, such as IQ, schooling, occupation, and income, and such family background variables as parents' educations, IQs, incomes, and occupations and number of siblings. In the second subsection I will review two studies which have attempted to employ the findings of statistical correlations to predict how individuals will perform in school and in the labour market. Third, as it is of some relevance for a limited number of personal injury cases, I will briefly comment on recent developments in the debate over the genetic versus environmental determination of IQ. Finally, I will summarize the main findings of the section as they pertain to the assessment of damages.

1. Statistical Correlations

For various reasons, psychologists, sociologists, economists, and educationists are all concerned with the correlations, if any, between individuals' socioeconomic and genetic backgrounds and their performances in the labour market when they become adults. In the last 20 years, a consensus has grown up among researchers in these fields that background variables affect the adult's performance in roughly the following way: Background variables, such as the size of the family, the parents' IQs, and the socioeconomic standing of the family, have a strong influence on IQ. IQ and background then influence the educational attainment of the individual. IQ, background, and education largely determine occupational attainment. And, finally, IQ, background, education, and occupation together combine to influence earnings.

In this Section, I will review the statistical findings concerning the determinants of each of IQ, education, occupation, and earnings separately. First, however, I offer a short bibliography of the studies which I have found to be of greatest general value in the construction of this Section.

Effects of Family Background on Adult Performance: Statistical Sources

Bayley, N., "Learning in Adulthood: The Role of Intelligence", in Klausmeier, H., and C. Harris, *Analyses of Concept Learning* (New York: Academic Press, 1975), pp. 117-35.

Behrman, J. R., Z. Hrubec, P. Taubman and T. J. Wales, *Socioeconomic Success*, (New York: North-Holland, 1980).

Blake, Judith, "Number of Siblings, Family Background, and the Process of Educational Attainment" (1986), 33 (2) *Social Biology* 5-21.

Bowles, S., "Schooling and Inequality from Generation to Generation" (1974), 82 *Journal of Political Economy* S219-42.

Bowles, Samuel, and Valerie Nelson, "The 'Inheritance of IQ, and the Intergenerational Reproduction of Economic Inequality' " (1974), 61 *Review of Economics and Statistics* 39-51.

Brittain, J. A., *The Inheritance of Economic Status* (Washington: Brookings Institution, 1977).

Corcoran, Mary, C. Jencks and M. Olneck, "The Effects of Family Background on Earnings" (1976), 66 *American Economic Review, Papers and Proceedings* 430-35.

Desai, S., P. L. Chase-Lansdale and R. T. Michael, "Mother or Market? Effects of Maternal Employment on the Intellectual Ability of 4-Year-Old Children" (1989), 26 (4) *Demography* 545-61.

Duncan, O. D., D. L. Featherman and B. Duncan, *Socioeconomic Background and Achievement*, (N.Y.: Seminar Press, 1972).

Fitzgerald-Krein, S., "Growing up in a Single Parent Family: The Effect on Education and Earnings of Young Men" (1986), 35 *Family Relations* 161-68.

Fitzgerald-Krein, S. and A. H. Beller, "Educational Attainment of Children From Single-Parent Families: Differences by Exposure, Gender, and Race" (1988), 25 (2) *Demography* 221-34.

Heer, David M., "Effects of Sibling Number on Child Outcome" (1985), 11 *Annual Reviews in Sociology* 27-47.

Hetherington, E. Mavis, K. Camara and D. Featherman, "Achievement and Intellectual Functioning of Children in One-Parent Households;" in Janet T. Spence, ed., *Achievement and Achievement Motives: Psychological and Sociological Approaches* (San Francisco: W. H. Freeman Company, 1983), pp. 205-76.

Hill, M. S., "Parental Family Income and the Socioeconomic Attainment of Children" (1987), 16 *Social Science Research* 39-73.

Jencks, C., *Inequality* (New York: Basic Books, 1972).

Kiker, B. F. and C. M. Condon, "The Influence of Socioeconomic Background on the Earnings of Young Men" (1981), 16 *Journal of Human Resources* 94-105.

Leibowitz, Arleen, "Home Investments in Children" (1974), 82 *Journal of Political Economy* S111-31.

Morgenstern, Richard D., "Direct and Indirect Effects on Earnings of Schooling and Socio-Economic Background" (1973), 60 *Review of Economics and Statistics* 225-33.

Mott, F. L. and R. J. Haurin, "Being an Only Child: Effects on Educational Progression and Career Orientation" (1982), 3 (4) *Journal of Family Issues* 575-93.

Parsons, D. O., "Intergenerational Wealth Transfers and the Educational Decisions of Male Youth" (1975), 89 *Quarterly Journal of Economics* 603-17.

Rumberger, R. W., "The Influence of Family Background on Education, Earnings, and Wealth" (1983), 61 (3) *Social Forces* 755-73.

Sewell, W. H. and R. M. Hauser, *Education, Occupation, and Earnings* (New York: Academic Press, 1975).

Siebert, W. S., "Careers Open to Talent? Family Background and Pay in America and Britain" (1986), Discussion Paper, Series B, No. 86, University of Birmingham 10-28.

Stafford, F. P., "Women's Work, Sibling Competition, and Children's School Performance" (1987), 77 (5) *The American Economic Review* 972-80.

Taubman, Paul, *Sources of Inequality in Earnings* (New York: North-Holland, 1975).

Taubman, Paul and Jere R. Behrman, "Effects of Number and Position of Siblings on Child and Adult Outcomes" (1986), 33 (2) *Social Biology* 22-34.

Tomes, Nigel, "The Family, Inheritance, and the Intergenerational Transmission of Inequality" (1981), 89 (5) *Journal of Political Economy* 928-58.

Venti, S. F. and D. A. Wise, "Individual Attributes and Self-Selection of Higher Education" (1983), 21 *Journal of Public Economics* 1-32.

Wachtel, P., "The Returns to Investment in Higher Education: Another View," in F. T. Juster, ed., *Education, Income, and Human Behavior* (New York: McGraw-Hill, 1975), 151-70.

Whimbey, A., *Intelligence Can Be Taught* (New York: E. P. Dutton, 1975).

Wolfe, John R., "The Impact of Family Resources on Childhood IQ" (1982), 17 *Journal of Human Resources* 213-35.

Second, for those who are not familiar with modern statistical methods, I might note that the studies cited in this Section generally employ one of two statistical techniques. These are "partial correlation" and "multiple regression." In a typical partial correlation analysis, the investigator might ask whether there was a tendency for sons from high-income families to have high incomes themselves. The statistic which is employed for this purpose takes on values which fall between 0 and 1, with a value greater than (approximately) 0.30 usually signifying the presence of a significant relationship.

Multiple regression, on the other hand, recognizes that a variable such as individual earnings will be influenced by a whole host of variables, many of which will interact with one another. For example, the "truly" important determinant of son's earnings may not be family income, but father's IQ. But, as these two variables are themselves highly correlated, partial correlation will not be able to disentangle their effects. In multiple regression analysis, this disentanglement is achieved by correlating son's earnings with both father's IQ and family income, simultaneously. The result is a formula such as:

$$SInc = 10,000 + 100(FIQ) + 0.1(PInc)$$

where SInc represents son's income, FIQ represents father's IQ and PInc represents parent's income. (The equation is read in the following way: if father's IQ is 120 and parent's income is $30,000, son's income is predicted to be: $10,000 + 100 \times (120) + 0.1 \times (30,000) = 25,000$.) In addition, various statistical tests can be employed to determine whether each of the right-hand (explanatory) variables was significantly correlated with the left-hand (dependant) variable (here, son's IQ). Also, a statistic called R^2 can be calculated which identifies the percentage of the variation among individual values of the left-hand variable which can be "explained" by the right-hand equation. An R^2 of 0.35 (35 percent) or more is generally considered to be satisfactory, if not good, in studies of this nature.

(a) IQ

Table 4.1 summarizes the main findings of those researchers who have employed multiple regression analysis to predict individuals' IQs. It is significant that the two studies which were most successful in explaining the variance in IQ (i.e., the two with the highest R^2s) were those which included, as independent variables, the IQs of the individuals' parents. The only other variable which proved to be significant in most studies which employed it was birth order. The evidence in this case was that the oldest children in the family had the highest IQs. Also, the figures in Table 4.1 suggest that parental income is not a significant determinant of child IQ. Although some studies found a positive correlation between these variables, it is important to note that the two studies which included parental IQ as explanatory variables both found parental income to be insignificant. This suggests that in the other studies, parental income was acting as a proxy for parental IQ.

These findings are supported by two sources which cite simple correlation statistics between IQ and various background variables. Jencks (at p. 337) indicates that whereas the correlation between the IQs of 11 year old males and their fathers' IQs is 0.52, the correlation between childhood IQs and both fathers' educations and fathers' occupations is 0.35. Bayley (at p. 134) adds the information that girls' IQs are more closely correlated with their socioeconomic backgrounds than are boys', and that the correlation between IQ and background increases until the child reaches age 5 when the correlation stabilizes. That is, IQ at age 18 can be forecast with (approximately) the same confidence as IQ at age 5, using factors such as father's and mother's education, father's occupation, and family income.

Finally, in addition to the studies summarized in Table 4.1, a number of studies have looked in detail at the effects which various family status variables have on children's IQs. Desai et al., for example, found that mother's employment (in the labour market) had a statistically significant (negative) effect on child IQ *only* among boys whose families had high incomes and whose mothers had returned to work in the first year following birth. Among all other groups, they found no effect of maternal employment on IQ. Similarly, Stafford found that although mothers' market work time had a statistically significant (negative) effect on children's cognitive skills, this effect was very small and tended to be offset by the (positive) effect which mothers' income had on those skills.

In a survey of the literature, Hetherington et al. reported that the children of one-parent families, particularly boys, tended to score lower on standardized aptitude tests than did the children of two-parent families, but that these differences were usually small.

Finally, in an extensive survey of the literature, Heer reported that

TABLE 4.1

DETERMINANTS OF IQ: SUMMARY OF MULTIPLE REGRESSION ANALYSES

			Study Authors(s)				
	Behrman et al. (1980)	Kiker and Condon	Leibowitz		Scarr and Weinberg	Taubman (1975)	Wolfe
Group Considered	Male Twins	Young Men	Males (age 11)	Females (age 11)	Both Sexes	Males	Both Sexes
Independent Variables							
Father's schooling	n.s	n.s.	n.s.	n.s.	n.s	+	n.s.
Mother's schooling	+		+	n.s.	n.s	+	+
Father's IQ		+			+		
Mother's IQ					+		
Family income	n.s.		+	+	n.s.	+[a]	
Family socioeconomic status		n.s.			n.s.		
Father's occupation	+					+	
Religion – Jewish	+						+

TABLE 4.1 (Cont'd)

DETERMINANTS OF IQ: SUMMARY OF MULTIPLE REGRESSION ANALYSES

	Study Authors(s)						
	Behrman et al. (1980)	Kiker and Condon	Leibowitz		Scarr and Weinberg	Taubman (1975)	Wolfe
Group Considered	Male Twins	Young Men	Males (age 11)	Females (age 11)	Both Sexes	Males	Both Sexes
Independent Variables							
Race – black							–
Birth order		–	–	n.s.	–	n.s.	+ / –[b]
Number of siblings	–				n.s.	n.s.	–
Age	n.s.					n.s.	
Rural upbringing	–					n.s.	
Adults other than parents present in home							–
R^2	0.14	0.40	0.19	0.13	0.08	0.15	

Symbols: (+) variable significant, with positive effect; (–) variable significant, with negative effect; (n.s.) not significant; (blank) variable not included in regression.

[a] Taubman used a variable which he called "biography," which measured parental income and education as well as the subject's hobbies, sports, and education.

[b] The middle children in the birth order were found to have the lowest IQs.

TABLE 4.2

DETERMINANTS OF EDUCATIONAL ATTAINMENT: SUMMARY OF MULTIPLE REGRESSION ANALYSES

Study Author(s)

Independent Variables	Behrman et al. (1980)[a] Twin Brothers	Blake Males	Bowles Males 25-34	Bowles & Nelson Both Sexes[b]	Duncan et al. White Males	Hill & Duncan Males	Hill & Duncan Females	Kiker & Condon Young Men	Leibowitz Males	Leibowitz Females	Morgenstern Both Sexes	Parsons Young Men	Sewell & Hauser[c] Males	Taubman (1975) Males	Taubman & Behrman Males	Taubman & Behrman Females	Tomes Both Sexes	Veni & Wise Attend College[f]	Veni & Wise Graduate[g]
Father's schooling	+	+		+	+	+	+	+	+	+	+	+	+	+	+	+	+	+	n.s.
Mother's schooling	+					+	n.s.		+	+	+	+	n.s.	n.s.	+	+		+	n.s.
Father's occupation	+		+		+								+						
Parent's income				+		+	+	n.s.	n.s.	n.s.	+	+	n.s.	+[d]	+	+	n.s.	+	
Parent's socio-economic status	+			+		n.s.	+	+											
Father's IQ								n.s.											
Own IQ				+				+	+	n.s.			+	+				+[h]	+[h]
Number of siblings	–	–	–		–			+	–	–		–			–	n.s.	n.s.	+[h]	n.s.
Birth order										–					–	–			
Married	+																		

TABLE 4.2 (Cont'd)

DETERMINANTS OF EDUCATIONAL ATTAINMENT: SUMMARY OF MULTIPLE REGRESSION ANALYSES

Study Author(s)

Independent Variable	Behrman et al. (1980)[a]	Blake	Bowles	Bowles & Nelson	Duncan et al.	Hill & Duncan		Kiker & Condon	Leibowitz		Morgenstern Parsons	Sewell & Hauser[c]		Taubman (1975)	Taubman & Behrman		Tomes	Veni & Wise	
Group Considered:	Twin Brothers Males		Males 25-34	Both Sexes[b]	White Males	Males	Females	Young Men	Males	Females	Both Sexes	Males	Young Men	Males	Males	Females	Both Sexes	Attend College[f]	Graduate[g]
Religion – Jewish	+													n.s.	n.s.	n.s.			
Rural upbringing		n.s.												+				n.s.	n.s.
Age	−		−								+			−	+	+			
Motivation								+											
Sex – male											n.s.						e	+	n.s.
R^2	0.19	0.04	0.52	0.46	0.26	.33	.28	0.50	0.08	0.15	0.22	0.40	0.54	0.28	0.23	0.30		e	e

Symbols: See foot of Table 4.1.

[a] Taken from Table 6.1 of Behrman et al.

[b] Bowles & Nelson do not make clear the sex(es) of their subjects.

[c] Sewell & Hauser also found educational and occupational aspirations (expressed ex ante) to be significantly correlated with educational attainment.

[d] Taubman employed the "biography" variable described in footnote a of Table 4.1, *supra.*

[e] Not reported.

[f] The dependent variable is probability of attending college.

[g] The dependent variable is probability of graduating from college given that the individual had entered college.

[h] SAT scores were used instead of IQ.

most studies found a negative correlation between child IQ and family size. A particularly detailed study of this effect, by Mott and Haurin, found that, among boys, IQ tended to be highest for those individuals with three or fewer siblings; whereas, among girls, the individuals with the highest IQs were those who were the older of two children. Other girls in families of less than four children had the next highest IQs, followed by girls in families of four or more. It is also important to note that a number of studies have concluded that the effect of the number of siblings on cognitive ability decreases, the further apart are those siblings in age. (See, for example, Stafford, p. 979.)

(b) Education

From Table 4.2 it is seen that the background variables which correlate most consistently with the individual's educational attainment are: the individual's own IQ, his/her parents' educational attainment and social status, and the number of siblings. Parents' income may also be significant, but the evidence is mixed. Of these variables, it appears that "own IQ" has the greatest explanatory power, given the effect which inclusion of that variable has on the R^2 statistic.

Other information concerning education comes from Wachtel (at p. 168) who reported that the rate of return on investments in education was 68 percent greater (6.7 percent versus 3.6 percent) for those whose IQs fell in the top 25 percent of his sample than for those whose IQs were in the bottom 25 percent. He also found that the children of individuals in the top third of the socioeconomic scale obtained returns on investments in education which were 51 percent higher (6.2 percent versus 4.1 percent) than were earned by the children of individuals in the bottom third of the scale. Although Wachtel did not predict the relative educational attainments of the different groups in his sample, it is clear that he believed that higher rates of return would be associated with greater demand for education.

Heer, in his survey of the effect of number of siblings on child success concluded that the number of years of completed education increased as number of siblings decreased. And Mott and Haurin, in their detailed analysis of this issue, found that the probability that individuals would complete college was highest for those with one or two siblings, followed by only children, and then children with more than two siblings.

In two studies, (Krein and Krein and Beller), Sheila Krein has investigated the effect of living in a single-parent family on years of completed education. Her conclusion was that this effect was negative, particularly among boys who had lived in single-parent families in their pre-school years.

Finally, the studies by Bayley (at p. 135), Corcoran et al. (at p. 434), Duncan et al. (at p. 381), and Jencks (at p. 337) provide information concerning the simple correlation of educational attainment with other variables. These studies found that correlations between own education and father's education ranged from 0.40 to 0.43; correlations between own education and father's occupation ranged from 0.34 to 0.49; and, in the one study which reported it (Jencks), the simple correlation between education and IQ was found to be 0.58. Bayley, however, found the correlations between girls' IQs at various ages and their ultimate educational attainments ranged from only 0.10 at 14 years to 0.53 at 21 years; but between boys' IQs and their ultimate educational attainments were 0.70 at age 16, 0.67 at 18, 0.74 at 21, 0.68 at 26, and 0.79 at 36. Finally, Duncan et al. found a correlation of -0.33 between own education and number of siblings.

(c) Occupational status

From the five studies summarized in Table 4.3, three variables are seen to be significantly and consistently correlated with the individual's occupational status at maturity. They are: own IQ, own schooling, and father's occupation/socioeconomic status. Furthermore, the ability of equations which incorporate these variables to predict occupational status is remarkable. This is particularly so when it is recognized that the measure of occupational status in these studies is a 7- to 9-point scale which must, in at least some senses, be in large part arbitrary.

These findings were also supported by the studies which reported simple correlations among variables. Whimbey (at p. 137), for example, reported the following average IQs by occupation for army inductees: professional, 120; semi-professional, 113; clerical, skilled trades, retail businessmen, 108; semi-skilled, senior clerical, 104; slightly skilled, 96; day laborers, 95; rural landowners, farmers, 94. And Jencks (at p. 337) and Duncan et al. (at p. 38) reported that the correlation between: occupation and fathers' education was 0.32 to 0.35; occupation and fathers' occupation was 0.39 to 0.44; and occupation and own education was 0.64 to 0.65. Finally, Bayley found that the correlations between girls' IQs at various ages and their occupational standings were 0.38 at age 16, 0.46 at 15, 0.33 at 21, 0.21 at 26, and 0.04 at 36; whereas for boys the comparable correlations were 0.72 at 16, 0.74 at 18, 0.72 at 21, 0.69 at 26, and 0.75 at 36.

(d) Earnings

Not surprisingly, the twelve studies summarized in Table 4.4 indicate that the variables which are most closely correlated with labour market

Assessment of Personal Injury Damages

TABLE 4.3

DETERMINANTS OF OCCUPATIONAL STATUS: SUMMARY OF MULTIPLE REGRESSION ANALYSES

			Study Authors(s)			
	Behrman[a] et al. (1980) Twin Brothers		Bowles & Nelson[d]	Brittain	Duncan et al.[d]	Sewell & Hauser
Group Considered	Initial[b]	Mature[c]	Both Sexes	Males	White Males	Males
Independent Variables						
Father's schooling	+	n.s.		+	+	n.s.
Mother's schooling	+	n.s.				n.s.
Father's occupation	+	+		+	+	+
Parents' income			+			n.s.
Parents' socioeconomic status		+	+			
Own IQ			+			
Own schooling	+	+				+
Number of siblings	−	n.s.		−		+

TABLE 4.3 (Cont'd)

DETERMINANTS OF OCCUPATIONAL STATUS: SUMMARY OF MULTIPLE REGRESSION ANALYSES

	Behrman[a] et al. (1980)		Bowles & Nelson[d]	Brittain	Duncan et al.[d]	Sewell & Hauser
	Twin Brothers					
Group Considered	Initial[b]	Mature[c]	Both Sexes	Males	White Males	Males
Independent Variables						
Married	n.s.	n.s.				
Religion – Jewish	+	n.s.				
Rural upbringing	–	–				
Race – black				–		
Father left a will				+		
Age	+	n.s.				
Initial occupation		+				
R^2	0.30	0.30	0.58[e]	0.28	0.27	0.43

Symbols: (See foot of Table 4.1.)

[a] From Table 6.1 of Behrman et al.
[b] Initial occupation.
[c] Occupation at maturity.
[d] Occupation at age 35-44.
[e] R^2 for ages 45-54 was 0.48 for same independent variables.

TABLE 4.4

DETERMINANTS OF EARNINGS: SUMMARY OF MULTIPLE REGRESSION ANALYSES

Study Author(s)

Independent Variables	Behrman et al. (1980)[a]	Bowles	Bowles & Nelson	Brittain	Duncan et al.	Kiker & Condon	Tomes	Leibowitz	Morgenstern	Parsons	Rumberger	Sewell & Hauser	Siebert		Taubman[a] (1975)	Taubman[a] & Behrman		Tomes
Group Considered:	Male Twins: Mature Earnings	Males: 25-34	Both Sexes: Age 35-44	Males	White Males: Age 35-44	Males: Age 19-32	Males: Age 39	Both Sexes	Males: 18-24		White Males	Males: Approx. Age 25	U.K.	U.S.	Males	Males	Females	Both Sexes
Father's schooling	+	n.s.		+	+	n.s.	n.s.	+			n.s.	n.s.			n.s.	n.s.	n.s.	
Mother's schooling	+						–		n.s.			n.s.			+	n.s.	+	
Father's occupation	–			n.s.								n.s.	+	+				
Parents' income	+					+	n.s.		+			+		+	+[b]	+	+	
Parent's socioeconomic status						n.s.												
Parent's wealth											+							
Father's IQ						n.s.	n.s.											
Own IQ	+		+			n.s.				+	n.s.	n.s.			+			
Own schooling	+		+			+		+	+		+	+	[c]	[c]	+			+
Own occupation	+					+						+						
Rural upbringing	n.s.																	
Married	+																	
Religion – Jewish	+			+											+	–	n.s.	+
Number of siblings	–			–							n.s.	n.s.				–	–	+

TABLE 4.4 (Cont'd)

DETERMINANTS OF EARNINGS: SUMMARY OF MULTIPLE REGRESSION ANALYSES

Study Author(s)

Group Considered:	Behrman et al. (1980)[a] Male Twins: Mature Earnings	Bowles Males: 25-34	Bowles & Nelson Both Sexes: Age 35-44	Brittain Males	Duncan et al. White Males: Age 35-44	Kiker & Condon Males: Age 19-32	Leibowitz Males: Age 39	Morgenstern Both Sexes	Parsons Males: 18-24	Rumberger White Males	Sewell & Hauser Males: Approx. Age 25	Siebert U.K.	Siebert U.S.	Taubman (1975) Males	Taubman[a] & Behrman Males	Taubman[a] & Behrman Females	Tomes Tomes Both Sexes
Independent Variables																	
Birth order														n.s.	n.s.	n.s.	
Race – black			–			n.s.											
Father left a will				+													
Age	–								+					+	+	+	
Health problem										–		–	n.s.				
Experience (work)						+	+	+		–							
Sex – male								+									
R²	0.24	0.15	0.24	0.24	0.09	0.43	0.07	0.27	0.31	0.15	0.08	0.38	0.40	0.10	0.18	0.06	[d]

Symbols: See foot of Table 4.1.

[a] Equation (1) from Taubman's Table 6.

[b] Taubman employed a composite variable called "biography". See footnote a of Table 4.1, *supra*.

[c] Siebert's equations hold the effect of education constant.

[d] Not reported.

earnings are those which are associated with the individual, specifically: own schooling, own occupation, work experience, and, to a lesser extent, own IQ. It is interesting that even after these factors had been accounted for, every study also found that at least one of the socioeconomic background variables — father's schooling, parents' income, parents' wealth, or parents' socioeconomic status — had a separate, significant impact on adult earnings. As these variables have already been shown to be important determinants of IQ and education, it is somewhat surprising that they also show up as having independent effects on earnings. One hypothesis which is consistent with this evidence is that parents with high socioeconomic status instill in their children values and modes of thought which are useful to them even after they have left home and school. Corcoran et al. (at p. 435), for example, concluded their study by suggesting that

> Unmeasured parental characteristics also exert considerable impact on son's earnings, independently of test scores and educational attainment. The unmeasured characteristics that create these effects are almost uncorrelated with measured advantages that we and other investigators have found to influence men's earnings. This suggests that parents may influence children's preferences for cash versus psychic income.

Finally, Jencks (at p. 337), Corcoran et al. (at p. 434), and Duncan et al. (at p. 35) report the following correlations between earnings and: father's education, 0.21 to 0.23; father's occupational status, 0.10 to 0.26; own IQ, 0.36 to 0.37; own education, 0.35 to 0.41; and own occupation, 0.44.

2. Intergenerational Correlations

Brittain and Venti and Wise have both developed tables which indicate the levels of education and income which the children of parents of varying socioeconomic backgrounds can expect to attain. The most important of their findings have been reproduced here, in Tables 4.5, 4.6., and 4.7. The first two of these Tables represent predictions of education and income attainment based upon equations which the two sets of authors have developed. Both indicate that significant differences in educational attainment can be expected between the children of low income/low socioeconomic status families and the children of high income/high socioeconomic status families. In addition, the estimates made by Venti and Wise suggest that variations in parents' education are more important in predicting variations in the child's education than are variations in parental income.

Tables 4.5 and 4.7, from Brittain, also provide information concerning the intergenerational transmission of socioeconomic status. Whereas Table 4.5 contains predictions of son's status based on parents' status, Table 4.7 contains data from two surveys of sons and their parents. It is informative to compare the two Tables. From the second row of Table 4.5, it is seen that the median 1976 income among sons was $17,000. Thus, the prediction that there was a 91.9 percent chance that sons from the top 20 percent of families would have incomes above $15,000 implies that approximately 85 percent of those sons would have incomes which were above the median (i.e., above $17,000). This contrasts with the findings, from Table 4.7, that 27 out of 28, or 96 percent, of the sons from the top 20 percent in the sample of 144 and 46 out of 50, or 88 percent, of the sons from the top 20 per cent in the sample of 253, placed in the top half of the socioeconomic scale (as measured by the Croy variable). Similarly, Brittain predicted that approximately 20 percent of sons from the bottom 20 percent of families would have incomes which were above the median. Table 4.7 indicates that, in the sample of 144, this value, for socioeconomic status, was actually 21 percent, whereas in the sample of 253 it was 28 percent.

TABLE 4.5

EXPECTED INCOME AND EDUCATIONAL ATTAINMENT OF SONS FROM VARIOUS SOCIOECONOMIC BACKGROUNDS: CLEVELAND, 1965-1966

	Socioeconomic Rank of Parents				
	Top 10%	Top 20%	Median	Bottom 20%	Bottom 10%
Predicted Years of Education[a]	15.9	15.2	12.9	10.6	9.9
Predicted 1976 Income ($,000)	28.2	25.2	17.0	11.5	10.3
Probability That 1976 Income is Greater Than:					
$50,000	6.2	3.3	0.2	c	c
35,000	28.1	18.9	2.6	0.1	c
25,000	62.6	50.8	14.9	1.8	0.8
15,000	95.5	91.9	63.3	23.6	15.6
10,000	99.7	99.4	92.4	64.8	53.2
5,000	b	b	b	98.8	97.4

Source: Education estimates are from Brittain, Table 2-5, at p. 62. Income estimates are from Brittain, Table 2-4, at p. 58.

[a] From Brittain's "extended sample".
[b] Greater than 99.5 percent.
[c] Less than 0.5 percent.

TABLE 4.6

SIMULATED EFFECTS OF PARENTS' INCOME AND EDUCATION
ON COLLEGE ATTENDANCE AND COMPLETION

Parents' Income[a]	Probability of Attendance		Probability of Completion	
	Parents: Less than high school[b]	Parents: College or more[c]	Parents: Less than high school[b]	Parents: College or more[c]
$ 6,000	11	33	38	50
9,000	13	35	43	54
12,000	14	38	47	58
15,000	15	40	51	62
18,000	17	43	55	66

Source: Venti and Wise, Table 5, at p. 21.

[a] Average parental income was $11,186 with a standard deviation of $5,380.

[b] 26.9 percent of mothers and 32.4 percent of fathers had less than high school education.

[c] 11.4 percent of mothers and 18.0 percent of fathers had college education or more.

Another way of viewing the data in Table 4.7 is to ask what percentage of sons deviated by a significant extent from the socioeconomic ranking of their parents. To answer this question I have added the last two columns of Table 4.7. There it is seen that almost half of all sons remained within one rank of their parents and that almost two-thirds remained within two ranks. Although these results may not appear to be particularly remarkable, it must be remembered that differences in income, occupational status, and residential quality among adjoining "tenths" of the population will be very small, particularly among those in the middle ranks. Thus, a relative movement of as much as 2 or 3 ranks may not imply a very large absolute change in economic well being.

3. Genetics Versus Environment

Economists and psychologists have been interested for some time in the effects of genetics and environment on the child's development. In the economic literature this concern has primarily been with the joint effects of genetics and home environment on the IQ, education, and (adult) income of the child. Psychologists, on the other hand, have primarily concerned themselves with the relative effects of genetics and environment on IQ. As the courts are generally not concerned with the question of whether behaviour is taught or inherited, but only with the problem of predicting behaviour, the psychological literature is of lesser interest than the economic. For this reason, I will deal with the latter first.

(a) Joint effects

In Section I, I summarized the results of a large number of studies of the intergenerational transmission of wealth. Although most of these studies appeared to suggest that genetics and family environment are very important determinants of adult success, most did not attempt to estimate the joint effects of these two variables. Two papers which attempted to estimate this effect have been written by Behrman and Taubman. In the first, Behrman and Taubman (1976), at p. 435, they concluded that

> ... *genetics plus common environment* account for 79 percent of the variance in education, 20 percent of the variance in SES in initial occupation, 45 per cent of the variance in SES in later occupation and 53 percent of the variance in subsequent earnings. [Emphasis in original.]

(SES is socio-economic status.) And in 1977, Behrman, Taubman, and Wales, at p. 73, summarized their study by noting:

> All our models indicate that the total of genetic and family environment account for more than half of the total variance in earnings around age 50.

In less technical terms, these authors were suggesting that there is a very strong correlation between an individual's level of success as a mature adult and the combination of childhood home environment and genetic inheritance.

(b) Separate effects

For over a century, psychologists (and, more recently, economists and educationists) have been asking whether it is genetics or environment which is the major determinant of IQ. As a general rule, this question is not of great importance in personal injury cases. The reason for this is that the courts are simply interested in predicting the child's adult IQ — or, more specifically, his or her adult earnings potential. Thus, if they are told, as Behrman et al. suggest (above), that over 50 percent of the variance in adult earnings can be explained by genetics and environment together, they need not concern themselves with the relative contributions of those two factors. An exception to this approach occurs when the child in question has been raised by individuals other than the natural parents, for example, when the child has been adopted or when the natural parents have been divorced and the natural parent with whom the child lives has remarried. In these cases, it may be of some interest to consider the genetics-environment controversy.

TABLE 4.7

TRANSITION MATRICES RELATING THE ECONOMIC STATUS RANKS, IN TENTHS, OF SUCCESSIVE GENERATIONS, FOR SON'S STATUS MEASURE CROY,[a] CLEVELAND AREA SAMPLE, 1965-66

Rank of Parent	Rank of Sons										Mean Rank of Son	Percentage of Sons Who Deviate from Parents by *More than*	
	1 (top)	2	3	4	5	6	7	8	9	10		1 Rank	2 Ranks
	Sample of 144 married sons of male decedents ($r_s = 0.600$)[b]												
1	7	4	2	1	—	—	—	—	—	—	1.14	21.4	7.1
2	1	3	4	4	1	1	—	—	—	—	2.71	35.7	14.3
3	—	2	5	1	2	1	2	1	—	—	3.29	42.9	28.6
4	2	1	2	1	—	4	1	1	1	2	4.97	80.0	46.7
5	—	4	—	—	1	3	2	2	2	1	5.43	73.3	60.0
6	—	—	1	3	3	1	3	3	1	—	5.50	53.3	13.3
7	1	1	1	1	3	1	1	1	3	2	5.70	80.0	40.0
8	1	—	—	1	2	2	2	1	3	2	6.36	57.1	28.6
9	—	1	—	2	3	—	1	2	1	4	6.45	50.0	57.1
10	—	—	—	—	—	2	1	3	2	6	8.07	42.9	21.4
Average												53.7	31.7

TABLE 4.7 (Cont'd)

TRANSITION MATRICES RELATING THE ECONOMIC STATUS RANKS, IN TENTHS, OF SUCCESSIVE GENERATIONS, FOR SON'S STATUS MEASURE CROY,[a] CLEVELAND AREA SAMPLE, 1965-66

| Rank of Parent | Rank of Sons | | | | | | | | | | Mean Rank of Son | Percentage of Sons Who Deviate from Parents by More than | |
	1 (top)	2	3	4	5	6	7	8	9	10		1 Rank	2 Ranks
					Sample of all 253 sons ($r_s = 0.518$)[b]								
1	14	2	4	5	—	—	—	—	—	—	1.50	36.0	20.0
2	4	2	7	3	2	3	3	—	1	—	3.58	48.0	36.0
3	1	8	1	2	3	3	2	1	3	1	4.30	56.0	40.0
4	3	3	4	1	—	3	3	3	2	3	4.94	68.0	56.0
5	1	4	—	3	6	3	3	4	2	—	4.88	50.0	42.5
6	—	2	3	4	1	4	7	3	1	1	5.27	53.8	26.9
7	—	1	2	3	4	3	2	6	1	4	6.00	57.7	38.5
8	2	—	1	1	4	3	—	3	2	9	6.66	80.0	32.0
9	1	1	—	4	3	2	4	5	1	4	6.06	60.0	44.0
10	1	—	—	1	3	1	3	5	5	6	7.18	56.0	36.0
Average												56.6	37.2

Source: Brittain, Table 3-10, at p. 109.

[a] Croy is a weighted average of three variables: RATE, OCC and LOGY. In turn, RATE is a measure of residential quality, on a scale of one (low) to seven (high); OCC is an occupational classification, also on a scale of one (low) to seven (high); and LOGY is the logarithm of annual family income.

[b] Spearman coefficient of rank correlation.

After conducting an extensive survey of the literature on this topic, I believe that the following two conclusions — and little more — can be drawn:

(a) The preponderance of evidence suggests that both genetics and environment are important as determinants of IQ, although the proportions into which the relative influences can be divided are not at all certain.

(b) Individuals tend to select their mates from among those who are of similar age, education, and IQ to themselves; while adoption agencies may select as adoptive parents individuals who are similar to the biological parents. That is, the nature-nurture distinction may be irrelevant for the purposes being considered here.

The "evidence" for the first of these conclusions derives from a number of sources. In addition to the studies summarized in Table 4.1, above, I would recommend the following readings:

Bouchard, Thomas, and Matthew McGue, "Familial Studies of Intelligence: A Review" (1981), 212 *Science* 1055-58.

Duyme, Michel, "School Success and Social Class: An Adoption Study" (1988), *24 Developmental Psychology* 203-09.

"The Great IQ Debate" (December 24, 1983), 289 *The Economist* 80-8.

Munsinger, H., "The Adopted Child's IQ: A Critical Review" (1975), 82 *Psychological Bulletin* 623-59.

Scarr, S. and R. Weinberg, "IQ Test Performance of Black Children Adopted by White Families" (1976), 31 *American Psychologist* 726-39.

Scarr, S. and R. Weinberg, "The Influence of 'Family Background' On Intellectual Attainment" (1978), 43 *American Sociological Review* 674-92.

Schiff, M., M. Duyme, A. Dumaret, and S. Tomkiewicz, "How Much Could We Boost Scholastic Achievement and IQ Scores? A Direct Answer From a French Adoption Study" (1982), 12 *Cognition* 165-96.

Teasdale, T.W., and David Owen, "Social Class and Mobility in Male Adoptees and Non-Adoptees" (1984), 16 *Journal of Biosocial Science* 521-30.

The first type of study to cast light on the genetics-environment question is that which employs multiple regression analysis to identify the determinants of IQ. These studies were surveyed in Section II.1(a) of this Chapter, where it was found that parental IQ had a much higher correlation with child's IQ than did measures of parental socioeconomic status. If the latter measure can be interpreted as a proxy for "environment", these findings suggest that genetics is more important than environment. However, an alternative possibility is that parents with high IQs provide better environments for their children, regardless of their socioeconomic status, than do parents with low IQs.

For this reason, the major source of information concerning the effects of environment on IQ has come from studies of children who were raised from birth in homes other than those of their natural parents; that is, from studies of adopted children. A useful survey of the 17 adoption studies which had been reported up to 1975 is contained in Munsinger. Perhaps the most important conclusion of Munsinger's survey is that the correlation between the IQs of adopted children and their adoptive parents is much lower than that between children and their biological parents.

Although Munsinger concludes from this that genetics is more important than environment, the studies he cites are not sufficiently free from bias and error, in my view, to provide strong support for this conclusion. First, if the effects which parents had on their adoptive children were on-going, it would be appropriate to test the correlation between the parents' and childrens' IQs when the latter reached adulthood, or at least, when they reached their late teens. Most studies, however, tested the adopted children before they were ten. Second, very few of the studies reported by Munsinger had information about the relationship between the IQs of the biological and adoptive parents. At least as important as the correlation between adoptive parents' and childrens' IQs is the change in that correlation over the time in which the child lives with its adoptive parents. An estimate of this change might be derived by comparing the correlation between the IQs of adoptive parents and children with the correlation between the IQs of the adoptive parents and the biological mothers or, preferably, the biological siblings.

A number of recent studies have taken this approach. Scarr and Weinberg in their 1976 study, for example, found that 130 black/interracial children adopted by advantaged white families had IQs which were more than 1 standard deviation (21 points[1]) above the mean for otherwise similar children who were living with their biological parents —although the adoptive children's IQs were (on average) 6 points below those of "natural" children in the adoptive families.[2] Very similar results were also found by Teasdale and Owen.

In their study, Schiff et al. (results also reported in Duyme), identified 32 children of unskilled biological parents who had been placed, by the age of 4 months, into families in the top 13 percent of the socioeconomic scale. Two interesting results were obtained. First, on average,

---

[1] The 21 point differential refers to the 111 children adopted before age 1. The differential between the IQs of black children living with their biological parents and those who were adopted into white homes after age 1 was approximately 7 points (97.5-90).

[2] The 6 point differential refers to the children adopted before age 1. The differential between the IQs of the 65 children adopted after age 1 and the IQs of the natural children was approximately 19 points (116.7-97.5).

the IQs of the adopted children were approximately 10 points higher than the population average, 12 points higher than the average for the children of unskilled workers, and 3 points lower than the average for the children of upper-middle-class parents. Second, for 20 of the adopted children, the researchers were able to locate natural siblings who had been raised by their biological mothers. The average difference between the IQs of these two groups of children proved to be (approximately) 16 points (110.6 versus 94.2) on the basis of an individually-administered test, and 12 points (106.8 versus 95.1) on the basis of a group test. Thus, the Schiff et al. study provides strong evidence of environmental influence on IQ.

On the other hand, a second study by Scarr and Weinberg (1978), found that information about the biological mother was a much more significant factor in the prediction of the IQs of 150 adopted children than was information about the adopting parents. There was an important distinction between this study and most of those considered by Munsinger, the Schiff et al., and the 1976 Scarr and Weinberg studies, however. Whereas in the latter two the adoptive parents were selected for their obvious differences from the biological parents, in the former the adoptive and biological parents were found to be similar. This leads to the possible conclusion that significant improvements in childrens' IQs can be obtained if they are taken from particularly "deprived" environments and placed in particularly "enriched" environments, but that any lesser degree of alteration of environment will have only limited ability to overcome the effects of genetics on IQ.

The second proposition which I put forward at the beginning of this subsection was that the IQs of the child's adoptive parents and those of the biological parents might be sufficiently closely related that the importance of the genetics-environment distinction would be weakened considerably. That adoptive parents might have similar characteristics to biological parents, because of matching by adoption agencies, is confirmed by numerous studies of adopted children. In this light, I would particularly recommend Munsinger, Bouchard and McGue, and Scarr and Weinberg (1975). There is also strong evidence to suggest that individuals tend to select spouses whose IQs are similar to their own (see, especially, Bouchard and McGue) and, therefore, that the spouse of a parent who remarries will have a similar IQ to the child's natural parent.

4. Summary

The main findings of the studies reviewed in this Section have been summarized in Table 4.8. Beside each of IQ, education, occupation, and income has been listed, in roughly descending order of importance, the characteristics that have been found to be most closely and consistently correlated with that factor. Thus, for example, it is my interpretation that the best predictor of the child's IQ is the IQ of the parents, followed by the child's place in the family's birth order and the number of siblings.

TABLE 4.8

Correlates with IQ, Education, Occupation, and Income: Summary of Literature Survey

Factor	Correlated Characteristics
IQ	— Parents' IQs
	— Birth order
	— Number of siblings
Education	— Father's schooling
	— Own IQ
	— Mother's schooling
	— Parents' incomes
	— Number of siblings
	— Birth order
Occupation	— Own schooling
	— Own IQ
	— Father's occupation/socioeconomic status
	— Rural upbringing
	— Number of siblings
Income	— Own schooling
	— Own occupation
	— Work experience
	— Age
	— Parents' income/wealth
	— Number of siblings
	— Sex

Source: Tables 4.1, 4.2, 4.3, 4.4, supra.

Following from the analysis of this Section, there would appear to be three techniques which could be employed to determine the foregone earnings of an injured child. The first of these would employ the first two sets of data in Table 4.8 to predict the ultimate level of educational attainment of the child (had the injury not occurred). Data concerning the correlation between education and income — for example, from the Census — could then be employed to predict the plaintiff's future level of earnings. Second, in a similar vein, the information in

Table 4.8 could be employed to predict the type of occupation for which the plaintiff would have been suited. Reference to the sources of occupational earnings data cited in the first section of this Chapter could then be made in order to identify the average earnings of individuals in that occupational category. For example, if it had been predicted that the child would have become a skilled tradesperson, an average of the earnings of carpenters, electricians, mechanics, plumbers, and welders might be used.

A third approach which could be employed would be to ignore (most) differences among child plaintiffs, and instead to award compensation on the basis of the average wage of all Canadians. Use of this approach can be defended on two grounds: First, it may be seen to be "unfair" that children whose adult earnings would have been lower than average, simply because they came from disadvantaged families, should receive lower than average damage awards. Second, it might also be argued that our ability to predict adult earnings is so limited that the cost of attempting to do so cannot be justified. In the analysis which follows, I will comment on both of these arguments. Before doing so, however, I believe that it is important to review the types of circumstances in which child plaintiffs come before the courts.

These circumstances are of two general types: those in which the child has been left unable to earn income, usually as the result of injuries to the brain, and those in which the child's capacity to work has been reduced or compromised, usually as the result of a major physical injury such as an amputation or spinal cord injury. In the former circumstance, the task of the court is strictly to identify the value of the earnings the plaintiff would have enjoyed in the absence of the injury. Because there is now no alternative source of income, the entire value of these earnings become compensable loss. In such a circumstance, I find myself inclined to the view that equity requires that most plaintiffs be treated as though they were equal, that is, average,[3] particularly if they have suffered sufficient brain damage that they are unable to appreciate fully the nature of their situations. The only exceptions which it seems reasonable to make in such circumstances involve those children who had shown a particular aptitude, before the accident, which clearly set them apart from other children.

In the circumstance in which the plaintiff retains some earning capacity, the arguments are much less clear. The reason for this is that

---

[3] This is the argument which was made by Lewis Klar in his "Annotation" to *Houle v. Calgary (City)* (1983), 26 Alta. L.R. (2d) 34, 24 C.C.L.T. 275, 44 A.R. 271 (Q.B.). Varied on other grounds (1985), 38 Alta. L.R. (2d) 331, 60 A.R. 366 (C.A.). Leave to appeal to S.C.C. refused (1985), 20 D.L.R. (4th) 15n, 63 A.R. 79. Klar, however, did not restrict his argument to cases in which the plaintiff was prevented from earning an income. (*Houle* concerns a young amputee. See C. J. Bruce, "The Calculation of an Infant's Lost Earnings" (1984), 22 Alta. L. Rev. 291-93.)

the claim for damages in these cases is based upon the difference between projected pre-accident and post-accident earnings. If both such levels were to be predicted to be equal to the average earnings for all Canadians, there would be no difference between them and, therefore, no damages. As it is clear that the plaintiff's injuries have reduced his/her earning capacity, however, this conclusion cannot be supported.

Accordingly, some projection of earning capacity must be made. One approach might be to assume that the plaintiff would have earned the average income had he/she not been injured and then to subtract from that the income he/she is now (after the accident) expected to earn. But this approach can easily be shown to be inequitable. Compare the following two cases: In case A, the plaintiff could have been expected to enter an occupation earning $40,000 per year had she not been injured. With her injury, she is now expected to average only $30,000 per year. Her "true" loss is $10,000. But, if the average income for Canadians in $25,000, a method of damage calculation which contrasted her post-injury earnings with average earnings would award her nothing. In case B, assume that the injury has reduced the plaintiff's annual earnings from $22,000 to $20,000. Comparison of post-accident earnings with the overall average of $25,000 would produce a damage award of $5,000 per year even though the "true" loss is $2,000. It is not at all clear that this differentiation between cases A and B is equitable; it almost certainly would not be considered to be so were it to be applied to adult plaintiffs.

It is my view, therefore, that damages should be based upon the difference between projections of the plaintiffs pre- and post-accident earnings streams. This raises the question, alluded to earlier, of whether the information available to the expert is of sufficient quality to allow these predictions to be made. I would respond affirmatively to this question. First, my understanding of the studies surveyed in subsections II.1, II.2, and II.3 of this Chapter is that there is a significant correlation between various socioeconomic and personal attributes of the child, particularly after age 4, and expected success as an adult. Clearly, the information available in childhood is not sufficient to predict adult behaviours with certainty. Some daughters of labourers will become doctors; and some sons of lawyers will become waiters. However, the degree of uncertainty which remains is not, in my view, so much greater than that which remains with respect to other values routinely projected by the courts — such as the future earnings of adults or the level of "contingencies" — that projections should be rejected out of hand. Second, it must be remembered that many of the same factors which enter the projections of pre-accident earnings will also enter the projections of post-accident earnings. Thus, even though both projections may be erroneous, the direction of those errors will tend to be the same. As a result, the estimate of the loss, which is the difference between the two earnings streams, can be expected to be much more accurate than is the estimate of either stream alone.

Finally, in the introduction to this Summary, I suggested that there were two methods of forecasting future income: one based on projections of the child's educational attainment and one based upon projections of the child's ultimate occupational choice. In my view, the former is preferable to the latter. The main reason for this is that the statistical basis for the prediction of adult success is not sufficiently precise in most cases to allow one to identify with any degree of certainty the occupation which a child would have entered had he/she not been injured. The best that can be accomplished, I believe, is to forecast the approximate level of educational success. This approach may have to be modified somewhat, however, in those cases in which the change in earnings resulting from a physical injury is not associated with a change in educational attainment. The child who would have dropped out of school after grade 12 had she not been injured may still complete grade 12 after her injury, for example; but this does not mean that she has suffered no earnings loss. A better measure of that loss may be the difference in earnings levels between her pre- and post-accident occupations. In no case, however, would I recommend that the forecast of earnings be based upon average incomes within a specific, narrowly-defined occupation such as plumber or lawyer. The better approach would be to identify a broad category of occupations, such as tradesperson or professional.

III. YOUNG ADULTS

An unfortunate fact of life is that a very high percentage of seriously injured plaintiffs are between the ages of 18 and 25. Although individuals in this age group have often completed their educations and entered the labour market, it is usually the case that their future career patterns have not been clearly established. It is not uncommon, for example, to encounter young male plaintiffs who have dropped out of school before completing grade 12 and who have since drifted from one unskilled job to another. The question in these cases is whether the additional information which is available concerning them, compared to children, is of use in forecasting their future earnings. I have been able to identify two literatures which cast light on this question. These literatures review the correlations between adult labour market success and (i) aspirations expressed before the individual left school and (ii) early experiences in the labour market. I will consider these two literatures in turn in subsections 1 and 2, respectively.

1. Aspirations

A number of studies have investigated the correlation between the career plans, or aspirations, of high school students and the occupations which they actually adopted when they entered the labour force. Six such studies are:

Bartling, H. C. and A. B. Hood, "An 11 Year Follow-Up of Measured Interest and Vocational Choice" (1981), 28 *Journal of Counselling Psychology* 27-35.
Gottfredson, L. S. and H. J. Becker, "A Challenge to Vocational Psychology: How Important Are Aspirations in Determining Male Career Development?" (1981), 18 *Journal of Vocational Behavior* 121-37.
Holland, John and Gary Gottfredson, "Predictive Value and Psychological Meaning of Vocational Aspirations" (1975), 6 *Journal of Vocational Behavior* 349-63.
Noeth, R. J. and D. A. Jepsen, "Predicting Field of Job Entry from Expressed Vocational Choice and Certainty Level" (1981), 28 *Journal of Counselling Psychology* 22-26.
Sewell, W. H. and R. M. Hauser, *Education, Occupation and Earnings* (New York: Academic Press, 1975).
Whitney, Douglas, "Predicting from Expressed Vocational Choice: A Review" (1969), 48 *Personnel and Guidance Journal* 279-86.

Among these, the Sewell and Hauser study (at p. 100) simply indicated that occupational aspirations expressed in high school (1957) were significantly correlated with occupational attainment 7 years later (1964) and with earnings 10 years later (1967). The Noeth and Jepsen study further suggested that vocational choices made in high school were better predictors of occupation entered, the more certain was the individual concerning that choice. In particular, they found that career choices made in high school were correct predictors of occupations actually entered two years after graduation for 43 percent of those who were "very sure choosers," 38 percent of "fairly sure choosers," and 28 percent of "choosers who were not sure".

Bartling and Hood found that when university students' expressed choices were congruent with their measured interests, expressed choice was a "good" predictor of occupation 11 years later in 60.4 percent of cases and provided a completely erroneous prediction in only 19.8 per cent of cases. On the other hand, when interests and expressed choices were not congruent, expressed choice was a good predictor in 32.5 percent of cases and erroneous in 40.6 percent. Women's expressed choices predicted their occupations slightly better than did men's choices. Holland and Gottfredson also found that aspirations were better predictors of future occupation when those aspirations were consistent with the individual's interests (as measured by Holland's Self-Directed Search, an instrument which is widely used by vocational psychologists in Canada).

Gottfredson and Becker provided information from which it is possible to compare the usefulness of "current job" and "aspiration" as predictors of field of job 5 years later for males of varying ages. Their data indicate that among men 15 to 20-years-old, aspiration has a stronger correlation with the job held 5 years later than does the job held in the present. Neither, however, is strongly correlated with later job. Among those who were 17 or 18 in 1966, for example, the correlation between aspiration in 1966 and job held in 1971 was only 0.28. Among 21 to 24-year-olds, current job was a better predictor of later job than was aspiration, furthermore, the correlations were quite high. Among those who were 23 or 24 in 1966, for example, there was a correlation of 0.49 between job held in 1966 and job held in 1971. Similar results were reported by Whitney in his survey of the pre-1969 research, although Whitney's findings suggest a stronger correlation between aspirations and occupations than reported by Gottfredson and Becker.

Finally, I have been able to identify three studies which provide information concerning the sources of young people's aspirations. These studies are: the Sewell and Hauser book cited in Section II.1 plus

Duncan, O. E., D. L. Featherman and B. Duncan, *Socioeconomic Background and Achievement* (New York: Seminar Press, 1972).
Ginzberg, E., S. Ginsburg, S. Axelrad and J. L. Herma, *Occupational Choice* (New York: Columbia University Press, 1951).

Sewell and Hauser (at p. 99) found that high school aspirations were positively and significantly correlated with measures of: parents' income, own IQ, high school grades, teachers' encouragement, parents' encouragement, friends' plans, and college plans. Duncan et al. (at p. 108) found that the occupational expectations of high school seniors were positively correlated with measures of the status of their fathers' occupations. (The regression coefficient of anticipated occupation on father's occupation was 0.31.)

The study by Ginzberg et al. (especially at pp. 149-51) contains a number of interesting conclusions. First, they found that both males and females began to make "realistic" evaluations of occupational choice at ages 11 or 12. Second, boys from high income families expected to go to college but did not expect to earn more than their fathers or enjoy a higher socioeconomic status than did their fathers. Boys from low income families, on the other hand, did not expect to go beyond high school or trade school, but they did aim for jobs which were more secure and paid more than those held by their fathers. Finally, they also found evidence that children of both sexes adjusted their aspirations to correspond with their perceptions of their own abilities.

2. Early Work Experiences

Because of the difficulty of obtaining reliable data, little information is available concerning the relationship between individuals' early work experiences and their experiences as mature adults. Six studies which present such information, and the groups which each surveyed, are:

Becker, B. and S. Hills, "The Nature and Consequences of Teenage Unemployment in the School to Work Transition Period" in S. Hills, ed., *Market Defenses — Early Work Decisions of Today's Middle-Aged Men* (Columbus, Ohio: Center for Human Resource Research, Ohio State University, 1983), pp. 23-65. (Males, 8-10 years after leaving school.)

Behrman, J., Z. Hrubec, P. Taubman and T. Wales, *Socioeconomic Success* (New York: North-Holland, 1980). (Male twins born in the United States between 1917 and 1927; surveyed between 1965 and 1974).

Corcoran, M., "The Employment and Wage Consequences of Teenage Women's Nonemployment" in Freeman, R. B. and D. A. Wise, eds., *The Youth Labor Market Problem* (Chicago: University of Chicago Press, 1982), pp. 391-423. (Young women who left school permanently in 1966, 1967, or 1968 with less than 14 years of education and who reported their work experiences in each of the next four years.)

Ellwood, D. T., "Teenage Unemployment: Permanent Scars or Temporary Blemishes?" in Freeman, R. B. and D. A. Wise, eds., *The Youth Labor Market Problem* (Chicago: Unversity of Chicago Press, 1982), pp. 349-89. (Young males comparable to the females in Corcoran's study, *ibid.*)

Ornstein, M., *Entry into the American Labor Force* (New York: Academic Press, 1976). (Males surveyed eight years after taking first job.)

Raelin, J. A., *Building a Career* (Kalamazoo, Mich.: W. E. Upjohn Institute for Employment Research, 1950). (Males 14 to 24-years-old in 1966 and females 14 to 24-years-old in 1968; both surveyed in initial year and each subsequent year, except 1974, until 1975.)

The studies by Behrman et al. (at p. 162), Ornstein (at p. 117), and Raelin (at p. 119) all show that the occupation of the individual's first job, in conjunction with IQ and education, is significantly correlated with the occupation of the individual's job at maturity. Indeed, in Behrman et al., a regression which employed only first occupation and education as the independant variables was able to "explain" almost as much of the variance in mature occupational status as was a regression which employed first occupation and education in conjunction with 10 other independant variables. (The R^2 values were 0.25 and 0.30, respectively.) Raelin (at pp. 144-49) also found that first job characteristics were more closely correlated with mature job characteristics among those from families of high socioeconomic status and among those with college educations than among those from families of low socioeconomic status and those with less than high school education.

Ornstein (at p. 167) and Raelin (at p. 119) both showed that there was only a weak correlation between the characteristics of the individual's first job and the wage earned at maturity. More particularly, when Raelin estimated the relationship between mature earnings and a limited number of independant variables, including characteristics of the first job, the latter proved to be significant. But, when he added age, sex, and schooling to his regression, the characteristics of the first job became insignificant. Apparently, the latter variables merely act as proxies for age, sex, and schooling when these are omitted, but have no significant explanatory power of their own.

Finally, Becker and Hills, Ellwood, and Corcoran investigated the effects of early unemployment experiences upon later wages and employment. Ellwood and Corcoran both found that males and females who experienced a period of time "not employed" or "unemployed" in the first year of the survey were more likely to experience a similar period 3 and 4 years hence than those who had not experienced such a period in the first year. Among males, for example, those who had experienced some unemployment in year 1 had a probability of 0.35 of experiencing unemployment in year 4, whereas those who did not experience unemployment in year 1 had only a 0.172 probability of unemployment in year 4. The comparable probabilities for females were 0.24 and 0.19. More importantly, however, Ellwood and Corcoran both found that the correlation between the lengths of time spent unemployed in the first and fourth years was extremely low, particularly for women. For men, this correlation was only 0.08, while for women it was 0.00. In short, Ellwood felt able to conclude that

> ... the long-run impact [of early unemployment experiences] is relatively small. Even thirty weeks out of work have virtually no impact after one or two years. For this group of youngsters [the male sample] there is no evidence of a long-term cycle of recurring periods without employment induced by an early episode out of work...[4]

On the other hand, both Ellwood and Corcoran found that total number of weeks worked in the preceding four years was positively and significantly related to the wage earned in the fourth year. Thus, although a period of unemployment in the early years did not necessarily presage unemployment in later years, it did result in a reduction

---

[4] Ellwood, D.T., "Teenage Unemployment: Permanent Scars or Temporary Blemishes?" in Freeman, R.B. and D.A. Wise, eds., *The Youth Labor Market Problem* (Chicago: University of Chicago Press, 1982) p. 374.

of the number of weeks worked and, therefore, in the amount of wage advancement enjoyed by the individual. Similarly, Becker and Hills found that the number of weeks of unemployment experienced by young men in their first two years out of school was negatively correlated with wages earned eight to ten years later. At the same time, however, they found that those young men who had changed jobs two or more times during their first two years out of school, but who had experienced no unemployment in that period, had significantly higher wages eight to ten years later than did their counterparts.

To conclude, it appears that information concerning individuals' first jobs may be useful in the prediction of the types of occupations which will be followed later in life. Information concerning the number of weeks without work or the wage rate earned during the first year, however, is of only limited value in predicting later unemployment or wages, except to the extent that all unemployment results in a reduction in experience and, therefore, a reduction in wages.

IV. THE SELF-EMPLOYED

Assume that the plaintiff (or the deceased) was the owner of a business. Three special problems arise when determining the value of lost earnings. First, the amount of money being withdrawn from the company, as personal income, may not have represented the value of the earnings derived from the company. The plaintiff, for example, may have been reinvesting his or her earnings by simply leaving them in the company; or may have been drawing down previous investments by taking a salary which exceeded current earnings. Second, it is often difficult to distinguish between the earnings which the plaintiff (or deceased) was receiving as a return on investment in the company and those which he or she was receiving as payment for personal services. Finally, the techniques for predicting the growth of wage income, which will be described in Chapter 5, normally do not apply to the prediction of the growth of business income. Each of these problems will be considered here in a separate subsection.

1. Salary Versus Earnings

Assume that the deceased's income from his or her company in the four years prior to death had been $30,000, $35,000, $39,000, and $44,000 at a time when the rate of inflation was approximately 10 percent per annum. It might appear that a reasonable prediction of his/her future income stream would be that it would have grown at the rate of inflation.

However, assume also that in the four years preceding death, the reported profits of the deceased's company had been $40,000, $28,000, $10,000, and $12,000. The prediction of steady income growth is now less easily defended. On the one hand, it could be argued that the deceased had been withdrawing ever larger amounts from the company in well-founded anticipation of a turnaround in its fortunes — after all, it is difficult to argue that these actions were taken in a deliberate attempt to deceive the court. On the other hand, it could equally be argued that the deceased was merely trying to extract as much income from the company as possible, before declaring bankruptcy; or that he/she was simply a poor manager of the company's funds.

The simplest method of resolving this problem, I suggest, is to discount the evidence of the deceased's income in the years preceding death. Rather, the techniques developed in Section 2, below, should be applied to determine the value of the deceased's services to the company. The techniques identified in Section 3 should then be employed to predict the growth of the company's income into the future. The growth rate of the deceased's "true" earnings can then be derived from the latter figure.

2. Investment Versus Labour Income

If the deceased (or plaintiff) owned a firm with significant assets (including goodwill) part of the earnings of the firm — and, therefore, part of the income of the owner — can be thought of as a return on the money invested in the company, regardless of the source of that investment. For example, assume that the individual in question had paid $200,000 for an existing firm 10 years ago. Through hard work and skillful management, he/she had built up its market value to $1,000,000 by the time of the accident. It is the $1,000,000, and not the $200,000, which is now invested in the company. At any time the firm could have been sold for $1,000,000 and, at the very least, the proceeds invested in interest-bearing bonds. Therefore, it can be presumed that the plaintiff would not have continued operating the business if it had returned less than the interest on $1,000,000. This part of the earnings of the firm may be thought of as the return on investment.

That this is a useful approach can be seen by asking what would happen to the "investment" portion of the firm's earnings should the owner be incapacitated. The answer is "nothing". The owner or his or her heirs can sell the firm and invest the proceeds, thereby maintaining the imputed investment income portion of the company's assets. These earnings are not affected by the presence or absence of the owner and, therefore, do not form a part of the claim for damages.

The claim for damages arises from the restriction which has been placed on the owner's ability to contribute labour and managerial skills to the operation of the firm. It is the lost value of these services which must be identified, therefore. In order to do this, the imputed investment income must be identified for each year and this figure must be deducted from the total value of the business' income in the relevant year.

The first step in the identification of investment income is to value the firm's net assets. In the year in which the firm was purchased, this is done by deducting from the purchase price of the firm (and its assets) the value of the mortgage(s) against that price. In subsequent years, changes in this net value can then be approximated[5] by adding to the initial value: (i) changes in the market value of the assets (such as land and buildings) which the firm held at the beginning of the year;[6] (ii) expenditures which increase the firm's holdings of inventory and assets; and (iii) payments which reduce the principal on mortgages held against the firm's assets.[7] In this process, a net value of the firm can be estimated for each year. By applying the prevailing interest rates to these values, a stream of annual investment incomes can be imputed.

The second step is then to determine the annual level of profit generated by the firm. This is done by subtracting from the firm's annual revenue only those expenses which do not increase the net value of the firm. (See the list in the preceding paragraph.) For example, a farmer would deduct the costs of seed and fertilizer, utility rates, the wages of farm workers other than him or herself, and interest payments. To this is added (subtracted) the change in the market value of those assets which were held at the beginning of the year. The value which is determined in this way is the increase (decrease) in the owner's net wealth which arose because the business was operated in the year in question (instead of being sold at the beginning of that year).

For example, assume that on January 1, 1992, a farmer owned a farm valued at $1,000,000. Against this farm there was a mortgage of $400,000. During 1992, he earned $200,000 revenue and paid: $20,000 for wages, $50,000 for operating costs, $45,000 for interest on his mortgage, $20,000 to reduce the principal on his mortgage, and $40,000

---

[5] The following operations can only approximate changes in the value of the firm because they exclude the effects of "goodwill".

[6] As an example of the importance of asset-appreciation, I was involved in a case in which the owner of a small horse-racing operation had declared an average annual income of $3,000 over the three years preceding a disabling accident. During those three years, however, the plaintiff had, through astute purchases, training, and selection of races, increased the value of his stable by more than $30,000. To the extent that the accident in question reduced the plaintiff's ability to increase this value further, it can be said that he had suffered a loss of $30,000 per three-year period, or $10,000 per year (in addition to the loss of declared income of $3,000 per year).

[7] Of course, if the value of assets falls, holdings of inventory or assets are reduced, or the principal owing on mortgages increases, those changes should be deducted from the net value of the firm.

for a new piece of equipment. Assume also that by January 1, 1993 the value of the farm (including the value of the new equipment) had increased to $1,100,000. By my calculations, the farmer's income for the year, before deducting investment income, was not $25,000 (i.e., the $200,000 revenue minus the various costs listed above). Rather, if he had sold the farm on January 1, 1992, he would have received $600,000 (= $1,000,000 − $400,000 (mortgage)). By operating it for one more year he has earned $25,000 cash, has increased the value of his assets by $100,000, and has reduced the principal on his mortgage by $20,000. Thus, if he were to sell his farm on January 1, 1993, he would have $145,000 more than he would have had a year earlier. His net wealth has been increased by that amount.

On the other hand, if the farm had been sold on January 1, 1992, the farmer could have invested the $600,000 net proceeds. Assuming that the interest rate on such an investment would have been 10 per cent, he has "lost" $60,000 investment income. Therefore, the net income for 1992 is calculated by deducting the imputed investment income from the change in net wealth calculated above. It is this net income figure which I suggest should form the basis of the evaluation of a claim for lost earnings.[8]

When this approach is followed, it becomes apparent that the market value of the firm has a direct effect on the assessment of damages only in the unusual situation in which the incapacitation of the owner affects the market value. I suggest that this is an unusual situation because, in an outright transfer of ownership, the original owner has no involvement in the firm following its sale. Therefore, whether the owner is alive or dead should not be relevant to the determination of the market value. One exception occurs when the incapacitation of the owner-operator forces sale at a particularly inopportune time. Another exception occurs when the new owners would have been willing to pay a premium had the original owner remained for a short period to ensure the smooth transfer of operations. In each of these cases, there may be a claim for a reduction in market value.

Otherwise, the determination of the market value of the firm should have little direct impact on the damage claim. Although the death of an owner-operator may lead the surviving members of the family to sell the firm earlier than would have occurred had the owner lived, the

---

[8] Additional information concerning the estimation of farmers' incomes can be found in C. Bruce and W. Kerr, "Estimating Farm Income to Determine Compensation in Death or Disability Cases" (1987), 9 *Journal of Agricultural Taxation and Law* 254-63; and in D. Kalesknikoff, M. Painter, and G. Young, *Assessing Income Losses of Grain Farmers* (available from Doug Kalesnikoff, C.A., Forensic Accounting Services, 805 CN Towers, Saskatoon, Saskatchewan, S7K 1J5)

interest which can be earned on the proceeds does not represent an "unjust gain". Rather, as I noted above, that interest would have formed a part of the firm's normal earnings had it not been sold. As this interest has been deducted from net profit in the evaluation of damages, it has already been accounted for, and has not been "double counted".

At the same time, the plaintiff cannot argue that if the owner had lived the firm would have increased in value and that this increase has now been lost through its early sale. On the one hand, if the gain in value was expected to arise from market forces, for example, making the land on which a farm was located more valuable, that gain will have been "capitalized" in the firm's market value. On the other hand, if the gain was expected to have arisen from reinvestments made by the owner, that gain cannot be said to have been lost by the plaintiff; for the approach I have outlined above compensates the plaintiff directly for those earnings which would have been reinvested.

3. Future Earnings

If at least 20 quarters of earnings data are available concerning the firm in question, it should be possible to base a forecast of future earnings growth on a statistical technique known as multiple regression. This technique, which can be applied by most economists and statisticians, identifies the correlation between a single "dependant" variable and one or more "independant" variables. In this case, the owner's, or firm's, earnings can be made the dependant variable and such factors as the level of consumer expenditure, the unemployment rate, and the real rate of interest can be made independant variables. If a strong correlation between the dependant and independant variables can be found, and if the values of the independant variables can be forecast with some confidence, then the multiple regression equation can be used to forecast the dependant variable — here, earnings.

If the data are not adequate to construct a multiple regression estimate, a number of alternatives are available. First, it may be possible to obtain a study which forecasts the average rate of growth of firms in the industry in question. Second, and more plausibly, it may be possible to obtain a forecast of the rate of growth of the industry as a whole. In this case, if one can identify the relationship between the rate of growth of industry sales and the number of firms entering the industry, it should be possible to identify the effect which industry growth will have on the firm's growth. Third, the industry growth rate itself can be used as an estimate of the individual firm's growth. Finally, if little else is available, it may be reasonable to argue that a proprietor's earnings will grow at a rate similar to the growth rate of the earnings of wage earners who have a similar level of education. The reason for this is that if the rates of growth of the incomes of these two groups began to differ significantly, we would expect there to be a movement of individuals from one group to the other. This would tend to reduce growth in the in-migrant sector and increase it in the out-migrant sector.

5

RATES OF GROWTH OF EARNINGS

The rate at which an individual's income grows can, notionally, be broken down into four sources. These are: (i) annual increases due to inflation; (ii) annual increases due to advances in the economy as a whole (usually called "productivity" increases); (iii) annual increases due to factors specific to the individual, such as merit increases, job changes, and changes in hours worked; and (iv) irregular increases due to promotions.

In the pre-trial period, information concerning the inflationary and productivity-based increases can generally be obtained from two sources. First, the individual's employer or union will often be able to identify the increases which the plaintiff would have received, or the increases which a similar employee has actually received. Second, actual percentage increases in average weekly earnings, by industry, are available from the Statistics Canada publication *Employment, Earnings, and Hours*, (Cat. No. 72-002). For example, if the individual had been working as a construction labourer in Ontario, earning $12 per hour in 1988, it might be possible to estimate his 1989 and 1990 potential earnings by increasing that $12 per hour figure by the average rate of increase experienced by workers in the Ontario construction industry between 1988, 1989 and 1990.

With respect to the remaining two sources of earnings growth and with respect to all future increases in earnings, however, less precise sources must be relied upon. Each of the four sources will be considered in a separate section in this Chapter.

I. INFLATIONARY INCREASES

In addition to those increases which arise from personal advancement, most wages increase from year to year in line with the increase in the consumer price index. Thus, the first step in forecasting the nominal (money) level of future earnings is to forecast the rate of price inflation. Numerous agencies provide publically available forecasts of this variable — many of them for many years into the future. Some of the more reliable of these agencies are listed here. (Where the forecasts are published in regularly recurring publications, the names of those publications are provided in brackets.)

Canadian Labour Market and Productivity Centre
66 Slater St.
6th Floor
Ottawa, Ont.
K1P 5H1
(Quarterly Labour Market & Productivity Review)

Conference Board of Canada
255 Smyth Rd.
Ottawa, Ont.
K1H 8M7

Economic Council of Canada,
P.O. Box 527
Ottawa, Ont.
K1P 5V6
(Annual Review)

Informetrica
Box 828
Station B
Ottawa, Ont.
K1P 5P9

Institute for Policy Analysis
University of Toronto
140 St. George St.
Suite 707
Toronto, Ont.
M5S 1A1

At the time of writing of this book, (1991) it seems unlikely that any reputable agency will forecast a long-run inflation rate outside of the range of 1-5 percent. As the calculation of the lump-sum value of future losses of earnings, in personal injury cases, will *not* be sensitive to choices of rates within that range, *any* such number can be chosen with confidence when making such calculations. However, "grossed up" values of losses of dependency, in fatal accident cases, and of future costs of care *are* sensitive to the choice of an inflation rate. Accordingly, in these cases, it may be desirable to seek expert advice, or to refer to one of the agencies identified above, when selecting this rate.

II. INDUSTRY- AND ECONOMY-WIDE INCREASES IN WAGES

Over the last century, in most industries and in most occupations, wages have risen more quickly than prices, allowing workers to purchase more goods and services than could their predecessors — "real wages" have risen. In order for this situation to continue over the long-run, it is necessary that output per worker, or "productivity" increase also. Accordingly, it has become common in the legal system to refer to wage increases which result from industry- or economy-wide changes as "productivity increases." When applied to the average wage for all workers in the economy, this term is appropriate. However, when it is applied to particular workers within specific occupations, it is so misleading that, in my view, it should be abandoned.

The primary reason for this can be seen with a simple example. Assume that there are two occupations which compete with one another for workers — let us call them waitresses and secretaries. Assume further that in one of these occupations, say secretarial work, there is ongoing technological advance whereas in the other there is none. What will happen if the wages in the secretarial field increase while those in the waitress field do not? Many of those workers who would otherwise have become waitresses will now become secretaries. This increase in supply of secretaries will reduce the rate of increase of wages in that occupation and increase the rate of advance of wages in the waitressing occupation. Hence, even though waitressing has been assumed to enjoy no increase in productivity, its wages will increase more rapidly than the rate of increase of prices. Indeed, casual observation suggests to us that since the 1940s the salaries of such workers as waitresses, parking lot attendants, construction labourers, and security guards have kept pace with the salaries of other workers in the economy even though there is little evidence of productivity increases in those occupations.

As this type of process tends to operate at every level of the labour market, in the long-run we expect the wages in most occupations to increase at the same rate, approximately the rate of increase of output per worker for the economy as a whole. It would only be in occupations in which there were restrictions on entry or a long-run decrease in demand that the growth of wages might deviate from the economy-wide average in the long-run. Hence, the first element of the real rate of increase in wages in any occupation is the average real rate of growth of wages in the economy as a whole.

In the short-run, however, while the labour market adjusts, the rate of growth of wages in any particular occupation may deviate from the economy-wide average. In the case discussed above, for example, secretaries' salaries might increase more quickly than waitresses' salaries for five or ten years after the change in technology, while the labour market adjusts to the new reality. Thus, as the short-run can often last for as much as ten or fifteen years, it may be important to predict how the rate of growth of wages in the plaintiff's occupation will deviate from the economy-wide average — as well as forecasting that economy-wide rate. In the discussion which follows, I will review forecasts of both the economy-wide real rate of increase of wages and of occupation-specific deviations from that average.

1. Economy-wide Increases in Wages

I would suggest that one of the governmental or private agencies which specialize in forecasting long-run developments in the economy be referred to in order to obtain forecasts of the economy-wide long-run real rate of increase of wages. A list of the most important of these agencies was provided in Section I of this Chapter, above. Most such agencies are currently predicting rates of growth in the order of 0.50 to 1.50 percent per annum. These rates are lower than those which were experienced in the 1950s, 1960s, and early 1970s, but higher than those which Canada has experienced since the the mid-1970s. There are two sources for this optimism. The first is the signing of the free trade agreement with the United States and the general movement toward reductions in trade barriers throughout the world. The second source is the conclusion which has been reached by a number of economists that the slow-down in productivity growth in the mid-1970's was due in large part to the rapid increase in energy prices. As energy costs rose relative to the price of labour, they hypothesize, firms increased their use of labour relative to that of other inputs. In turn, this decreased output per worker. This explanation offers some hope that, as firms adjust to higher energy prices and as the rate of growth of those prices slows, output per worker will rise once again. Some of the most important studies with respect to this last issue include:

Griliches, Zvi, "Productivity Puzzles and R&D: Another Nonexplanation" (1988) 2 *Journal of Economic Perspectives* 9-22
Jorgenson, Dale, "Productivity and Postwar U. S. Economic Growth" (1988) 2 *Journal of Economic Perspectives* 23-42
Rao, P. S., *Factor Prices and Labour Productivity* Discussion Paper No. 194 (Ottawa: Economic Council of Canada, March 1981).
Stuber, Gerald, "The Slowdown in Productivity Growth in the 1975-83 Period: A Survey of Possible Explanations", (October 1986) No. 43, *Bank of Canada Technical Reports*.

2. Occupation-specific Changes in Wages

Very few reliable sources of predictions concerning changes in relative wages among occupations are available. The only source which I feel can be recommended in Canada is the Canadian Occupational Projection System (COPS) which is being developed by Employment and Immigration Canada. At the time of the writing of this book, the most useful publication from the COPS office is:

Canada. Employment and Immigration, *Job Futures, Occupational Outlooks*, 1990 ed., vol. 1 (Ottawa: Employment and Immigration, 1990).

This publication identifies hundreds of individual occupations and provides forecasts of supply and demand conditions for each of them. Local offices of Employment and Immigration Canada should also have provincial forecasts of supply and demand conditions in most occupations.

III. INDIVIDUAL EARNING PATTERNS

The wage structure is very much like an escalator. The speed at which the stairs are moving is the average rate of growth of wages in the economy. Some people get on one step and stand still while the escalator carries them along to retirement age. For them, the real rate of growth of wages is simply the economy, industry, or occupational average rate (discussed in Section II, above). Most people, however, begin to move from stair to stair as soon as they get on. The general pattern which they follow is that they move up fairly briskly at first, then as they approach middle age their ascent begins to slow until, in their mid-fifties, most begin to drop backward a few steps. For these people, the rate of movement of the escalator is merely a base rate of progression, on which their personal rate of progress is compounded. It is this personal rate of progress, which is normally represented in terms of an "age-earnings profile," which I wish to consider in this Section.

Years of empirical investigation have shown that the most reliable predictors of an individual's future age-earnings profile are education, occupation, sex, and past performance. Thus, once the court has determined where, in each of these categories, the plaintiff (or deceased) falls, what remains to be done is to obtain as much empirical information as possible concerning the "typical" age-earnings profile for that individual. I will summarize some recent findings concerning each of the four relevant categories separately.

1. Education

There are two reliable sources of Canadian data concerning earnings patterns by education. These are the Survey of Consumer Finances

(Statistics Canada) and the Census. Table 5.1, which has been calculated from Survey of Consumer Finances data for males working full time, indicates clearly that the age-earnings profile becomes more and more steeply-sloped as individuals become more educated.[1] Whereas those with high school education (9-13 years) can expect their incomes to rise by a little less than 1 percent per year (above the average rate for their occupations) from their mid-twenties to their mid-forties, those with university degrees can expect their incomes to grow at more than 2 1/2 percent per year over the same 20 year period. All groups, however, can expect a slow decline in their annual incomes from age 50 to retirement.[2]

Table 5.2 presents comparable data taken from the 1981 Census.[3] Unfortunately, as Census data are presented in 10 year age intervals, they are less useful than the data offered in Table 5.1. On the other hand, the finer degree of detail concerning educational attainment provides additional confirmation of the positive correlation between level of educational attainment and rate of earnings growth. The only significant deviation from this correlation arises with respect to those holding trade certificates. A very high percentage of these individuals belong to unions which offer very little room for age- or experience-based earnings increases.

---

[1] All of the "age-earnings" profiles tabulated in this Section are based upon cross sectional studies. Thus, the implicit assumption is being made that the difference in earnings between each pair of age groups derives solely from personal advancement and not from temporal alterations in the wage structure. In terms of the analogy introduced at the beginning of this Section, I am assuming that today's young workers are stepping on to the same escalator as the experienced workers are already riding and that the "step" on which the new workers begin is the same step entered by previous workers (although, in the meantime, that step has moved up with the rest of the escalator). This assumption will not hold for short periods of time. However, age earnings profiles have been sufficiently stable over the long term that results based on reference to a number of different sources — such as those presented below — can, I believe, be relied upon with some confidence.

[2] Jacob Mincer, *Schooling, Experience, and Earnings* (New York: National Bureau of Economic Research, 1974) provides some evidence that the age-earnings profiles of different educational goups do not differ from one another quite as dramatically as Table 5.1 would appear to indicate. His data, from the 1960 U. S. Census, indicates that relatively uneducated men experience their highest rates of wage growth between ages 15 and 24.

[3] Although the 1986 Census has similar data, I have presented the 1981 data here because it provides a more detailed breakdown by educational category than does the 1986 data. However, those who are interested in 1986 Census data are referred to Tables 5.5 and 5.7, *infra*.

TABLE 5.1

ANNUAL RATES OF GROWTH OF EARNINGS[a]: CANADIAN MALES, BY AGE AND EDUCATION, 1971/73 and 1978/81

Age Groups Between Which Rates of Growth Have Been Calculated	Education							
	Less Than 9 Years		9-13 Years		Some Post-Secondary		University Degree	
	1971/73 (%)	1979/81 (%)	1971/73 (%)	1979/81 (%)	1971/73 (%)	1979/81 (%)	1971/73 (%)	1979/81 (%)
25-29/30-34	1.36	-0.12	2.19	1.37	3.96	2.60	4.89	4.22
30-34/35-39	1.24	1.29	0.91	1.33	2.09	1.59	3.82	3.42
35-39/40-44	0.31	-0.07	1.07	0.89	0.61	1.04	1.79	1.04
40-44/45-49	0.19	1.41	-0.57	-0.36	0.85	0.63	0.91	1.51
45-49/50-54	-1.23	-0.92	-0.63	0.44	-1.27	0.01	-1.40	-0.52
50-54/55-59	-1.17	-0.33	-0.30	-1.45	-0.41	-1.93	-0.75	-1.49
55-59/60-64	-1.59	-1.36	-0.83	-1.08	-2.55	0.37	0.40	-0.63
25-29/45-49	0.77	0.63	0.90	0.81	1.87	1.34	2.84	2.54
45-49/60-64	-1.34	-0.87	-0.59	-0.69	-1.40	-0.52	-0.58	-0.88

Source: Canada. Statistics Canada, *Survey of Consumer Finances* (Ottawa: Statistics Canada) (unpublished).

a All figures represent *annual* rates of growth of annual earnings of full-year, full-time male workers.

TABLE 5.2

ANNUAL RATES OF GROWTH OF EMPLOYMENT INCOME
BY EDUCATION: MALES, CANADA, 1980

Highest Level of Education	Comparison Age Groups		
	25-34/35-44	35-44/45-54	45-54/55-64
	(%)	(%)	(%)
Less Than Grade 9	2.02	0.14	− 1.14
Grades 9-13, No Diploma	2.02	0.41	− 1.04
Grades 9-13, Diploma	2.22	0.86	− 1.24
Trade Certificate	1.43	0.23	− 1.12
Non-University, No Diploma	2.31	0.30	− 0.79
Non-University, Diploma	2.20	0.53	− 0.92
Some University, No Diploma	3.12	0.87	− 1.23
Some University, Diploma	3.23	1.07	− 1.04
University, 1st Degree	4.55	1.97	− 0.73
University, Degree Beyond 1st	3.93	1.20	− 0.44

Source: Calculated from figures provided in Statistics Canada, *Population: Worked in 1980 — Employment Income by Selected Characteristics*, Cat. No. 92-931 (Ottawa: Statistics Canada) Table 1.

2. Occupation

There are many more sources of data available concerning occupational earnings profiles than educational earnings profiles, particularly among the "professional" occupations. With respect to professionals, I would recommend the following sources:

Muzondo T.R. and B. Pazderka, Research Monograph No. 5 in Consumer and Corporate Affairs Canada, Research Branch, Bureau of Competition and Policy, *Professional Licensing and Competition Policy* (Ottawa: Consumer and Corporate Affairs Canada, April 1979).

Canada. Pay Research Bureau, *Salary Trends in Canadian Industry*, (Ottawa: Pay Research Bureau) published occasionally.

Canada. Statistics Canada, *Salaries and Salary Scales of Full-Time Teaching Staff at Canadian Universities* (Ottawa: Statistics Canada) published annually.

Canada. Statistics Canada, *Salaries and Qualifications of Teachers in Public Elementary and Secondary Schools* (Ottawa: Statistics Canada) published annually.

Association of Professional Engineers, Geologists, and Geophysicists of Alberta, *The Value of Professional Services* (Edmonton) published annually.

Association of Professional Engineers of Ontario, *Report on Engineers' Salaries* (Toronto) published annually.

Table 5.3 provides the rates of growth of earnings between ages 26 and 45 and ages 45 and 60 for 15 professions described in the 1971 Census. Although the data employed to produce this Table was derived from

TABLE 5.3

ANNUAL RATES OF GROWTH OF EARNINGS[a] FOR SELECTED PROFESSIONAL OCCUPATIONS, CANADA, 1971

Occupation	Comparison Ages	
	26/45	45/60
	(%)	(%)
Group 1 (No Licensing Requirements)		
Agriculturalists	2.54	− 1.45
Chemists	3.01	− 0.96
Economists	3.01	− 0.96
Geologists	3.24	− 0.72
Mathematicians, Actuaries	2.77	− 1.21
Social Workers	3.01	− 0.96
Group 2 (Licensing Requirements)		
Architects	3.24	− 0.72
Dentists	3.48	− 0.48
Engineers — Chemical	3.24	− 0.72
— Industrial	2.54	− 1.45
— Mechanical	3.01	− 0.96
Lawyers	3.72	− 0.24
Optometrists	3.01	− 0.96
Physicians, Surgeons	3.95	0
Veterinarians	3.48	− 0.48

Source: Calculated from figures provided in Canada. Consumer and Corporate Affairs, *supra.* Figures for Group 1 are based on data in Table 6.2, while figures for Group 2 are based on data in Table 7.3 (1st ed.). All data, in turn, are derived from regressions estimated by Muzondo and Pazderka.

[a] Earnings have been adjusted for hours and weeks worked.

a statistical estimation procedure[4] (regression analysis) and, therefore, are not precisely indicative of the figures on which they were based, it is interesting to note how closely they reflect the findings of Tables 5.1 and 5.2. In addition, Table 5.4 suggests that the age-earnings profiles of engineers in different regions and time periods follow the general pattern of other university-trained professions.

Less information is available concerning non-professional occupations. Two sources, however, are:

Canada. Statistics Canada, *Employment Income by Occupation* (Ottawa: Statistics Canada) Cat. No. 93-116.
Canada. Pay Research Bureau, *Salary Trends in Canadian Industry* (Ottawa: Pay Research Bureau) published occasionally.

TABLE 5.4

ANNUAL RATES OF GROWTH OF ENGINEERS' EARNINGS, SELECTED SOURCES AND YEARS

Year and Region	Years Since Graduation	
	5/25	25/40
	(%)	(%)
Canada[a]		
1978	2.00	0
1980	1.93	− 0.22
1982	1.77	0.20
Alberta[b]		
1982	2.22	0.16
Ontario[c]		
1983	1.66	− 0.15

[a] *Source:* Calculated from figures provided in Pay Research Bureau, *supra*.
[b] *Source:* Calculated from figures provided in Association of Professional Engineers, Geologists, and Geophysicists of Alberta, *supra*.
[c] *Source:* Calculated from figures provided in Association of Professional Engineers of Ontario, *supra*.

---

[4] Muzondo and Pazderka first estimated an equation in which the earnings of individuals was the dependent variable. The coefficients on the independent variables in this equation were then applied to the average values of the independent variables for each occupation in order to obtain an estimate of the average earnings for each occupation. See pp. 142-45 of Muzondo and Pazderka, *supra*.

The first of these publications provides a detailed set of data drawn from the 1986 Census. Table 5.5, for example, summarizes some of the more important findings with regard to males. (A "finer" breakdown of age groups is not provided as Statistics Canada offers only 15-24, 25-44, and 45-64.) Comparable data concerning females are found in Table 5.7. The Pay Research Bureau publication does not provide age-earnings profiles, but does contain a wealth of information concerning wage scales and pay practices in many occupations.

TABLE 5.5

ANNUAL RATES OF GROWTH OF MALE EARNINGS BETWEEN AGES 25-44 and 45-64, BY OCCUPATION AND EDUCATION: CANADA 1985

Occupation	Less than Grade 9	Grades 9-13 No Diploma	Education High School	Trades/ Other Diploma	University Degree
Managerial, Administrative	0.72	1.05	1.25	1.07	1.82
Natural Sciences, Engineering, Mathematics	0.93	0.63	0.80	0.75	1.39
Social Sciences	1.05	0.68	1.02	0.82	1.76
Teaching	0.33	1.36	1.15	0.70	1.01
Medicine and Health	0.35	0.66	0.87	0.58	1.38
Clerical	0.41	0.49	0.52	0.58	1.02
Sales	0.22	0.54	0.76	0.54	0.95
Service	0.33	0.26	0.02	− 0.06	0.45
Farming	− 0.47	0.13	0.35	0.28	0.07
Forestry	0.39	0.38	0.96	0.21	1.45
Mining, Oil and Gas	− 0.27	0.44	0.52	0.23	0.75
Processing	0.66	0.65	0.59	0.47	0.38
Machining	0.38	0.56	0.45	0.36	− 0.16
Product Fabricating, Assembling, and Repair	0.48	0.66	0.56	0.23	0.26
Construction	0.15	0.49	0.53	0.21	0.73
Transport	0.15	0.49	0.78	0.85	1.01
Material Handling	0.61	0.55	0.52	0.70	0.84

Source: Canada. Statistics Canada, *Employment Income by Occupation*, Cat. No. 93-116 (Ottawa: Statistics Canada, 1989).

3. Sex

Comparison of the Census data for male earnings growth in Tables 5.2 and 5.5 with the comparable data for females in Tables 5.6 and 5.7, respectively, indicates that in virtually every occupation, at every education level, and at every age, the wages of females grow more slowly than do those of males. The one major exception is found in the later age groups, between 45-54 and 55-64.

TABLE 5.6

ANNUAL RATES OF GROWTH OF EMPLOYMENT INCOME BY EDUCATION: FEMALES, CANADA, 1980

	Comparison Age Groups		
Highest Level of Education	25-34/35-44	35-44/45-54	45-54/55-64
	(%)	(%)	(%)
Less Than Grade 9	1.33	0.43	−0.12
Grades 9-13, No Diploma	0.99	0.48	−0.44
Grades 9-13, Diploma	0.39	0.28	−0.28
Trade Certificate	0.71	0.71	−0.31
Non-University, No Diploma	0.43	0.36	0.10
Non-University, Diploma	−0.05	0.44	−0.12
Some University, No Diploma	1.12	0.14	−0.29
Some University, Diploma	1.09	0.45	−0.20
University, 1st Degree	1.97	0.79	−0.11
University, Degree Beyond 1st	2.42	1.43	−0.61

Source: Same as for Table 5.2.

Both of these findings can be explained by the same phenomenon, *viz.*, the greater proclivity of females than males to interrupt their work careers. Economic theory predicts that wages will increase with both formal and informal training. As the latter is primarily determined by experience, the prediction, therefore, becomes that those who gain the greatest amount of work experience between two ages will have obtained the largest increase between starting and concluding salaries. In turn, this implies that if women spend a greater amount of time out of the labour force between the ages of 25 and 44 than do men, their earnings at age 44 should have increased by a lesser amount relative to their earnings at age 25 than should men's earnings.

Furthermore, economic theory predicts that some of the experience and training gained before leaving the labour market will have been

TABLE 5.7

ANNUAL RATES OF GROWTH OF FEMALE EARNINGS BETWEEN AGES 25-44 and 45-64, BY OCCUPATION AND EDUCATION: CANADA 1985

Occupation	Less than Grade 9	Grades 9-13 No Diploma	High School	Trades/ Other Certificates	University Degree
Managerial, Administrative	0.28	0.39	0.60	0.44	0.96
Natural Sciences, Engineering, Mathematics	0.61	0.34	0.58	0.04	0.90
Social Sciences	0.65	0.10	0.03	0.10	0.61
Teaching	0.58	0.48	0.56	0.58	0.76
Medicine and Health	0.32	0.26	0.62	0.24	0.94
Clerical	0.35	0.20	0.22	0.22	0.29
Sales	− 0.10	− 0.21	− 0.14	− 0.10	0.39
Service	0.35	0.42	0.28	0.04	0.08
Farming	− 0.43	− 0.21	− 0.64	− 0.22	− 1.14
Processing	0.35	0.32	0.16	0.11	0.79
Machining	0.49	0.60	0.00	0.46	2.97
Product Fabri- cating, Assem- bling, and Repair	0.23	0.40	0.16	− 0.12	− 0.44
Construction	0.41	0.79	− 0.62	0.65	0.16
Transport	− 0.17	0.31	− 0.01	− 0.47	1.11
Material Handling	0.65	0.43	0.17	0.15	0.56

Source: Canada. Statistics Canada, *Employment Income by Occupation*, Cat. No. 93-116 (Ottawa: Statistics Canada, 1989).

lost or, in economic terms, will have "depreciated" during the work interruption. As a result, women's wages will be lower than men's, on average, not just because they have less experience than men but also because some of their experience will have been lost to them.

Finally, theory also predicts that, as individuals advance in their careers, they will find fewer and fewer opportunities to add to their knowledge. Therefore, the further an individual is from the point at which his career began, the more slowly should his earnings increase (or the more rapidly should they decrease). Concomitantly, if women delay the start of their careers, relative to men, their earnings should rise more rapidly than do men's in the later years of their working lives — say, ages 50-65 — as less time has elapsed between those years and the beginnings of their careers than will be the case for men.

Support for the latter hypothesis is found in the last columns of Tables 5.2 and 5.6, where it is seen that the earnings of women 45-64 decline less rapidly than do the earnings of men in that same age group. Support for the preceding two hypotheses is also found in a series of American studies based upon the National Longitudinal Survey (NLS) and the Panel Study of Income Dynamics (PSID). The two most authoritative, studies in this vein are:

Corcoran, M., G. J. Duncan, and M. Ponza, "A Longitudinal Analysis of White Women's Wages," (1983) 18 *Journal of Human Resources* 497-20.
Mincer, J. and H. Ofek, "Interrupted Work Careers" (1982) 17 *Journal of Human Resources* 3-24.

The findings of these studies are best represented through the use of Figure 5.1, which has been adapted from Figure 1 in Corcoran et al. (at p. 508). The solid line in Figure 5.1 represents the hypothetical real earnings path of a worker who remains in the labour force throughout the 15 year period described on the horizontal axis. The dashed line represents a situation in which the individual works for 5 years, drops out for 3 years, and then returns to the labour force at the same wage and growth of wages as was experienced before the work interruption. Finally, the dotted line represents a situation in which the 3 year work interruption results in the worker returning to the labour force with a lower level of earnings than experienced upon leaving, but in which a relatively rapid rate of growth of earnings after the return allows the worker to regain the earnings path indicated by the dashed line within 5-6 years.

Both Mincer and Ofek, and Corcoran et al. found that it was the dotted line in Figure 5.1 which best fits the data. That is, although there appeared to be some depreciation of skills during women's absences from the labour market, causing them to re-enter the market at lower wages than they had enjoyed when they left, this depreciation was quickly overcome through a relatively rapid growth of wages in the immediate post re-entry period. Thus, if the rate of increase in the wages of women who have experienced a work interruption are calculated between years 5 and 15 in Figure 5.1, i.e., between points A and C, the resulting estimate will be the same whether or not there was depreciation in their skills during the interruption. Furthermore, the change in wages between years 5 and 15 along the "work-interruption" (dotted) path will be less than the comparable "no interruption" (solid) path only by the loss in growth suffered during the interruption. No long run reduction in annual rate of growth of wages during the working years, i.e., the slope of the wage path, will be encountered, nor will the depreciation suffered during the interruption produce any long term impact.

FIGURE 5.1

EFFECTS OF WORK INTERRUPTION ON REAL WAGES

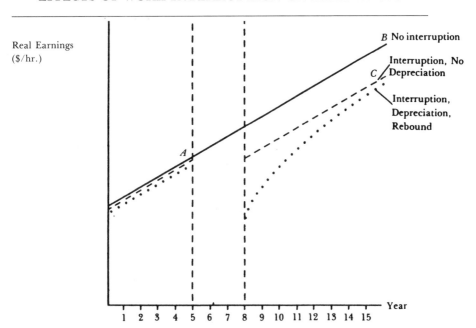

Adapted from: M. Corcoran, G.J. Duncan and M. Ponza, "A Longitudinal Analysis of White Women's Wages" (1983) *18 Journal of Human Resources* 497-520.

The Corcoran et al. and Mincer and Ofek studies suggest that the relatively low rates of growth of female earnings between ages 25-34 and 35-44 can be explained by the longer work interruptions experienced by women, on average, than by men. These studies also suggest that whereas male earnings might increase in a relatively smooth progression between 25-34 and 35-44, female earnings will follow a much more complex pattern — a pattern in which earnings initially rise at the same rate as do those of comparable males, then fall after a work interruption, rise more rapidly than do those of males, and finally rise at the same rate as do the earnings of comparable males.

4. Past Performance

An important, additional piece of information which must not be neglected is the plaintiff's (or deceased's) work record to the date of the accident. Particularly if the individual has been steadily employed for 10 years or more, the pre-accident record will provide important indications of the potential deviation of the individual's future wage growth from the average for his or her education/occupation/sex cohort.

IV. PROMOTIONAL ADVANCES

Most individuals' "advancements through the ranks" can be captured by an annual rate of growth factor, such as those discussed in Section III, above. This is because most "promotions" do not produce significant, discontinuous increments in salary. In my own profession, for example, most individuals are not promoted from Associate Professor to Full Professor until their salary as Associate exceeds the salary at the "floor" of the Full Professor rank. Hence, there is normally no discontinuous increase in salary at that time. There is, however, a small number of occupations in which promotions are associated with significant salary increases. When sufficient information is available to predict when such promotions can be expected to occur, it may be desirable to include such information, rather than to capture the increase in an annual growth rate which is constant across a number of years. In general, information concerning promotion-related wage increases is not available from statistical agencies. Rather, it must be collected from either the plaintiff's employer or trade union.

6

POSITIVE CONTINGENCIES

The wage and salary figures discussed in Chapters 4 and 5 included only what are usually called "straight-time" earnings. In addition to these earnings, most employees also receive various fringe benefits from their employers and many employees also earn overtime and shift-differential pay. As these benefits, which the courts refer to as "positive contingencies," are an integral component of the employee's compensation, their loss, due to death or injury, forms a legitimate element of the plaintiff's claim for damages. Although information concerning both of these factors is best obtained from the plaintiff's employer, often this is not possible — for example, if the plaintiff's injuries are such that he/she will now have to retrain and seek new employment. In this Chapter, I review a number of sources of information concerning fringe benefits and overtime/shift differential earnings.

I. FRINGE BENEFITS

If the injured party could have been expected to work for a particular employer (had the accident not occurred) it will often be possible to obtain from that employer an accounting of the annual value of fringe benefit expenses which would have been incurred. More commonly, however: the employer is unwilling (or unable) to provide such an accounting; the injured party did not have steady employment with a single firm; or the effect of the injury has been such that the party must enter a new occupation and has not obtained steady employment in that occupation at the time of trial. In these situations, the expert must rely upon average data drawn from various statistical sources. Four such sources are available at relatively low cost. They are:

Canada. Pay Research Bureau, *Employee Benefits and Working Conditions. — Canada* (Ottawa: Pay Research Bureau) published irregularly.

Canada. Statistics Canada, *Employee Compensation in Canada. — 1978*, Cat. No. 72-619 (Ottawa: Statistics Canada, 1980).[1]

---

[1] In the late 1960's and early 1970's Statistics Canada published a series of studies concerning compensation practices in a number of industries. The catalogue numbers, industries, and years of coverage of these publications are:

Canada. Statistics Canada, *Estimates of Labour Income* Cat. No. 72-005
(Ottawa: Statistics Canada) published annually.
Peat Marwick Stevenson & Kellogg, *Employee Benefit Costs in Canada*
(Toronto) published every second year.[2]

Tables 6.1-6.4 offer examples of the types of information available from these publications. Although the same categories, approximately, appear in each Table, the bases on which the percentages are

TABLE 6.1

EMPLOYEE BENEFIT COSTS AS PERCENTAGE OF
STRAIGHT-TIME PAYROLL: CANADA, 1989

Expenditure Category	Manufacturing	Non-Manufacturing
CPP/QPP	1.7	1.8
Unemployment Insurance	2.8	3.1
Workers' Compensation	2.7	1.6
Private Pension Plan	4.0	5.4
Insurance (Life, Health,		
Disability, Dental, etc.)	6.7	6.2
Profit Sharing and		
Bonus Plans	4.5	3.0
Miscellaneous		
(Inc. Severance Pay)	2.7	4.3
Total	25.1	25.4

Source: Peat, Marwick, Stevenson & Kellogg, *Employee Benefit Costs in Canada,*
1989 (Toronto).

- 72-510 *Manufacturing,* 1968
- 72-511 *Mines, Quarries, and Oil Wells,* 1969
- 72-610 *Finance, Insurance, and Real Estate,* 1970
- 72-611 *Transportation, Communication, and Other Utilities,* 1970
- 72-612 *Manufacturing,* 1971
- 72-613 *Mines, Quarries, and Oil Wells,* 1972
- 72-615 *Trade,* 1972
- 72-616 *Education, Libraries, and Museums,* 1974
- 72-617 *Services to Business Management,* 1975

[2]   Although there are many other, similar publications by private firms, none are readily
available to the public. It is for this reason that I have excluded them from the listing in the text. Three of these publications are: Hay Associates Canada, Toronto,
Remuneration Comparison, published annually (55 University Ave., Suite 1800,
Toronto, M5J 2H7); A. G. Lennox & Associates, *Western Canadian Oil/Gas Compensation Survey,* published annually (Suite 412, 630-4th Ave. SW, Calgary, T2P
0J9) and Towers, Perrin, Forster, & Crosby, *BENSUR* (Benefits Survey), published
annually (800 Dorchester Blvd. West, Suite 3010, Montreal, H3B 1X9).

TABLE 6.2

WAGE-EARNERS: EMPLOYEE COMPENSATION AS PERCENTAGE OF PAY FOR TIME WORKED,[a] CANADA, 1978

Expenditure Category	All Industries	Commercial	Non-Commercial
Paid Absence			
Paid Holidays	4.4	4.3	5.1
Vacation Pay	6.5	6.5	6.2
Sick Leave Pay	0.9	0.7	2.5
Other	0.2	0.2	0.3
Total	12.0	11.7	14.0
Miscellaneous Payments			
Floating COLA	0.9	1.0	0.0
Bonuses	0.2	0.2	0.0
Severance Pay	0.2	0.1	0.7
Other	0.7	0.7	0.4
Total	2.0	2.1	1.1
Welfare and Benefit Plans			
Provincial Medicare	0.8	0.8	0.8
Workmen's Compensation	2.1	2.3	0.6
Unemployment Insurance	1.7	1.7	1.9
Canada/Quebec Pension	1.3	1.3	1.4
Private Pension	4.3	4.1	5.3
Private Life/Health	2.0	2.1	1.3
Other	0.7	0.8	0.6
Total	12.9	13.0	11.9
Total — Excluding Paid Absence	14.9	15.1	13.0

Source: Derived from figures provided in Statistics Canada, Table 8.

[a] Includes overtime but excludes "paid absences."

calculated differ among them. To make the figures in the Tables comparable, I have, in each case, presented an estimate of the cost of all fringe benefits, other than pay for time not worked (e.g., holiday pay and sick leave pay) as a percentage of straight-time pay alone.[3] Three results stand out in these Tables. First, the value of fringe benefits,

[3] For an explanation of the reasons for selecting the particular statistic, see the discussion which follows in the text.

TABLE 6.3

MEAN ANNUAL EMPLOYER EXPENDITURE BASED ON ESTABLISHMENTS PARTICIPATING IN PAY RESEARCH BUREAU SURVEY, 1984

	Percent of Straight-Time Payroll		
	Office	Non-Office	Combined
PAY FOR STRAIGHT-TIME WORKED**	81.9%	81.6%	82.2%
Paid Time Away From Duty			
— Paid Holidays	4.4	4.2	4.3
— Paid Vacations	7.2	7.9	7.4
— Paid Sick Leave	2.1	1.3	1.7
— Paid Personal Leave	0.6	0.5	0.5
— Paid Rest Periods	3.8	4.3	3.9
STRAIGHT-TIME PAY	100.0	100.0	100.0
Pay Supplements			
— Overtime and Holiday Work Pay	2.2	7.8	4.1
— Shift-Work Compensation	0.2	1.4	0.6
Financial Benefits			
— Severance Pay	0.2	0.0	0.1
— Retirement Allowances	0.6	0.3	0.5
GROSS PAY***	105.4	111.6	107.5
Legislated Benefits			
— Workers' Compensation	0.9	2.0	1.3
— Unemployment Insurance	1.9	2.4	2.1
— Canada/Quebec Pension Plans	1.1	1.3	1.2
Group Life Insurance and Related Plans	0.6	0.5	0.5
Health Insurance Plans			
— Provincial Health Care****	0.4	0.7	0.5
— Quebec and Manitoba Health Care	0.9	0.8	0.9
— Supplementary Health Insurance	0.3	0.5	0.4
— Dental Care Plans	0.6	0.7	0.6
Salary Continuation Plans			
— Sickness Indemnity Insurance	0.0	0.5	0.2
— Combined Sick Leave & Sickness Indemnity	0.1	0.7	0.3
— Long-Term Disability Insurance	0.4	0.5	0.4
— Supplementary Unemployment Insurance	0.0	0.1	0.0

TABLE 6.3 (Cont'd.)

MEAN ANNUAL EMPLOYER EXPENDITURE BASED ON
ESTABLISHMENTS PARTICIPATING IN PAY RESEARCH BUREAU
SURVEY, 1984

	Percent of Straight-Time Payroll		
	Office	Non-Office	Combined
Private Pension Plans	7.1	6.4	6.8
Fringe Benefits*	14.3	17.1	15.2
Fringe Benefits Plus Overtime and Shift-Work	16.7	26.3	19.9

* Legislated benefits, group life insurance, health insurance, salary continuation, plus private pension.

Source: Pay Research Bureau, *Employee Benefits and Working Conditions: Canada, 1984* (Ottawa: Pay Research Bureau, 1985) Tables 29-B, 30-B and 31-B.

as a percentage of pay for time worked, is not less than 10.6 percent in any of them. Second, fringe benefits have been increasing as a percentage of straight-time pay over time. Third, there are very significant differences among the four estimates. Whereas the Statistics Canada survey reported in Table 6.4 reports that "supplementary income" had risen to only 11.4 percent of labour income (excluding supplementary income) by 1990, the Pay Research Bureau and Peat Marwick Stevenson & Kellogg surveys both suggest fringe benefits of approximately 25 percent of straight-time earnings. In part, these differences reflect the fact that the Statistics Canada figures exclude profit sharing, bonus plans and severance pay, which account for approximately 8 percent of the other surveys' fringe benefit packages. However, I also suspect that the results also reflect the Pay Research Bureau and Peat Marwick Stevenson & Kellogg surveys' reliance on large firms. It is well known that large firms offer more liberal fringe benefit packages than do small firms. Hence, the figures in Tables 6.1 and 6.3 may be reliable indicators of the fringe benefit packages available at large firms, whereas the figures in Tables 6.2 and 6.4 may more accurately reflect fringe benefits offered at the "average" firm.

A number of cautions must be offered with respect to the use of tables such as those presented here. First, if evidence is to be led as to the value of fringe benefits as a percentage of "earnings," one must be certain that the earnings figure being employed in court is comparable to the one which was employed to construct the statistics which are being cited. For example, the "straight-time pay" figure, on which most percentages in Tables 6.1 and 6.3 are based, excludes overtime; whereas

TABLE 6.4

SUPPLEMENTARY INCOME AS A PERCENTAGE OF NET LABOUR INCOME: CANADA, 1983-1990

Year	Supplementary Income as Percentage of Net Labour Income
1983	10.6%
1984	10.7
1985	10.8
1986	10.8
1987	10.9
1988	11.0
1989	10.6
1990	11.4

Source: Derived from information in Statistics Canada, *Estimates of Labour Income*, Cat. No. 72-005 (Ottawa: Statistics Canada, 1991) Table 1, published annually.

TABLE 6.5

AVERAGE WEEKLY OVERTIME EARNINGS, AS A PERCENTAGE OF "STRAIGHT-TIME PAY": CANADA, 1990

Industry	Salaried Workers	Hourly Workers
Forestry	0.93%	13.34%
Mines, Quarries, and Oil Wells	3.67	14.20
Manufacturing	2.15	9.16
Construction	0.73	8.50
Goods Producing Industries	2.13	9.38
Transportation, Commerce, Utilities	3.41	9.37
Trade	0.95	3.12
Finance, Insurance, Real Estate	1.02	2.24
Commercial Business and Personal Service	0.72	2.34
Service Producing Industries	0.94	3.37
INDUSTRIAL AGGREGATE	1.15	6.06

Source: Statistics Canada, *Employment, Earnings, and Hours*, Cat. No. 72-002 (Ottawa: Statistics Canada, 1990) Table 2.1.

the "pay for time worked" base employed in Table 6.2 includes over-time. If the annual earnings figure which is led in court includes overtime, the figures in 6.1 and 6.3 will slightly overstate the value of fringe benefits.

Second, consistency must be maintained with respect to the treatment of pay for time not worked, such as holidays and sick leave. It would be double-counting to assume that the plaintiff had been working 52 weeks per year and then to add into the earnings for that period pay for holidays and vacations. To avoid this, I recommend that estimates of annual earnings not be reduced by a factor for holidays, sick leave, vacations, etc. Rather, it is simpler to assume that the employee receives his or her regular salary during these periods and then to exclude such payments from estimates of the value of fringe benefits. Hence the figures offered in the last line of each of Tables 6.1-6.3 are based on straight-time earnings, inclusive of holiday and vacation pay.

Finally, the manner in which employer payments for unemployment insurance are to be incorporated depends upon the way in which unemployment benefits are to be treated. For example, assume that it has been predicted that the individual's lifetime earning capacity would have been reduced by 10 percent because of spells of unemployment. Assume also, that it has been recognized that this loss will be offset to a certain extent by unemployment insurance benefits. It might, for example, have been assumed that the 10 percent incidence of unemployment would have led to only a 6 percent reduction in income. If this approach has been taken, then it would be inappropriate also to include an allowance for the employer's contributions to unemployment insurance in the fringe benefit calculation; for that would be to double compensate the employee, once for the employer's contribution and again for the payment of the benefits. In this case, the employer's contribution to the unemployment insurance plan would have to be omitted. Only if the *unreduced* unemployment contingency is to be used to calculate future loss of income should the employer's contribution to the plan be included in fringe benefits.

II. OVERTIME AND SHIFT DIFFERENTIAL PAY

In addition to straight-time pay, many employees receive additional income from overtime work or from shift differential pay. Table 6.3 reports reliable data concerning both of these sources of income, while Tables 6.5 and 6.6 report some recent data concerning overtime pay, by major industry group.

Both the Pay Research Bureau study, reported in Table 6.3, and the Statistics Canada data, reported in Table 6.5, suggest that overtime pay represents a greater percentage of total compensation for hourly rated workers involved in physically-oriented occupations than it does for salaried, office workers. Among the former, overtime pay can be expected to add 10-15 percent to "straight time" pay; whereas among the latter it would not be expected to add more than 2-4 percent in most cases. Finally, Table 6.6 suggests that the basis of this difference among sectors is variations in hours of overtime worked, rather than in variations in the size of the overtime differential.

TABLE 6.6

AVERAGE WEEKLY HOURS, BY INDUSTRY, HOURLY PAID WORKERS: CANADA, 1990

Industry	Excluding Overtime	Overtime
Forestry	36.02	3.28
Mines, Quarries, and Oil Wells	36.28	3.89
Manufacturing	36.17	2.03
Construction	36.31	1.83
Goods Producing Industries	36.24	2.09
Transportation, Commerce, Utilities	35.33	2.11
Trade	27.57	0.49
Finance, Insurance, Real Estate	25.86	0.37
Commercial Business and Personal Service	26.30	0.42
Service Producing Industries	27.57	0.58
INDUSTRIAL AGGREGATE	30.37	1.08

Source: Statistics Canada, *Employment, Earnings, and Hours*, Cat. No. 72-002 (Ottawa: Statistics Canada, 1990) Table 3.1.

7

NEGATIVE CONTINGENCIES

When evaluating an individual's potential stream of earnings, allowance must be made for the possibility that the individual might not be employed during certain periods. In this Chapter I will consider three classes of situations in which this possibility might arise. First, the individual may not be a member of the labour force, in spite of being old enough to work, either because he or she has chosen some other activity or because a disability has prevented him/her from working. Second, the plaintiff may have entered the labour force but have been unable to locate a job; that is, he or she may be unemployed. And, finally, he or she may have died.

Individuals are classified as being members of the labour force if they are employed — including those on holiday, sick leave, and strike — or unemployed — comprising those who were available for work and: were actively seeking employment; were expecting to be called back to a job from which they had been laid off; or were waiting to begin a job which had been promised to them. The percentage of individuals in the working age population, where the latter excludes institutionalized individuals and members of the armed forces, who are members of the labour force is called the labour force participation rate. In this Chapter, I will begin by reviewing the data concerning the determinants of this rate. This will lead to an analysis of long-term disability, one of the reasons why participation rates might be less than 100 percent. These analyses will be followed by a section which deals with unemployment. Finally, brief mention will be made of mortality rates. Retirement age will be considered in Chapter 9.

I. LABOUR FORCE PARTICIPATION RATES

Table 7.1 identifies the major changes in labour force participation rates, by sex, for various age groups since the 1931 Census. A number of important factors are evident from this Table. First, males aged 20-24 have participation rates which are approximately 15-20 percent lower than the comparable rates for males 25-54. Second, all but a very small percentage of males 25-54 are members of the labour force. Third, the participation rates of males 55-64 and 65 + have declined at a steady rate in the past 20 years. Finally, the participation rates of females over

20, although appreciably lower than those of males in the same age groups, have been rising rapidly, particularly in the age groups 25-34 and 35-44. In the following subsections I will discuss the trends in male participation rates only briefly and then will turn to a more extensive review of the determinants of female participation rates. Finally, I will also comment on some forecasts of labour force participation.

Those who are interested in a more detailed examination of the issues discussed in this Section are advised to refer to:

Bruce, Christopher J., *Economics of Employment and Earnings* (Toronto: Nelson), 1990, Chapter 11.

TABLE 7.1

LABOUR-FORCE PARTICIPATION RATES BY AGE AND SEX, CANADA, SELECTED YEARS 1931-1991

	15-24[a]	25-34	35-44	45-54	55-64	65 +
Males						
1931[b]	80.6	97.7	—	95.9	—	55.7
1941	79.0	97.7	97.9	96.2	89.0	47.0
1951	75.5	96.4	96.7	94.5	85.7	38.6
1961	61.9	94.1	94.3	91.9	81.9	28.4
1971	65.3	92.6	92.8	90.3	80.1	23.6
1981	73.1	95.2	95.1	92.0	76.9	16.3
1986	72.4	94.3	94.6	91.2	70.6	13.7
1991	71.7	93.5	94.2	90.8	63.0	11.3
Females						
1931[b]	36.6	21.4	—	12.0	—	6.2
1941	41.3	24.9	16.2	12.9	10.8	5.5
1951	42.5	24.2	21.8	20.4	14.5	5.1
1961	41.2	29.6	31.1	33.4	24.4	6.7
1971	49.3	44.5	43.9	44.4	34.4	8.3
1981	64.8	66.0	64.4	55.9	35.5	5.4
1986	66.8	73.6	72.1	62.4	35.9	4.2
1991	67.4	77.5	79.5	69.3	35.9	3.7

[a] Until 1975, the youngest age group was 14-24.
[b] The third figure in the 1931 row represents the participation rate for workers 35-64.

Sources: Census of Canada, various years; and Statistics Canada, *The Labour Force*, Cat. No. 71-001 (Ottawa: Statistics Canada, August 1991). May 1991 figures were chosen in order to maintain comparablity with the Census figures, which relate to May and early June.

1. Male Participation Rates

Virtually all of the difference between the male participation rates listed in Table 7.1 and a 100 percent participation rate can be explained by three variables: education, long-term disability, and retirement. With respect to education, for example, it is known that at the time of the last Census, 1986, the number of individuals enrolled full-time in post-secondary institutions of education was approximately 20 percent of the total population of individuals 15-24. Although many 15 to 24-year-olds are still in secondary schools and although some post-secondary students are older than 24, these figures strongly suggest that approximately 20-25 percent of 18 to 24-year-olds are full-time students. As the participation rate of 20 to 24-year-old males is approximately 20 percent less than that of those 25-34, it can be presumed that enrolment in educational institutions accounts for most of this difference. That long-term disability represents a second major constraint on the labour force participation of males, particularly among those over 45, will be shown in Section III, *infra*. Third, it will be shown in Chapter 9 that a significant portion of the male population over 55 leave the labour force through retirement.

A fourth factor which sometimes also proves to be of use in the forecasting of male participation rates is marital status. For example, Table 8.2 indicates that single men aged 15-64 had much lower participation rates than married men, especially after age 35. Furthermore, from the fact that divorced and widowed men also had lower participation rates than married men, it appears that it is the absence of a spouse which "causes" men to remain out of the labour force, rather than some third factor (such as disability) which causes them both to be single and to be out of the labour market.

2. Female Participation Rates

Although education, disability, and retirement influence female participation rates in much the same way they affect male rates, additional variables must be introduced to explain why (i) female rates are lower than male and (ii) female rates have shown steady growth over the last three decades. The purpose of this subsection will be to review the literature which has dealt with these two questions.

The following studies (among others) have attempted to identify the factors which influence female labour force participation rates in Canada:

Allingham, J., and B. Spencer, *Women Who Work: Part 2*, Special Labour Force Studies, Series B. Part 2 (Ottawa: Dominion Bureau of Statistics, 1968).

Boothby, D., "The Continuity of Married Women's Labour Force Participation in Canada" (1984) 17 *Canadian Journal of Economics* 471-80.

Bruce, C., "The Effect of Young Children on Female Labour Force Participation Rates: An Exploratory Study" (1978) 3 *Canadian Journal of Sociology* 431-40.

Nakamura, A., and M. Nakamura, "A Comparison of the Labour Force Behaviour of Married Women in The United States and Canada, With Special Attention to the Impact of Income Taxes," (1981) 49 *Econometrica*, 451-90.

Nakamura, A., M. Nakamura, and D. Cullen, *Employment and Earnings of Married Females* (Ottawa: Statistics Canada, 1979.)

Officer, L., and P. Andersen, "Labour Force Participation in Canada" (1969) 2 *Canadian Journal of Economics* 278-87.

Ostry, S., *The Female Worker in Canada* (Ottawa: Dominion Bureau of Statistics, 1968).

Prescott, D., R. Swidinsky, and D. Wilton, "Labour Supply Estimates for Low-Income Female Heads of Households Using Mincome Data," (1986) 19 *Canadian Journal of Economics*, 134-41.

Skoulas, N., *Determinants of the Participation Rate of Married Women in the Canadian Labour Force: An Econometric Analysis* (Ottawa: Statistics Canada, February 1974.)

Spencer, B., "Determinants of the Labour Force Participation of Married Women: A Micro-Study of Toronto Households" (1973), 6 *Canadian Journal of Economics* 222-38.

Spencer, B. and D. Featherstone, *Married Female Labour Force Participation: A Micro Study*, Special Labour Force Studies, Series B, No. 4 (Ottawa: Dominion Bureau of Statistics, December 1970).

Stelcner, M., and J. Breslaw, "Income Taxes and the Labor Supply of Married Women In Quebec," (1985) 51 *Southern Economic Journal*, 1053-72.

These studies, and other similar ones conducted in the United States, consistently find six variables to be significantly correlated with the female labour force participation decision. These are: age, education, income of other family members, marital status, age of youngest child, and number of children.

A number of interesting points concerning the effect of age on women's participation rates can be seen by comparing the 1981 and 1991 data in Table 7.1. Consider, for example, the group aged 35 to 44 in 1991. This group is composed of virtually the same set of women who comprised the 25 to 34-year-old group in 1981. (The primary differences between the two result from immigration and emigration.) Yet we observe that the participation rate of these women increased from 66 percent to 79.5 percent. Similarly, the participation rate of those who were 15-24 in 1981 increased from 64.8 to 77.5 percent by 1991; and the participation rate of those who were 35-44 in 1981 increased from 64.4 to 69.3 percent by 1991. These figures suggest two important predictions concerning future developments in the labour force participation of Canadian women. First, it would be incorrect to use the current participation rate of women, say, 45-54 to predict what the participation of women currently 35-44 will be ten years from now. Rather, if the trends observed between 1961 and 1991 continue into the future, we would expect that the participation rates of 45 to 54-year-olds ten years from now will be higher than today's participation rate of 35 to 44-year-olds — and similar predictions might be made concerning women currently 15-24 and 25-34. Second, that a woman has not been in the labour force at a particular age does not necessarily imply that she will remain outside of the labour force when she is older. As is seen from Table 7.1, the participation rates of given cohorts of women have increased as they have aged, up to age 55.

These observations are not inconsistent with the findings of a number of studies which have followed given sets or "panels" of women as they have aged.[1] These studies generally find that the best predictor of whether a particular woman will be in the labour force in the future is whether she was in the labour force in the past. That is, women who have been working are likely to continue to do so, regardless of whether the participation rates for women older than them are lower than the participation rate of the age groups of which they are currently members.

Boothby, Bruce, Nakamura et al., Skoulas, and Spencer all found evidence that the most highly educated women had the strongest attachments to the labour force.[2] As education has been seen to be highly correlated with income, the interpretation which is usually given to this finding is that women are more strongly attracted to the labour force, the greater are their potential earnings.

With the exception of Officer and Andersen, the studies cited above found that women's participation rates fell as the incomes of other family

---

[1] See, especially, A. Nakamura and M. Nakamura, *The Second Paycheck* (New York: Academic Press, 1985); A. Nakamura, M. Nakamura, and D. Cullen, *Employment and Earnings of Married Females* (Ottawa: Statistics Canada, 1979); D. Boothby, "The Continuity of Married Women's Labour Force Participation in Canada" (1984) 17 *Canadian Journal of Economics* 471-80; and F. Mott and D. Shapiro, "Complementarity of Work and Fertility Among Young American Mothers," (1983) 37 *Population Studies*, 239-52.

[2] Participation rates of women aged 25-44 who have post-secondary education are almost as high as the equivalent rates for all males in that age group. In May 1991, for example, the participation rate for women 25-44 with a post-secondary certificate or diploma was 90.8 percent and for women in this age group with a university degree it was 92.1 percent; the participation rate for all males 25-44 in that month was 93.8 percent. (Source: Statistics Canada, *The Labour Force*, Cat. No. 71001 (Ottawa: Statistics Canada, May 1991) Tables 1 and 8.)

members rose, *ceteris paribus*. This provides a potential explanation for the observation, in Table 7.2, that single women have higher participation rates than widows and divorcees, and that the latter have higher rates than married women. Whereas single women have no income from other family members, divorced and widowed women will often obtain at least some income from their former spouses. In turn, however, that income will generally be less than that which married women share with the spouses with whom they are living.

TABLE 7.2

Labour Force Participation Rates by Age, Sex, Marital Status: Canada, 1986

Canada	Single	Married	Separated	Widowed	Divorced
Male					
15-19	48.1	73.6	52.3	48.5	54.4
20-24	88.8	95.2	94.1	73.7	91.4
25-34	90.6	96.9	93.9	88.3	92.9
35-44	84.4	96.6	92.7	87.9	90.3
45-54	74.9	93.9	86.4	82.6	83.2
55-59	62.9	84.1	73.1	69.3	71.2
60-64	47.2	62.3	48.7	48.6	51.7
65 +	17.1	15.3	13.3	8.4	14.4
Female					
15-19	44.8	62.1	49.2	29.6	59.2
20-24	84.8	75.4	68.6	51.3	69.4
25-34	85.5	70.3	74.8	65.5	76.9
35-44	82.7	70.3	78.6	68.1	78.9
45-54	75.7	60.5	71.2	59.9	73.7
55-59	63.3	41.7	53.4	44.4	61.0
60-64	45.9	24.0	36.9	28.5	47.1
65 +	9.5	4.7	6.3	3.5	9.7

Source: Statistics Canada, *Population and Dwelling Characteristics: Labour Force Activity*, Cat. No. 93-111. (Ottawa: Statistics Canada, March 1989)

Finally, there is mixed evidence with respect to the effect which young children have on female labour force participation. On the one hand, the studies referenced in footnote 1 tend to suggest that married women who had been working prior to the birth of their first child have a strong tendency to return to work within one to two years of the birth of that child. That is, these studies find that the presence of children in the home, particularly those over 2-years-old, has very little influence on the participation rates of married women. Statistics Canada data show, for example, that the participation rate of married women with children less than 3-years-old is approximately 65 percent.[3] On the other hand, Statistics Canada data for married women indicate that the participation rates of women whose youngest children are between the ages of 3 and 5 are approximately 8-9 percent lower than those of women whose youngest children are between the ages of 6 and 15. These data suggest that although most women return to the work force in the first two years following the birth of a child there is a large number who delay re-entry until their youngest child is of school age.

These studies lead one to conclude that the best predictor of a female plaintiff's future labour force participation is her current participation, unless she has a child under the age of six. My recommendation, therefore, is that the average participation rates drawn from Tables 7.1 and 7.2 should not be applied to individual women. Rather, if a woman has a history of labour force participation, her future attachment to the labour force must be assumed to be much stronger than that implied by the average figures, unless evidence has been led which would lead one to believe otherwise. And, conversely, if she does not have a history of labour force participation, it must be assumed that her future degree of attachment to the labour force would have been much lower than that for the average woman.

The only situation in which it appears appropriate to employ the averaged data of Tables 7. 1 and 7.2 is that in which the (female) plaintiff had not revealed her degree of attachment to the labour market before becoming injured. This situation would most commonly arise if the plaintiff had had her first child at a relatively early age and her youngest child was still less than 6, or if she was a minor at the time of her injury. Even in these situations, however, it would be inappropriate to employ the current labour force participation rates as forecasts of future rates. As Table 7.1 demonstrates clearly, there has been a long run trend to ever-increasing female participation. Those 30-year-old women who today have higher participation rates than did 30-year-olds 20 years ago, can be expected to have higher participation rates 20 years from now than do 50-year-olds today.

---

[3] Among women whose youngest child was under three-years-old in May 1991, the participation rate of those whose husbands were working was 66.4 percent, whereas the comparable rate of those whos husbands were not working was 54.7 percent. (Source: Statistics Canada, *ibid.*, Table 8.)

3. Forecasts of Labour Force Participation

Section I of Chapter 5 lists a number of agencies which offer public
forecasts of trends in the Canadian rate of price inflation. As a rule,
these agencies also make available forecasts of labour force participation rates.

As I argued in subsection 2, it is my view that any such forecast
should take into account the trends which have been observed with
respect to particular cohorts over the last three decades. It would be
unreasonable to forecast a participation rate of 65 percent for 35 to
44-year-old women ten years from now if 25 to 34-year-old women currently have a participation rate of 77.5 percent. Experience shows that
the participation rates of 25 to 34-year-old women *increase* as they pass
the child-bearing ages, not decrease. Indeed, as the participation rates
of all female cohorts have been increasing over time, it would seem
reasonable to assume that female participation rates will *approach* the
male rates over the long run.

II. LONG-TERM DISABILITY

One of the reasons that individuals may not be "available for work"
and, therefore, may not contribute to the labour force participation
rate statistic is that they are suffering from a disability. To the extent
that such disabilities restrict the individual's ability to earn income, they
represent negative contingencies which must be taken into account when
calculating foregone income. As I shall assume that short-term ailments
will not generally result in income loss, as they are covered by employer
sickness benefits, in this Section I will concentrate on long-term disabilities.

For many years, no reliable source was available concerning the
disability rate among Canadians. Fortunately, this deficiency has been
rectified with the publication of:

Wilkins, R. and O. B. Adams, *Healthfulness of Life* (Montreal: Insti-
    tute for Research on Public Policy, 1983).

The most important findings from Wilkins' and Adams' research are
summarized in Table 7.3. There it is seen, for example, that among
males, 5.8 percent of 25 to 44-year-olds and 19.2 percent of 45 to 64-year-
olds suffer a major disability; while, among females, 7.1 percent of 24
to 44-year-olds and 17.9 percent of 45 to 64-year-olds are disabled. The
similarity between these figures and the (implied) figures for male non-
participation in the labour force, seen earlier in Table 7.1, imply that

a major determinant of male non-participation before age 65 is ill health. Furthermore, the disability figures displayed in Table 7.3 also serve to suggest an upper limit to female labour force participation, particularly in the 45 to 64-year-old group.

TABLE 7.3

PERCENTAGE, AND CHANGE IN PERCENTAGE, OF POPULATION WITH MAJOR ACTIVITY RESTRICTION: BY AGE AND SEX, CANADA 1978

Age/Sex	Institution-alized %	Change[a]	Cannot Do Major Activity %	Change[a]	Restricted In Major Activity %	Change[a]	Total %	Change[a]
Male								
0-14	0.2	—	0.0	—	2.3	—	2.5	—
15-24	0.3	0.1	0.6	0.6	2.2	(0.1)[b]	3.1	0.6
25-44	0.3	0.0	1.1	0.5	4.4	2.2	5.8	2.7
45-64	0.6	0.3	8.2	7.1	10.4	6.0	19.2	13.4
65-74	2.3	1.7	14.2	6.0	20.4	10.0	36.9	17.7
75+	11.2	8.9	11.1	(3.1)[b]	23.2	2.8	45.5	8.6
Female								
0.14	0.1	—	0.0	—	1.4	—	1.5	—
15-24	0.1	0.0	0.5	0.5	2.5	1.1	3.1	1.6
25-44	0.2	0.1	0.4	(0.1)[b]	6.5	4.0	7.1	4.0
45-64	0.5	0.3	2.5	2.1	14.9	8.4	17.9	10.8
65-74	2.6	2.1	3.8	1.3	27.4	12.5	33.8	15.9
75+	17.5	14.9	5.7	1.9	27.5	0.1	50.7	16.0

Source: R. Wilkins and O.B. Adams *Healthfulness of Life* (Montreal: Institute for Public Policy, 1983) at p. 60.

[a] The difference between the figure in the column headed "%" and the preceding figure in that column.
[b] Bracketed terms are those with negative values.

The Wilkins and Adams figures do not, however, provide a direct estimate of the probability that the average plaintiff would have been disabled at a particular age. The reason for this is that whereas most plaintiffs were not disabled before the accident which is being litigated, some of the members of the age groups described in Table 7.3 were disabled before entering that age group. For example, assume that the plaintiff was injured on her 45th birthday. Table 7.3 indicates that 17.9

percent of all females 45-64 are seriously disabled. Does this imply that
there was a 17.9 percent chance that the plaintiff would have become
disabled between her 45th and 65th birthdays, had she not been involved
in the accident which is being litigated? The answer is "no." It will be
noted that 7.1 percent of 25 to 44-year-olds are seriously disabled also.
If this percentage of 44-year-olds carried that disability into their 50's
and 60's, then the disability rate among 45 to 64-year-olds which arose
from disabilities incurred after their 45th birthdays would be 17.9 −
7.1 = 10.8. In such a case, it would be the 10.8 percent figure which
should be applied to the 45-year-old plaintiff, not 17.9 percent.

Although Wilkins' and Adams' data do not allow us to determine
with certainty whether the disabled in the 25 to 44-year-old age group
will continue to be disabled when they reach their 50's and 60's, it should
be noted that all three categories of restrictions listed in Table 7.3 result
from long-term disability. For this reason, I have considered it to be
useful to include the columns headed "change" in Table 7.3. These
columns indicate the increases in disability rates between congruent age
groups. Thus, if all who are disabled in one group continue to be so
when they enter the next group, this column approximates the level
of disability, within each age group, among those who were not disabled when they entered that group.[4]

More direct evidence concerning the probability of becoming disabled during a particular year is available from an American study by
H. Luft. Luft's primary findings are summarized in Table 7.4. Although
his figures refer to all long-term health problems and, therefore, include
disabilities which do not seriously inhibit work, they are useful in the
sense that they provide information concerning the relative incidences
of disability among different age groups. Luft's study also provides useful
information concerning the incidences of disability by education, income,
and sex.

Canadian data concerning disability by income group are available from Wilkins and Adams. Their data, presented in Table 7.5, indicate that those in the lower income brackets are more likely to suffer
from disabilities than are those in the upper brackets. In part, this must
be due to the fact that many people have relatively low incomes because

---

[4] If all disabled individuals — as defined by the last two columns of Table 7.3 — continue to be disabled permanently, the "change" column in Table 7.3 will overestimate the change in the disability rate. Consider: if 7.1 percent of 25 to 44-year-old
females are disabled, it is likely that many more than 7.1 percent of 44-year-olds
are disabled, because the disability rate is cumulative as the age group ages. Assume,
for example, that the percentage was 12 percent and that all of these women continued to be disabled until they were (at least) 65. Then 12 percent of those women
45-64 who were disabled would be women who became disabled before age 45. In
this case, the increase in disability during the 45-64 year period would be only 17.9
− 12.0 = 5.9 percent.

TABLE 7.4

INCIDENCE OF DISABILITY[a] BY SEX AND BY AGE, EDUCATION, AND INCOME AT TIME OF ONSET OF DISABILITY: UNITED STATES, 1967

	Educational Attainment and Age								
	0-8 Years			9-12 Years			13 + Years		
Income and Sex	18-34	35-54	55-64	18-34	35-54	55-64	18-34	35-54	55-64
White Males									
<$2000	.002	.039	.104	.013	.012	.064	.003	.010[b]	.035[b]
$2-4000	.021	.034	.057	.013	.026	.109	.011	.017	.020[b]
$4-6000	.015	.027	.045	.009	.014	.041	.010	.014	.035[b]
$6-8000	.029	.021	.037	.007	.013	.018	.012	.013	.039
$8-10000	.003	.019	.020	.003	.007	.018	.005	.011	.030
$10000 +	.033	.017	.059	.003	.007	.019	.005	.009	.023
White Females									
<$2000	.041	.061	.048	.021	.019	.039	.010	.010	.047
$2-4000	.034	.029	.077	.014	.024	.023	.002	.002	.064
$4-6000	.013	.029	.031	.007	.013	.015	.004	.017	.050
$6-8000	.014	.017	.037	.006	.010	.036	.006	.005	.017
$8-10000	.024	.024	.044	.007	.007	.003	.008	.010	.011
$10000 +	.026	.017	.031	.009	.008	.020	.008	.006	.020

Source: Reprinted with permission from H. Luft, *Poverty and Health* (Cambridge, Mass.: Ballinger, 1978) at pp. 82-83. Copyright 1978, Ballinger Publishing Company.

a Number of individuals becoming disabled per year. "Disability" is defined to be any long-term health problem which limits the kind or amount of work (or housework) that can be done.

b Based on small sample.

probability of becoming disabled to pre-disability income, indicates that that probability decreases somewhat as incomes rise. In addition, older individuals, who have relatively high incomes, also have relatively high disability rates. (See Table 7.3.) This should have the effect of raising reported disability rates in the higher income groups. That disability rates in those groups remain lower than those among the lower income groups, in spite of this bias, adds weight to the inference that poor Canadians tend to work in relatively risky occupations.

Although not all long-term disabilities are work-related, they may result, for example, from factors such as heart attacks and cancer, it must be recognized that there are considerable differences in risk rates among industries and occupations. For this reason, Tables 7.6 and 7.7, which provide information concerning the distribution of fatality and injury rates among industries and occupations, are presented here. As one would expect, Table 7.6 indicates that the industries with the highest fatality rates are forestry, fishing, and mining. However, this Table also indicates that fatality rates may be an inaccurate measure of the relative riskiness of the various industries as it shows that injury rates in manufacturing and construction are proportionately much higher than their fatality rates and that injury rates in fishing are proportionately much lower than their fatality rates. Table 7.7 also reveals the expected distribution of injury rates among occupations, with the most physically demanding occupations — such as forestry, machining, and

TABLE 7.5

PERCENTAGE OF YEARS OF TOTAL LIFE EXPECTANCY DURING WHICH INDIVIDUALS CAN EXPECT TO SUFFER MAJOR ACTIVITY RESTRICTION: BY SEX AND INCOME LEVEL, CANADA 1978

| Income Level (by Fifths) | Extent of Constraint on Major Activity | | | |
| | Cannot Do | | Restricted In | |
	Males	Females	Males	Females
	(%)	(%)	(%)	(%)
Lowest	13.1	2.5	9.4	14.4
Second	5.8	2.8	8.1	12.5
Third	3.0	1.5	7.8	12.1
Fourth	2.6	1.0	8.3	12.5
Highest	1.6	0.5	5.6	8.1
Average	4.7	1.8	7.9	11.7

Source: Figures were calculated from data presented in Table 5.4 of Wilkins and Adams (at p. 98).

materials handling — having the highest rates and the least physically demanding — such as managerial, natural sciences, and teaching — having the lowest rates.

TABLE 7.6

Fatality and Time-Loss Injury Rates by Industry, Canada

Industry	Fatality Rates per 100,000 Workers 1979-1987	Time-Loss Injury Rates Per 1,000 Workers 1982-1956
Agriculture	11.2	42
Forestry	111.1	155
Fishing	152.0	57
Mining	74.4	69
Manufacturing	7.7	93
Construction	30.7	117
Transportation	20.1	57
Trade	4.0	47
Finance	1.1	6
Service	2.4	31
Public Administration	7.5	43
TOTAL	9.4	54

Source: Labour Canada, *Employment Injuries and Occupational Illness*, (Ottawa: Labour Canada, 1990) Table 6; and Statistics Canada, *The Labour Force*, Cat. No. 71-001 (Ottawa: Statistics Canada, March 1988).

Additional information concerning relative industrial disability rates is sometimes available from Workers' Compensation Boards, although most publish very little. In Alberta, for example, the WCB provides information, classified by 50 industries, on the number of permanent injury awards, number of fatal accident claims, and estimated payrolls. Using an estimate of average annual earnings, the payroll figure can be employed to develop an estimate of covered employees per sector. In turn, these figures can be combined with the disability figures to obtain disability rates. Although these rates may not be accurate in an absolute sense, they can be expected to provide reasonable estimates of relative rates.

Finally, Table 7.8 indicates that (in the United States) individuals who have worked for their present employer for less than one year are substantially more likely to suffer employment-related injuries and illnesses than are individuals who have worked for four or more years.

TABLE 7.7

Time-Loss Injury Rates by Occupation: Canada, 1982-1986

Occupation	Injuries per 1,000 Employed
Managerial, Administrative	2
Natural Sciences	8
Social Sciences	11
Teaching	8
Medicine and Health	47
Artistic and Recreational	10
Clerical	13
Sales	20
Service	44
Farming	49
Fishing, Hunting, and Trapping	104
Forestry and Logging	193
Mining and Quarrying	102
Processing	136
Machining	163
Product Fabrication, Assembly, and Repair	81
Construction	116
Transport Equipment Operation	105
Materials Handling	158

Source: Statistics Canada, *The Labour Force*, Cat. No. 71-001 (Ottawa: Statistics Canada, March 1988) p. 104.

This finding suggests that slightly lower disability rates should be applied to individuals with stable work records than to those with unstable records.

To conclude, the findings of this Section indicate (i) that a large percentage of males over 25 who are listed as not participating in the labour force suffer from a major disability; (ii) physically demanding occupations, such as mining and logging, have much higher injury rates than do office-oriented occupations; and (iii) disability rates rise with age. The latter finding suggests that it is inappropriate to employ a single contingency factor to apply to the victim's entire life. Technically, a more desirable approach would be to recognize that the probability that the individual will suffer a disability is an increasing function of age.

TABLE 7.8

**RELATIVE INJURY EXPERIENCE BY DURATION
OF EMPLOYMENT AND SEX: UNITED STATES, 1978**

Employment Duration	Relative Incidence of Work-Related Injury and Illness[a]	
	Males	Females
1-3 months	2.02	1.33
4-6 months	1.33	1.00
7-12 months	1.63	1.30
2-3 years	1.09	0.96
4-5 years	0.80	0.86
6-10 years	0.76	0.90
11-25 years	0.53	0.80
26-35 years	0.30	0.53
36 years and over	0.13	0.25

Source: F. Siskind, "Another Look at the Link Between Work Injuries and Job Experience" (1982) 105 *Monthly Labor Review* 38-40.

[a] The figures in this Table represent numbers of compensable (by worker's compensation) injuries and illness per worker, relative to the average. Thus, the figure of 2.02 for males, 1-3 months indicates that an individual in that group is 2.02 times as likely to suffer an injury or illness as is the average male worker.

III. UNEMPLOYMENT

1. Average Rates

To the extent that those who are employed are not earning income,[5] unemployment must also be treated as a negative contingency to be set off against potential earnings. An extremely useful summary of Canadian unemployment statistics can be found in

McKitrick, Ross, *The Current Industrial Relations Science in Canada, 1989: The Economy and Labour Markets:Reference Tables* (Kingston, Ont.: Industrial Relations Centre, Queen's University, 1989), Table 32.

---

[5] Most unemployed workers receive unemployment insurance benefits — a form of income. The effects of these benefits on the contingency rate are discussed in Section IV.3 of this Chapter, *infra*.

Other information concerning average unemployment rates are contained in Tables 7.9-7.14. The data in these Tables are described in the following subsections, which have been categorized according to the major factors which influence unemployment rates.

TABLE 7.9

Unemployment Rates by Age and Sex: Canada

Age and Sex	1975	1981	1985	1989
Total				
15-19	14.9	16.2	18.7	13.1
20-24	9.9	11.2	15.1	10.1
25-34	6.1	7.0	10.8	8.1
35-44	4.4	5.1	7.9	6.1
45-54	4.5	4.7	7.2	5.3
55-64	4.3	4.4	8.2	6.3
Average	6.9	7.5	10.5	7.5
Male				
15-19	15.4	16.9	20.6	14.5
20-24	10.5	12.2	16.8	11.0
25-34	5.0	6.0	10.4	7.4
35-44	3.6	4.3	7.2	5.5
45-54	3.8	4.2	6.8	4.8
55-64	4.0	4.4	8.4	6.4
Average	6.2	7.0	10.3	7.3
Female				
15-19	14.4	15.4	16.7	11.5
20-24	9.1	10.0	13.2	9.1
25-34	8.0	8.4	11.3	8.8
35-44	5.9	6.3	8.8	6.9
45-54	5.7	5.5	7.8	5.9
55-64	4.9	4.3	7.7	6.0
Average	8.1	8.3	10.7	7.9

Sources: Canada. Statistics Canada, *Labour Force Annual Averages,* Cat. No. 71-529,and *Annual Averages,* Cat. No. 71-001 (Ottawa: Statistics Canada, 1989).

(a) Age and sex

Table 7.9 indicates that although there tends to be no significant difference between the average unemployment rates of males and females, there is a difference in the way that male and female unemployment rates are distributed among age groups. In particular, whereas males 15-24 had higher unemployment rates than females 15-24 in every time period reported in Table 7.9, males 25-64 had lower unemployment rates than comparable females in most periods.

The second pattern which is very clear in Tables 7.9 and 7.11-7.14 is that individuals 15-24 tend to have much higher unemployment rates than those 25-64. This pattern is more pronounced among males than females (Table 7.9) and among married than single individuals (Table 7.13). There is also some evidence that it is more pronounced among those with the greatest numbers of years of education (Tables 7.11 and 7.12).

TABLE 7.10

Unemployment Rates by Occupation, All Classes of Workers: Canada

Occupation	1975	1981	1985	1989
Managerial, Administrative	2.1	2.2	4.7	3.8
Natural Sciences	2.8	3.2	6.0	3.3
Social Sciences	3.6	4.8	6.8	5.0
Teaching	3.4	3.3	4.8	4.0
Medicine and Health	3.1	2.8	3.6	2.5
Artistic and Recreational	5.9	8.5	11.4	8.2
Clerical	5.5	6.3	8.9	6.9
Sales	4.3	5.2	8.0	6.0
Service	7.4	9.7	13.1	9.8
Agriculture	3.7	5.5	9.2	7.4
Forestry and Logging	21.3	23.4	30.8	23.5
Mining and Quarrying	8.9	9.3	12.7	9.9
Processing	9.6	9.7	12.6	9.3
Machining	7.1	7.5	11.2	7.2
Product Fabricating, Assembling, and Repairing	7.0	7.9	10.3	6.7
Construction Trades	10.8	12.1	18.9	12.4
Transport Equipment Operating	6.5	8.0	10.7	7.7
Materials Handling	10.9	11.6	15.3	11.2
Other Crafts, Equipment Operating	4.7	5.5	8.5	5.6
Average	**6.9**	**7.5**	**10.5**	**7.5**

Sources: Canada. Statistics Canada, *Labour Force Annual Averages,* Cat. No. 71-529, and *Annual Averages,* Cat. No. 71-001 (Ottawa: Statistics Canada, 1989.)

(b) Occupation

Table 7.10 reveals two patterns. First, certain occupations — particularly those involving physical labour or seasonal activity — consistently have higher unemployment rates than others. Second, the ratios of the unemployment rates in various occupations to the average unemployment rate show a remarkable degree of stability over the displayed time period. For example, among managerial workers unemployment rates have been approximately 30-40 percent of the average rate for all workers; among workers in teaching, and medicine they have been 40-50 percent of the average; among transport equipment operators they have roughly equalled the average; and among forestry and logging workers they have been almost three times the average.

TABLE 7.11

UNEMPLOYMENT RATES BY AGE, SEX, AND EDUCATION: CANADA 1971

Age and Sex	Education				
	Less than Grade 9	Grades 9-11	Grades 12 and 13	Some University	University Degree
Male					
15-19	22.9	22.8	20.4	13.9	11.9
20-24	14.2	11.2	9.2		
25-34	8.5	5.4	3.3	4.5	3.0
35-44	6.5	3.8	2.5	2.8	1.3
45-54	5.9	3.9	3.2	3.2	1.3
55-64	6.5	4.6	3.8	4.0	1.6
65 +	9.3	10.2	9.8	6.8	2.7
Average	7.9	8.1	6.6	7.7	3.4
Female					
15-19	21.9	26.5	21.7	13.5	11.2
20-24	13.3	10.8	7.4		
25-34	9.5	8.0	5.4	4.4	4.7
35-44	7.1	5.7	4.2	4.2	3.8
45-54	6.4	5.5	4.1	3.5	2.9
55-64	6.3	5.3	4.0	2.7	2.1
65 +	7.2	6.6	5.9	5.4	2.3
Average	8.3	10.3	8.0	8.1	6.0

Source: Canada. Statistics Canada, *Labour Force Activity — Work Experience*, Cat. No. 94-772 (Ottawa: Statistics Canada, 1975).

(c) Education

Tables 7.11 and 7.12 reveal a clear, and strong correlation between unemployment and education. Among males 25-64, for example, unemployment rates among the least educated group are approximately three to four times greater than among the most highly educated group; whereas among females 25-64 the least educated are approximately two to three times as likely to be unemployed as the most highly educated.

TABLE 7.12

Unemployment Rates by Age, Sex and Education: Canada, 1986

	Age and Sex							
Highest level of schooling:	15-24		25-44		45-64		Average	
	M	F	M	F	M	F	M	F
Less than Gr. 9	32.9	35.3	16.6	17.9	10.5	12.2	20.0	21.8
Gr. 9-13 no diploma	20.1	21.2	11.3	13.4	6.9	8.5	12.8	14.4
Gr. 9-13 diploma	14.3	14.4	7.1	10.0	5.9	7.7	9.1	10.7
Trades certificate	14.4	14.4	8.8	10.8	6.9	7.7	10.0	11.0
Some university no diploma	15.5	16.4	8.1	10.5	6.3	8.6	10.0	11.8
University with diploma	14.0	12.2	5.5	7.5	4.6	6.0	8.0	8.6
University degree	14.4	12.8	4.2	6.6	2.6	3.9	7.1	7.8

Source: Canada. Statistics Canada, *Labour Force Activity*, Cat. No. 93-111 (Ottawa: Statistics Canada, 1986).

(d) Marital status

From Table 7.13 it can be seen that married men, particularly those over the age of 20, have significantly lower unemployment rates than either single men or men who are widowed or divorced. Among women, on the other hand, the correlation between unemployment and marital status is weaker, with widowed and divorced women tending to have slightly higher unemployment rates than married women, and married women having higher rates than single women.

TABLE 7.13

Unemployment Rates by Age, Sex and Marital Status: Canada, 1986

Age	Single		Married		Separated		Widowed		Divorced	
	M	F	M	F	M	F	M	F	M	F
15-19	20.7	20.4	21.6	25.6	22.8	42.4	15.6	35.3	29.7	37.8
20-24	16.8	14.0	11.5	15.6	16.8	21.9	28.6	11.8	18.1	22.1
25-34	14.7	9.5	7.1	11.4	12.4	14.2	10.3	16.7	15.0	14.3
35-44	14.5	7.7	5.3	8.4	11.0	11.5	10.4	10.0	14.3	11.3
45-54	14.5	5.7	5.3	7.9	11.3	10.6	10.7	9.6	13.9	10.5
55-59	12.5	6.0	6.3	8.4	12.5	9.8	10.1	9.2	4.1	9.0
60-64	11.4	6.5	8.0	9.2	12.5	10.3	10.0	8.6	14.7	8.4
65 +	4.0	3.4	3.1	6.9	4.8	4.9	5.2	9.2	7.6	6.9

Source: Canada. Statistics Canada, *Labour Force Activity*, Cat. No. 93-111 (Ottawa: Statistics Canada, 1986) Table 3, p. 3-2.

(e) Area of residence

Finally, Table 7.14 indicates that there has not been a consistent relationship between unemployment and area of residence. Whereas urban dwellers, particularly women, had slightly higher unemployment rates than urban dwellers in 1971, that relationship was reversed in 1981. Comparable data was not available from the 1986 Census.

2. Individual-Specific Rates

The data summarized in Tables 7.9-7.14 relate to broad aggregates of individuals. Within those aggregates, one would expect there to be wide variations in the incidence of unemployment among individuals. A recent study prepared by Arun Roy and Matthew Robertson, of the Department of Employment and Immigration, considers this question. This study, which is entitled:

Roy, A. and M. Robertson, *The Distribution of Unemployment by Spell Frequency and the Relationship Between Past and Present Unemployment Experience in the Canadian Labour Market* (Presented at the Canadian Economics Association Meeting, University of Guelph, May 29, 1984) (unpublished).

used information from a 1975-1979 longitudinal sample of 885 workers to identify factors which were useful in predicting individuals' 1979

TABLE 7.14

UNEMPLOYMENT RATES BY AGE, SEX, AND AREA OF RESIDENCE: CANADA 1971 and 1981

	1971				1981			
	Urban		Rural		Urban		Rural	
Age	M	F	M	F	M	F	M	F
15-19	16.6	15.2	11.4	15.9	15.0	15.4	15.6	18.9
20-24					10.9	10.6	13.4	16.3
25-34	5.2	7.2	5.7	5.3	5.2	7.5	7.2	10.3
35-44	4.2	6.0	4.8	3.8	3.3	6.1	5.4	7.7
45-54	4.5	5.6	4.3	3.7	3.5	5.7	5.3	7.3
55-59	5.5	5.6	4.9	3.4	3.9	5.7	5.4	7.1
60-64					5.1	5.3	6.4	7.0
65 +	11.3	7.1	4.0	4.4	3.2	4.7	1.9	4.0

Source: 1971 figures calculated from Canada, Statistics Canada. *Labour Force Activity — Work Experience*, Cat. No. 94-773 (Ottawa: Statistics Canada, 1975). 1981 figures taken from Canada. Statistics Canada. *Population — Labour Force Activity*, Cat. No. 92-915 (Ottawa: Statistics Canada, 1984).

unemployment experiences. The variables which they found to be most significantly (positively) correlated with number of weeks unemployed in 1979 were: value and availability of unemployment insurance benefits, the level of unemployment in the individual's area of residence, and the cumulative number of weeks unemployed in the January 1975-September 1975 period. Of particular interest for the assessment of personal damages, is their further finding, that once allowance for these three factors had been made, the age, sex, and occupation of the individual had only a weak effect (if any) on the number of weeks an individual could expect to be unemployed. For example, of the seven occupational categories employed in the study, only two were found to have a statistically significant effect on unemployment. Workers in the clerical/sales category had higher than average unemployment rates, while those in the primary sector had lower than average rates, *ceteris paribus*.

Thus, the Roy and Robertson study suggests that the individual's own unemployment record is a much more important predictor of future record than is the unemployment rate of the group to which he or she belongs. A construction worker with a steady employment record, for example, is no more likely to have a high future rate of unemployment than is any other worker with a similar past record, in spite of the construction industry's relatively high unemployment rate. In short, if further studies provide support for the Roy/Robertson findings, the most important factors to be considered when predicting the plaintiff's future course of employment will be that individual's past employment/ unemployment record and the expected, average rate of unemployment.

3. Unemployment Insurance Benefits

That an individual is unemployed does not necessarily mean that he or she is receiving no income. Subject to various qualification requirements, discussed below, Canadians are eligible to receive up to 60 percent of their average weekly employment earnings while unemployed. Thus, an individual who was unemployed for 10 percent of a year could lose as little as 4 percent of annual earnings and the relevant contingency factor would become 4 percent instead of 10.

Table 7.15 summarizes the maximum weekly earnings insurable for purposes of unemployment benefits, and the maximum weekly benefits payable, for each year 1985-90. Statistics Canada[6] indicates that these maxima are raised each year in accordance with an index of wages and salaries paid in Canada. The experience over 1985-1990 appears to bear this out, as maximum weekly benefits rose approximately 2.3 percent per year faster than the rate of consumer price inflation.

TABLE 7.15

Maximum Weekly Insurable Earnings and Maximum Weekly Benefits Under the Unemployment Insurance Act: Canada, 1985-1990

Year	Maximum Weekly Insurable Earnings	Maximum Weekly Benefits
1985	$460	$276
1986	495	297
1987	530	318
1988	565	339
1989	605	363
1990	640	384

At the time of writing, 20 weeks of insurable employment in the previous 52 was required before "regular" unemployment benefits could

---

[6] See Canada. Statistics Canada, *Statistical Report on the Operation of the Unemployment Insurance Act* Cat. No. 73-001 (Ottawa: Statistics Canada) published annually.

be collected. Depending upon the rate of unemployment in the region where the applicant lived, "special" unemployment benefits could be collected with as little as 10-14 weeks of insurable employment in the previous 52.

Once eligibility had been determined and the individual had served a two-week waiting period, benefits equal to the lesser of 60 percent of the individual's insurable weekly earnings or $384 per week were paid. The length of the payment period was determined according to a three-phase system but in no circumstance did it exceed 50 weeks. In the "initial" phase, one week of benefits was paid for each week of insurable earnings, to a maximum of 25. In the second, "labour force extended" phase, one additional week of benefits was paid for each two weeks in excess of 26 accumulated during the qualifying period, to a maximum of 13. Finally, after benefits had been exhausted in the first two phases, a "regional extended" benefit was available for two weeks for every half point by which the local unemployment rate exceeded 4 percent, to a maximum of 32 weeks. For example, if the local rate of unemployment was 8 percent, the benefit period was extended by 16 weeks and if the local rate was over 11.5 percent, the benefit period was extended for (up to) 32 weeks.

Given that the length of this eligibility period exceeded the duration of unemployment of most workers,[7] it seems reasonable to assume that most individuals would have received 60 percent of their insurable earnings, or the maximum benefit permissible, for all but 2 weeks of each spell of unemployment. Thus, an individual who made $640 per week ($33,280 per year) or less (in "1990 dollars") who was expected to be unemployed for 9.62 percent of each year (i.e., 5 weeks) would have suffered a loss of earnings equal to 6.15 percent of her potential, full-employment income;[8] and a similar worker with an expected unemployment rate of 19.23 percent (i.e., 10 weeks per year) would have lost only 10 percent of her potential income.

IV. MORTALITY

The various techniques for incorporating assumptions about mortality were discussed in some detail in Section IV.2(a) of Chapter 1 and will not be reviewed again here. Instead, the primary function of this

---

[7] See A. Hasan and P. De Broucker,"Duration and Concentration of Unemployment" (1982) 15 *Canadian Journal of Economics* 735-56.

[8] An individual who is unemployed for 5 weeks will lose 100 percent of his or her income during each of the first 2 weeks, and 40 percent during each of the remaining 3 weeks. The net result is a loss of 2 + (0.4 x 3) = 3.2 weeks' earnings, or (3.2/52 =) 6.15 percent of 52 weeks' earnings.

Section will be to note that the pre-eminent source of information concerning Canadian mortality rates is:

Canada. Statistics Canada, *Life Tables, Canada and the Provinces, 1985-1987* (Ottawa: Statistics Canada, 1989).

The statistics contained in this publication relate to the average Canadian (of a particular age, sex, and province) and therefore may overestimate the life expectancy of a severely injured plaintiff. Thus, if the court wishes to award lower levels of damages to plaintiffs whose life expectancies have been reduced than to those with "normal" life expectancies, it will not be appropriate to employ life tables based on standard statistical sources. Unfortunately, it is usually very difficult to obtain information concerning the life expectancies of individuals with various diseases or disabilities. My experience has been that the most reliable sources of such information are actuaries and insurance companies. The latter often collect such data in order to set life insurance premiums. One published source, which is now rather outdated, unfortunately, is

Singer, Richard, and Louis Levinson, eds., *Medical Risks: Patterns of Mortality and Survival*, (Lexington, Mass.: Lexington Books, 1975).

This book summarizes hundreds of studies which have been conducted to determine the mortality rates associated with a whole host of possible disabilities. The final source for information concerning the plaintiff's life expectancy is medical testimony. Such testimony must be accepted with some scepticism, however, unless the expert demonstrates that his or her opinion has been based upon statistically reliable research.

8

EARNINGS PROSPECTS OF THE SEVERELY DISABLED

The purpose of this Chapter will be to review a number of sources which offer information concerning the effect of disability on earnings and employment. In Section I, I begin by considering a number of studies of the disabled in general. In Section II, I review two studies, each of which has considered a large number of different types of injuries. In the remaining Sections, I will summarize studies which have dealt with specific injuries, such as injuries to the spinal cord and to the head.

I. THE GENERAL CASE

A number of studies have attempted to identify the factors which influence the earnings prospects of disabled individuals in general. Two of the most important of these employ Canadian data. They are:

Canada. Statistics Canada. *Selected Socio-economic Consequences of Disability for Women in Canada*, Cat. No. 82-614, Vol. 2 (Ottawa: Statistics Canada, September 1990).
Gower, D., *Labour Market Activity of Disabled Persons in Canada*, Statistics Canada, Cat. No. 71-535, No. 1 (Ottawa: Statistics Canada, April 1988).

Both of these studies were based upon surveys which were undertaken by Statistics Canada — the first in conjunction with the 1986 Census, the second in conjunction with the Labour Force Surveys of October 1983 and June 1984. Tables 8.1 and 8.2 summarize information concerning the labour force activities of disabled and non-disabled populations from the Census survey. In Table 8.1 the percentage of male and female disabled individuals who are working is only about half as large as the percentage of non-disabled individuals. Furthermore, Table 8.2 indicates that the percentage of women employed tends to be highest among those whose disability is hearing-related and among young individuals, although in no category in Table 8.2 is the employment rate as high as the 60 percent rate, reported in Table 8.1, for all non-disabled females.

TABLE 8.1

Labour Force Characteristics of Disabled and Non-Disabled Canadians, Aged 15-64: 1985

Sex and Labour Force Activity	Non-Disabled	Disabled
Females		
Employed/Population	60.0%	30.7%
Unemployed/Labour Force	11.6	17.0
Males		
Employed/Population	79.8	49.7
Unemployed/Labour Force	9.4	14.2

Source: Canada. Statistics Canada. *Selected Socio-economic Consequences of Disability for Women in Canada*, Cat. No. 82-614, Vol. 2 (Ottawa: Statistics Canada, September 1990) Tables 8 and 9.

TABLE 8.2

Employment-to-Population Ratios, Females with a Disability, Aged 15-64, by Age Group, by Nature of Disability: Canada, 1986

Age Group	Nature of Disability				
	Mobility[a]	Agility[b]	Seeing[c]	Hearing[d]	Speaking[e]
15-24	29.8	34.2	25.0	41.4	20.0
25-29	42.4	41.8	36.1	55.0	40.8
30-34	51.7	43.5	19.8	50.8	36.5
35-39	41.9	46.0	52.5	43.8	42.4
40-44	34.4	35.5	17.0	52.7	23.6
45-49	38.6	39.2	41.8	42.8	27.0
50-54	22.0	26.0	17.3	17.4	n.a.
55-59	17.0	15.1	8.1	30.0	n.a.
60-64	5.4	5.3	2.6	5.8	n.a.
Total, 15-64	25.5	25.8	21.2	33.5	24.2

[a] Limited in ability to walk, move from room to room, carry an object for 10 metres, or stand for long periods.
[b] Limited in ability to bend, dress or undress oneself, get in and out of bed, cut toe-nails, use fingers to grasp or handle objects, reach or cut own food.
[c] Limited in ability to read ordinary newsprint or to see someone from 4 metres, even when wearing glasses.
[d] Limited in ability to hear what is being said in conversation with one other person or two or more persons, even when wearing a hearing aid.
[e] Limited in ability to speak and be understood.

Source: Canada. Statistics Canada. *Selected Socio-economic Consequences of Disability for Women in Canada*, Cat. No. 82-614, Vol. 2 (Ottawa: Statistics Canada, September 1990) calculated from figures in Table 6A.

Further information concerning the effect of disability on employment is reported in Table 8.3. The data there, drawn from the 1984 Labour Force Survey, indicates that the effects of disability on employment decline slightly as the individual's education increases.

TABLE 8.3

Employment-to-Population Ratios Among Disabled and Non-Disabled Persons, by Sex and Education: Canada, 1984

Education	Male		Female	
	Non-Disabled	Disabled	Non-Disabled	Disabled
Elementary or less	62.5%	24.5%	28.8%	9.4%
High School	73.0	42.2	50.4	23.8
Post-Secondary	77.0	53.4	61.7	40.4

Source: Gower, D., *Labour Market Activity of Disabled Persons in Canada*, Cat. No. 71-535, No. 1 (Ottawa, Statistics Canada, April 1988) calculated from Table IV.

TABLE 8.4

Median Employment Income and Total Income for Disabled and Non-Disabled Individuals Aged 15-64, by Sex: Canada, 1985

	Median Employment Income	Median Total Income
Males		
Non-disabled	$21,000	$20,855
Disabled	19,250	12,980
Females		
Non-disabled	$10,000	$10,000
Disabled, Total	8,360	8,175
Mobility[a]	8,360	8,040
Agility[b]	8,360	8,000
Seeing[c]	10,500	8,305
Hearing[d]	8,000	8,330
Speaking[e]	7,000	7,200

[a-e] See footnotes to Table 8.2

Source: Canada. Statistics Canada. *Selected Socio-economic Consequences of Disability for Women in Canada*, Cat. No. 82-614, Vol. 2 (Ottawa: Statistics Canada, September 1990) Figure 3 and Table 13.

In addition to information concerning the effects of disability on employment, the 1986 Census survey also contains information concerning the effects on income. Table 8.4 summarizes some of these data with respect to median *total* income and median *employment* income, the latter being calculated only for those with at least some employment income. It is seen in Table 8.4 that average income from all sources, for all disabled individuals, is considerably less than the comparable figure for non-disabled individuals; but that, among males who managed to *earn* at least some income, the disabled had only slightly lower incomes than the non-disabled. This Table seems to suggest, therefore, that for males the negative effects of disability are felt primarily through their effects on the ability to work, not on the income which can be earned if work is found. With respect to females, however, Table 8.4 seems to suggest that the incomes of disabled females are unaffected by employment. It would be useful to obtain further information concerning this factor, however, before drawing definitive conclusions.

In the United States, a survey similar to the two Canadian surveys cited above, was conducted in 1972. Some of the most important results of that survey are reported in Tables 8.5 and 8.6. First, what Table 8.5 indicates is that although the disabled in the less severe categories, occupationally disabled and secondary work limitation, were almost as likely as the non-disabled to have been employed at some time during the year, they were much more likely than the non-disabled to have worked less than 50 weeks during the year and were much more likely to have worked part-time.

Table 8.6 shows that this reduction in hours of work led to reductions in income. For example, differences between the average earnings of all disabled and all non-disabled are larger than the differences between the earnings of the disabled and the non-disabled who worked full-time. That is, part of the differences between the overall averages was due to differences in the distributions between full-time and part-time employments. However, Table 8.6 also reports that, even among those who were working full-time, incomes were lower among the disabled than among the non-disabled. It is also important to note from this Table, that among those who returned to their pre-accident employment, the disabled earned less than the non-disabled.

Finally, three academic studies which employ statistically-reliable techniques to analyse the effects of disability on employment are:

Bellante, D. M., "A Multivariate Analysis of a Vocational Rehabilitation Program" (1972), 7 *Journal of Human Resources* 226-41.
Luft, H. S., *Poverty and Health* (Cambridge, Mass.: Ballinger, 1975).
Schechter, E. S., "Commitment to Work and the Self-Perception of Disability" (1981), 44(6) *Social Security Bulletin* 22-32.

TABLE 8.5

Employment-to-Population Ratios by Extent of Employment, by Sex and Disability Status: United States, 1971

Sex and Disability Status	Percent Employed with Earnings	Extent of Employment[a]		
		Full Time 50-52 Weeks	26-49 Weeks	Part Time or Inter- mittent
White Males				
Severely disabled[b]	41.9%	24.4%	33.8%	41.8%
Occupationally disabled[c]	91.6	61.2	21.6	17.1
Secondary work limitations[d]	91.4	57.7	27.9	14.4
Not disabled	93.6	74.7	14.7	10.6
White Females				
Severely disabled[b]	18.0	14.8	11.3	73.9
Occupationally disabled[c]	53.4	29.6	11.4	58.9
Secondary work limitations[d]	54.4	50.2	22.7	27.1
Not disabled	57.5	47.5	17.1	35.3

[a] The figures in the second, third, and fourth columns add up to 100.0. That is, they represent the percentages of those who worked at some time during the year who worked the specified number of weeks or hours.

[b] Unable to work or unable to work regularly.

[c] Able to work regularly but unable to do the same work as before the onset of the disability.

[d] Able to work full-time, regularly, doing the same work as before the onset of the disability, but with some limitation to the kind or amount of work.

Source: Robert Ferguson, *The Impact of Disability on Employment and Earnings*, Disability Survey 72, Report No. 14 (Washington: U. S. Department of Health, Education, and Welfare, December 1979) Table D.

Bellante was able to contrast various characteristics of the clients of the Florida Division of Vocational Rehabilitation who were successfully "rehabilitated" with the characteristics of those clients who were not rehabilitated. In general, he found that the younger were these individuals and the greater was their education, the more likely were they to be able to obtain employment after they left Florida's rehabilitation program. He also found that individuals with dependants were more likely to obtain employment than single individuals and that those receiving welfare were (slightly) less likely to seek employment than those who were not. Finally, he found that individuals whose major disabilities were "visual," "speech and hearing," "digestive," or "genitourinary"

TABLE 8.6

Mean Annual Earnings of Those with Earnings by Extent of Employment, by Sex and Disability Status: United States, 1971

Sex and Disability Status	Total with Earnings	Full Time 50-52 Weeks	Full Time 26-49 Weeks	Part Time 26 Weeks or more	Part Time Inter- mittent
White Males					
Severely disabled[b]	$5,433	$9,638	$6,090	$2,571	$2,444
Occupationally disabled[c]	7,722	9,100	6,584	3,199	5,142
Secondary work limitations[d]	8,341	9,565	7,434	3,745	5,920
Not disabled	10,544	11,418	8,785	6,522	6,959
White Females					
Severely disabled[b]	2,177	4,829	3,394	1,692	1,287
Occupationally disabled[c]	2,700	5,054	3,642	1,685	808
Secondary work limitations[d]	4,231	5,668	3,799	2,217	1,772
Not disabled	4,544	6,020	5,259	2,732	1,640

[a] The figures in the second, third, and fourth columns add up to 100.0. That is, they represent the percentages of those who worked at some time during the year who worked the specified number of weeks or hours.

[b] Unable to work or unable to work regularly.

[c] Able to work regularly but unable to do the same work as before the onset of the disability.

[d] Able to work full-time, regularly, doing the same work as before the onset of the disability, but with some limitation to the kind or amount of work.

Source: Robert Ferguson, *The Impact of Disability on Employment and Earnings,* Disability Survey 72, Report No. 14 (Washington: U. S. Department of Health, Education, and Welfare, December 1979) Table E.

were most likely to obtain employment, followed by those whose disabilities were "amputation," "neoplasms," "allergies," "orthopedic," and "mental retardation." Those who suffered "mental disorders" or "blood, circulatory, and respiratory" disorders were the least able to obtain employment, *ceteris paribus.*

Luft used the results of the U.S. Survey of Disabled Adults and the Survey of Economic Opportunity to distinguish between those disabled men who were able to work and those who were not. He found that such socioeconomic factors as pre-disability income, age, and education were not significant determinants of employability when the nature of the individual's pre-disability employment and post-disability physical limitations were taken into account. His most significant finding was that individuals who had been employed in jobs requiring heavy labour before their accidents and who suffered disabilities which restricted their abilities to lift heavy weights had an unemployment rate which was 48 percent higher than the average of 24 percent for all disabled workers in the sample. Unemployment also tended to be high among urban residents (25 percent above the average), among those whose previous jobs had required climbing and who now experienced difficulty with stairs (18 percent above average) and among those whose previous jobs had required that they talk and whose speech was now impaired (43 percent above average).

Schechter, like Luft, used the Survey of Disabled Adults to identify the differences between those severely disabled adults who returned to work and those who did not. In his sample, the former group consisted of 537 individuals while the latter contained 4,963. He found that those who were most likely to have returned to work were those who: were supporting relatives outside the household, had been employed for 4 or more years before the onset of their disabilities, had no formal education, and were not receiving welfare. Also, men were found to be more likely to be employed than women and there was some evidence that married individuals were more likely to be working than those not married.

II. EMPLOYMENT BY CATEGORY OF DISABILITY

Two of the studies which I have been able to locate provide useful information concerning large numbers of categories of disability. These are:

Greenblum, J., "Effect of Rehabilitation on Employment and Earnings of the Disabled: Sociodemographic Factors" (1979), 42(8) *Social Security Bulletin* 11-37.

McBride, E., *Disability Evaluation*, 6th ed. (Philadelphia: J.B. Lipincott, 1963).

Greenblum's study is based upon a suvey of the clients dealt with by American state vocational rehabilitation agencies during 1971. These clients were referred to the various agencies if they demonstrated both "... a substantial vocational handicap and a potential for rehabilitation."[1] Those who successfully completed the agencies' programs and

---

[1] Greenblum, J., "Effect of Rehabilitation on Employment and Earnings of the Disabled: Sociodemographic Factors" (1979), 42(8) *Social Security Bulletin* at p. 12.

obtained at least 1 month employment in 1971 were classified as "rehabilitated." Those who had been accepted for the agencies' programs but whose files had been closed without "success" having been obtained were considered "not rehabilitated;" while those who were referred to the agencies but did not enter their programs were classified as "not accepted."[2] Although the distinctions among these three categories are not useful for the purposes of this book, Greenblum's study is of importance for the information which it provides about the relative employability of individuals with different disabilities.

Table 8.7 summarizes some of the most important findings of Greenblum's study, as presented in his Table 8. There it is seen that blindness is clearly the greatest bar to employment among the 19 disabilities considered. "Extremity loss," "heart and circulatory conditions," and "respiratory" problems were also associated with relatively low employment rates. On the other hand, "deafness," "mental retardation," and "epilepsy" had among the highest employment rates.

Also available from Greenblum's Table 8, but not included in my Table 8.7, are data concerning the average annual incomes of the various groups identified in Table 8.7 and the percentages of each group who were "rehabilitated." Among employed males, the lowest incomes were earned by those with: "mental retardation," "personality disorders," "drug addiction," "psychoses," "alcoholism," and "epilepsy." Among employed women, the lowest incomes were earned by those suffering: "mental retardation," "genitourinary" and "digestive" problems, "epilepsy," "personality disorders," and "psychoses."

Table 8.8 is provided as an indication of the type of detailed information available in Greenblum's Table 9. It shows clearly, as one might expect, that the younger was the individual at the time of the reference to a rehabilitation agency, the greater was the probability that he/she would later be able to obtain employment. For further information concerning any of the four disabilities listed in Table 8.8, or with respect to any of the other 15 disabilities also considered by Greenblum, I recommend that the reader refer to Greenblum's Table 9.

McBride's book is one of a number which have been written as guides to medical practitioners who are appearing before Workers' Compensation Boards and the courts to give evidence concerning the individual's impairment of work capacity. Of the many books I have seen, however, McBride's stands out in two ways. First, whereas most such books categorize injuries according to their effects on the physical

---

[2] Among men (women) the percentage of individuals in the three categories who were considered to be "'rehabilitated" were, among those suffering: "blindness," 57 (68); "deafness," 64 (70); "orthopedic impairments," 40 (48); "extremity loss," 64 (67); "epilepsy," 40 (46); and "speech impairments," 50 (55).

TABLE 8.7

Percentage Employed by Major Disabling Condition and Sex:
State Vocational Rehabilitation Agencies, United States, 1972

Major Disabling Condition	Rehabilitated[a]		Not Rehabilitated[b]		Not Accepted[c]	
	Male	Female	Male	Female	Male	Female
Blindness[d]	47.3	26.8	18.6	13.9	24.3	16.9
Other visual impairments	73.3	50.8	50.5	40.9	63.1	45.4
Deafness	77.4	56.3	58.6	35.2	66.8	46.5
Other hearing impairments	69.9	49.6	54.5	39.9	73.2	52.0
Orthopedic impairments[e]	73.7	52.6	44.2	32.3	55.6	39.9
Extremity loss[f]	64.7	35.9	27.0	19.3	45.9	28.1
Psychosis/psychoneurosis	72.1	57.6	43.1	36.0	50.2	42.1
Alcoholism	74.8	55.9	55.7	39.2	56.8	45.4
Drug addiction	73.9	58.2	55.2	44.6	65.2	50.4
Other personality disorders	81.3	65.3	63.9	49.4	70.0	54.4
Mental retardation	82.1	58.7	60.4	35.5	61.8	37.7
Epilepsy	79.2	58.0	45.0	36.2	52.1	39.1
Heart condition	65.1	49.2	29.3	24.6	40.8	35,4
Other circulatory	65.2	50.8	36.9	37.1	46.3	37.8
Respiratory	63.5	54.7	36.8	39.2	42.4	39.8
Digestive	77.6	59.1	49.0	44.4	66.9	51.7
Genitourinary	70.8	51.7	35.7	38.9	58.8	51.1
Speech impairments	82.1	65.2	48.2	33.3	65.8	49.4
All other	77.3	57.1	46.7	36.1	58.6	47.8

Source: J. Greenblum, "Effect of Rehabilitation on Employment and Earnings of the Disabled: Sociodemographic Factors" (1979), 42(8) *Social Security Bulletin* 11-37, Table 8.

a Those who successfully completed a plan for guidance, restoration, and training services and who were employed for at least 1 month in 1971.

b Those who did not successfully complete the plan described in footnote a.

c Those referred to the rehabilitation services but not included in the descriptions in footnotes a and b.

d Both eyes.

e Includes limbs, trunk, back, or spine. Excludes amputations.

f Includes congenital malformations.

capabilities of individuals, such as listing the loss of an arm as representing a 30 percent loss of the physical functioning of one's body, McBride categorizes injuries according to their effects on employment earnings. Second, whereas categorizations based on physical limitations apply equally to all individuals, McBride's system distinguishes among individuals on the basis of occupation. Thus, for example, he finds that loss of a foot is much more important for a truck driver than for an

TABLE 8.8

Percentage Employed by Age, Sex, and Selected Disabling Conditions, United States, 1972

Age and Major Disabling Condition	Rehabilitated[a]		Not Rehabilitated[b]		Not Accepted[c]	
	Male	Female	Male	Female	Male	Female
Blindness[d]						
Under 20	66.7	51.4	50.0	9.5	51.8	35.4
20-34	72.7	48.5	32.6	22.6	47.8	31.8
35-54	49.2	31.2	16.5	14.5	23.4	17.5
55 and over	28.8	10.2	8.6	6.8	9.9	7.2
Orthopedic impairments[e]						
Under 20	87.6	67.8	75.8	56.7	81.6	64.9
20-34	86.1	64.4	63.2	42.1	73.5	51.5
35-54	67.6	49.4	37.4	30.4	47.1	37.1
55 and over	43.3	33.2	15.5	15.1	25.1	21.5
Extremity loss[f]						
Under 20	86.0	57.1	50.0	[g]	73.6	53.3
20-34	86.4	59.4	52.5	33.8	66.7	45.9
35-54	69.0	39.1	26.3	22.6	46.0	28.7
55 and over	41.4	15.3	7.3	2.5	17.3	9.8
Mental retardation						
Under 20	88.7	58.5	68.7	39.8	70.8	39.4
20-34	81.2	60.0	60.0	35.0	63.5	39.8
35-54	66.6	57.1	38.1	31.0	32.6	28.4
55 and over	46.9	38.1	18.2	14.0	20.2	22.9

Source: T. Greenblum, "Effect of Rehabilitation on Employment and Earnings of the Disabled: Sociodemographic Factors" (1979), 42(8) *Social Security Bulletin* 11-37, Table 9

a-f See Table 8.7.

[g] Insufficient sample size.

engineer. Although McBride's system is, apparently, based on a subjective evaluation, and therefore cannot be considered to be reliable, it is useful for the great detail it provides — over 700 disabilities and over 25 occupations are listed. Table 8.9 is offered as a sample of the types of information listed in McBride's Tables 14 and 15.

III. SPINAL CORD INJURIES

Of the major disabilities encountered by the tort system, those involving damage to the spinal cord are among the most common. Briefly, these injuries may be classified as follows: the vertebrae of the human spine are generally divided into four segments which, in descending order, are referred to as the cervical, thoracic, lumbar, and sacral regions. A complete lesion of the spinal cord in the cervical region is called *quadriplegia*, while an incomplete lesion in this region is called *quadriparesis*. A complete lesion below the cervical region is said to result in *paraplegia*, while an incomplete lesion produces *paraparesis*. A complete lesion of the spinal cord at the third cervical vertebra, C3, or above will leave the individual with independent movement only in the head. Injury: below the C4 level allows independent breathing; below C5 allows shoulder and biceps movement; below C6 allows extension of the wrist; and below C8 allows finger movement. Injuries between the first and eighth thoracic vertebrae, T1 to T8 involve paralysis of the chest, trunk, abdomen, and leg muscles; while injuries at the T9 level or lower lead to impaired hip and leg function. Finally, as bowel and bladder functions are controlled by nerves in the sacral (the lowest) region, virtually all victims of spinal cord injury experience difficulty with the control of these organs. Indeed, infection of the bowel and bladder is, along with pressure sores, one of the most common problems associated with paraplegia and quadriplegia.

I have been able to identify ten studies of the employment status of the spinal cord injured which appear to be based on random samples and which use statistically-reliable techniques of analysis: These studies are:

DeJong, Gerben, Laurence Branch, and Paul Corcoran, "Independent Living Outcomes in Spinal Cord Injury: Multivariate Analyses" (1984), 65 *Archives of Physical and Medical Rehabilitation* 66-73

DeVivo, M. and P. Fine, "Employment Status of Spinal Cord Injured Patients 3 Years After Injury" (1982), 63 *Archives of Physical and Medical Rehabilitation* 200-03.

DeVivo, M., Richard Rutt, Samuel Stover, and Philip Fine, "Employment After Spinal Cord Injury" (1987), 68 *Archives of Physical and Medical Rehabilitation* 494-98.

De Yoe, F., "Spinal Cord Injury: Long-Term Follow-Up of Veterans" (1972), 53 *Archives of Physical Medicine and Rehabilitation* 523-29.

Dvonch, P., et al., "Vocational Findings in Postdisability Employment of Patients With Spinal Cord Dysfunction" (1965), 46 *Archives of Physical Medicine and Rehabilitation* 761-66.

El Ghatit, A. and R. Hanson, "Educational and Training Levels and Employment of the Spinal Cord Injured Patient" (1979), 60 *Archives of Physical Medicine and Rehabilitation* 405-06.

Geisler, W., A. Jousse, and M. Wynne-Jones, "Vocational Re-Establishment of Patients with Spinal Cord Injury" (1966), *Medical Services Journal*, Canada 698-710.

Guttman, Sir L., *Spinal Cord Injuries*, 2nd ed. (Oxford: Blackwell, 1976).

Jenik, F., W. Kuhn, and G. Zach, "Social and Vocational Reintegration of Paraplegic and Tetraplegic Patients in Switzerland" (1982), 20 *Paraplegia* 65-70.

Karp, Jeffrey, *A Discriminant Functions Analysis of Productivity-Related Variables Following Spinal Cord Injury*, (Vancouver, B.C.: Faculty of Eduction, Simon Fraser University, 1989) Unpublished M.A. Thesis.

Kiwerski, J. and T. Chrostowska, "Social and Professional Evaluation of Para and Tetraplegics" (1982), 20 *Paraplegia* 97-102.

Weidman, C., and A. Freehafer, "Vocational Outcome in Patients with Spinal Cord Injury" (1981), 47(2) *Journal of Rehabilitation* 63-5.

Young, J.S., et. al., *Spinal Cord Injury Statistics*, (Phoenix, Ariz.: Good Samaritan Medical Center, August 1982).

In addition, I have also obtained unpublished material from the Statistics Canada, Health and Activity Limitations Survey, (HALS); and those who are interested in the wide variety of occupations which are open to paraplegics and quadriplegics may be interested to read the dozens of case studies reported in

Crewe, Nancy, Gary Athelstan, and Ames Bower, *Employment After Spinal Cord Injury* (Minneapolis, Minn.: Medical Rehabilitation Research and Training Center, University of Minnesota, 1978)

The most important findings concerning employability are summarized in Table 8.10. There it is seen that the percentage of spinal cord injured who are in either full- or part-time employment varies from 13 to 77.8. However, of the five studies which found relatively low employment rates, two — DeVivo and Fine and Young et al. — surveyed individuals who had been injured for less than five years. Of the remaining studies, there appears to be a consensus that between 40 and 60 percent of spinal cord injured are employed, which should be compared with the general finding that approximately 50 percent of non-disabled females and 70 percent of non-disabled males are employed. Table 8.10 also indicates that employment rates among paraplegics are considerably higher than those among quadriplegics. Furthermore, two of the three studies which distinguished between part-time and full-time employment for both paraplegics and quadriplegics found that the ratio of full-time to part-time employment was greater for paraplegics than for quadriplegics.

A small amount of information concerning the effects of spinal cord injury on earnings is also available from Statistics Canada's Health and Activity Limitation Survey. These figures are reported in Table 8.11, where it is seen that, among those male spinal cord injured who earned at least some income, those with secondary education had average incomes which were only slightly lower than those of non-disabled males; but that those with university education had incomes which were significantly lower than were those of non-disabled males.

In addition, information is also available concerning the effects on employment of: age, education, pre-injury employment, area of residence, and disability payments.

Age:

Geisler et al. (at pp. 704-05) found that among "complete" quadriplegics, of those who had been injured between the ages of 11 and 20, 46.9 percent were either employed or at school. The comparable figure for those injured between 21 and 40 was 26.5 percent, and for those injured between 41 and 60 was only 11.8 percent. Among "complete" paraplegics, the comparable figures were 77.8 percent for those injured between 11 and 20, 50.2 percent for those injured between 21 and 40, and 40.6 percent for those injured between 41 and 60. Similarly, DeVivo and Fine (at p. 201) found that patients less than 24-years-old at the time of their injury were approximately four times more likely to be employed three years after their injury than were their older counterparts.

The age of the patient at the time of the survey was also found to be of importance. Dvonch et al. (at p. 762) found that of those patients who had been employed at some time since the onset of their disabilities, 66.7 percent of those between the ages of 20 and 39 were employed at the time of the survey, whereas only 50 percent of those between the ages of 40 and 59 were employed at that time. And Kiwerski and Chrostowska (at p. 100) found that whereas 42.7 percent of those who were 40-years-old or less were employed in either the competitive labour market or co-operatives for the disabled, only 25.5 percent of those between 41 and 60 were similarly employed.

TABLE 8.9

McBride's Disability Ratings[a] for Selected Injuries and Occupations

Disability		Pre-Disability Occupation							
	Cook	Die Press Operator	Engineer: Electrical	Farmer General	Machinist	Mechanic: Automobile	Plumber	Sewing Machine Operator	Truck Driver
Amputations									
Major arm: above elbow	59	58	57	59	61	61	60	59	61
Thumb	25	19	22	22	31	31	27	22	25
Foot	43	43	40	46	43	46	43	46	50
Whiplash: Recovery to 75% of normal									
Cervical region	14	14	14	20	17	23	23	14	20
Sacroiliac region	29	29	29	35	32	38	38	28	35

TABLE 8.9 (Cont'd)

McBride's Disability Ratings[a] for Selected Injuries and Occupations

					Pre-Disability Occupation				
Disability	Cook	Die Press Operator	Engineer: Electrical	Farmer General	Machinist	Mechanic: Automobile	Plumber	Sewing Machine Operator	Truck Driver
Head, Brain									
Paralysis cranial nerves:									
tenth nerve	37	33	35	35	43	43	43	35	40
twelfth nerve	17	13	15	15	23	23	23	15	29
Epilepsy: grand mal, severe seizures every 2-3 months	47	43	45	45	53	53	53	45	59
Hearing									
1 foot in each ear	58	54	58	51	62	62	58	47	58
10 feet in each ear	28	26	28	22	31	31	28	19	28

Source: E. McBride, *Disability Evaluation*, 6th ed. (Philadelphia: J.B. Lipincott) Chapter 5, Tables 14 and 15.

[a] Percentage *reduction* in ability to earn income.

Table 8.10

Employment-to-Population Ratios of the Spinal Cord Injured

Type of Injury and Employment Status	DeVivo et. al. (U.S.A.)	DeVivo & Fine (U.S.A.)	Devoe (U.S.A.)	Dvonch et. al. (U.S.A.)	El Ghatit (U.S.A.)	Geisler et. al. (Canada)	Gutmann (England) Employable[a] / Total[b]	Jenik et al. (Switzerland)	Karp (Canada)	Statistics Canada (Canada) Male / Female	Weidman & Freehafer (U.S.A.)	Young et al. (U.S.A.) 1 yr. after injury / 4 yrs. after injury
Quadriplegic												
Full-time			13.4				32.0	17.1				
Part-time			11.9				15.1	54.3				
Total employed			25.4				47.1	71.4		35.0 / n.a.	20.3	
Student/housewife			0.0				43.3				27.9	
Paraplegic												
Full-time			19.7				57.3	10.9				
Part-time			9.9				10.3	70.9				
Total employed			29.6				67.6	81.8		65.5 / 32.5	10.6	
Student/housewife			5.3				15.9				48.5	

Author(s) of Study and Country in Which Sample Taken

Table 8.10 (Cont'd)

Employment-to-Population Ratios of the Spinal Cord Injured

Type of Injury and Employment Status	DeVivo et. al. (U.S.A.)	DeVivo & Fine (U.S.A.)	Deyoe (U.S.A.)	Dvonch et. al. (U.S.A.)	El Ghatit (U.S.A.)	Geisler et. al. (Canada)	Gutmann (England) Employ-able[a]	Gutmann (England) Total[b]	Jenik et al. (Switz-erland)	Karp (Canada)	Statistics Canada (Canada) Male	Statistics Canada (Canada) Female	Weidman & Freehafer (U.S.A.)	Young et al. (U.S.A.) 1 yr. after injury	Young et al. (U.S.A.) 4 yrs. after injury
Total															
Full-time			17.8				53.3[e]	45.5[f]	13.3						
Part-time			10.5				11.1[e]	9.4[f]	64.5						
Total employed	19.4[c]	13.0	28.3	52.9[d]	50.2	45.8	64.3[e]	59.9[f]	77.8	40.3	50.2	n.a.	15.9	17.0	27.0
Student/housewife	18.8		3.7			5.3	20.3[e]	16.0[f]					32.4	12.0	19.0

a Excludes those individuals considered "physically unfit" and those "under treatment" in hospital. These individuals represented 14.7 percent of the sample.

b Includes the "physically unfit" and those "under treatment" in hospital.

c Sample taken 7 years after the injury. 29.9 percent of the sample had been employed at least some time during the 7 years.

d 55 of 104 patients (52.9 percent) had been employed some time since the onset of disability. Thus, the employment rate at the time of the survey was 52.9 percent or less.

e Excludes the "polio" and "miscellaneous" categories in Guttman's Table 45.

f Assumes that all 348 individuals identified as "physically unfit" or "under treatment" in hospital were spinal cord injury patients.

TABLE 8.11

Earnings of Spinal Cord Injured Males, Aged 15-64, as Percentage of Earnings of Non-Disabled Males, by Education Level: Canada, 1985

Age Group	Secondary Education	University Degree
35-64	90.8%	66.7%
Total, all ages	86.3	52.3

Source: Canada, Statistics Canada, *Health and Activity Limitation Survey* (Ottawa: Statistics Canada, 1986) Special Tabulation.

Education:

El Ghatit (at p. 406) found positive correlations between the percentage of spinal cord injured who were employed and both the pre-injury level of education and the amount of education obtained following injury. For example, whereas those with college educations both before and after injury had a 53.8 percent employment rate (post-injury), those with a high school education or less, pre- and post-injury, had a 36.7 percent employment rate. Those who had obtained their college degrees after their injuries, however, had an 86.9 percent employment rate.

Similarly, Geisler et al. (at p. 707) found that 67 percent of those with post-secondary education, 58 percent of those with secondary school education, and 37 percent of those with less than secondary school were employed. And Dvonch et al. (at p. 763) found that whereas 73.9 percent of those with high school education were employed, only 40.6 percent of those with a lesser amount of education were employed. Similar results can be seen in the case studies reported in Crewe, Athelstan, and Bower.

Pre-injury employment:

De Vivo and Fine's data indicated that those who were ". . . employed at the time of injury were 7.6 times more likely to be employed 3 years after injury than those who were unemployed at the time of injury."[3]

---

[3] DeVivo, M. and P. Fine, "Employment Status of Spinal Cord Injured Patients 3 Years After Injury" (1982), 63 *Archives of Physical and Medical Rehabilitation*, at p. 202.

Area of residence:

Geisler et al. (at p. 707) found that the employment rate of complete quadriplegics was approximately 25 percent, and of partial paraplegics was approximately 50 percent, regardless of where they lived. Among partial quadriplegics, however, the employment rate was approximately 40 percent in towns and cities compared with 24 percent in rural areas; and among complete paraplegics, the employment rate was approximately 50 percent in towns and cities compared with 36 percent in rural areas.

Disability payments:

DeJong and Weidman and Freehafer found that fear of losing their government disability payments was ". . . the primary reason (the spinal cord injured) had not returned to gainful work activities. All of the patients who were not in a vocational mode gave this as a major reason why they did not work."[4] However, as the payments from a court-awarded lump-sum (or from a structured settlement) do not vary with the employment income of the plaintiff, the employment levels of those who have received adequate awards will be unaffected by this factor. Also, DeVivo et al. found that the spinal cord injured were *less* likely to be employed, the fewer were the outside sources of income.

Summary:

Very few clearcut conclusions can be drawn from this review of the literature. The findings which appear to have the soundest support are that paraplegics are more likely to be employed than quadriplegics, that the probability of employment increases with education, and that those who had been employed at the time they became spinal cord injured were more likely to be employed after the injury than were those who had been unemployed at the time of the injury. With respect to the average effect of spinal cord injury on employment, it appears that, relative to the non-disabled, the probability of employment falls by approximately 10-20 percent for paraplegics and by approximately 20-30 percent for quadriplegics. In addition, it appears that, among those paraplegics who do obtain employment, income may be as much as 50 percent lower (on average) than the comparable incomes of the non-disabled.

---

[4] Weidman, C., and A. Freehafer, "Vocational Outcome in Patients with Spinal Cord Injury" (1981), 47(2) *Journal of Rehabilitation*, at p. 65.

IV. VISUAL IMPAIRMENT

Two major studies of the blind are of particular relevance to Canada. They are:

Canada. Statistics Canada, *Blindness and Visual Impairment in Canada*, Cat. No. 82-615, Vol. 3, (Ottawa: Statistics Canada, November 1990).

Greenland, C., *Vision Canada, Vol I.* (Toronto: Canadian National Institute for the Blind, 1976).

In addition, two European studies may also be helpful to determine employment after the onset of visual impairment:

Greenhalgh, R. and J. Gill, "Employment Problems of Those With Visual Disability" (1978), 98 *Transactions of the Ophthalmological Society of the United Kingdom*, 249-51.

Jeppsson-Grassman, E., "Returning to Work After the Onset of Visual Impairment" (1989), 83 (5) *Journal of Visual Impairment*, 241-44.

The Statistics Canada study is not only the most useful source of Canadian data, it contains some of the most reliable figures concerning the visually impaired to be found anywhere in the world. Perhaps the most important information contained in this study concerns the effect of visual impairment on employment. As Table 8.12 indicates, the proportion of the visually impaired population between the ages of 15 and 64 who are employed is less than half of that of the non-disabled population. And among those aged 30-64, the percentage of both the male and female populations of visually impaired who are employed is only *one third* of that of the non-disabled populations.

TABLE 8.12

Employment Rates of Visually Impaired and Non-Disabled Populations, Age 15-64: Canada, 1985

Age Group	Percentage Employed			
	Males		Females	
	Non-Disabled	Disabled	Non-Disabled	Disabled
15 to 29	68.1%	44.5%	59.0%	30.0%
30 to 64	87.7	30.2	60.7	20.0
15 to 64	79.8	32.7	60.0	21.2

Source: Statistics Canada, *Blindness and Visual Impairment in Canada*, Cat. No. 82-615, Vol. 3, (Ottawa: Statistics Canada, 1990) Table 15.

The Statistics Canada study also provided information concerning the education of the visually impaired population. However, it is clear that the summary statistics are heavily influenced by the age distribution of the visually impaired. That is, although the overall statistics show that the average visually impaired individual has a much lower education than does the average non-disabled Canadian, statistics concerning the educational attainment of the visually impaired, by age group show that the 15 to 29-year-old visually impaired have similar education levels to the population at large. The overall statistics appear to result from a concentration of the visually impaired in the older age groups, where both non-disabled and disabled have relatively low educational levels. Nevertheless, the Statistics Canada study did suggest that among those whose onset of vision loss was at an early stage of education, a disproportionate percentage failed to complete secondary education. Also, as is seen in Table 8.13, the visually impaired tend to have lower incomes than do the non-disabled population even when level of education is accounted for.

TABLE 8.13

Income Distribution by Education, Visually Impaired and Non-Disabled Populations: Canada, 1985

Level of Education	Income Group		
	$0-$10,000	$10,001-$30,000	Over $30,000
0-8 Years			
— Visually Impaired	76.3%	22.5%	1.2%
— Non-disabled	54.9	36.7	8.1
Secondary			
— Visually Impaired	63.5	29.4	6.9
— Non-disabled	54.3	34.8	10.5
Post-secondary			
— Visually Impaired	46.9	47.7	5.1
— Non-disabled	41.6	40.4	17.7
Certificate/Diploma			
— Visually Impaired	44.8	40.5	14.3
— Non-disabled	32.6	46.4	20.6
University Degree			
— Visually Impaired	24.9	44.2	28.9
— Non-disabled	20.7	33.6	45.5

Source: Statistics Canada, *Blindness and Visual Impairment in Canada*, Cat. No. 82-615, Vol. 3, (Ottawa: Statistics Canada, 1990) Table 14.

In the Greenland study, the staff of the CNIB regional offices were asked to identify the employment status of individuals between the ages of 20 and 64, living in their regions in September 1975, who were registered as being blind. The findings of this survey, along with comparable employment figures for Canadians on average, are presented in Table 8.14. There it is seen that the employment rate for those registered as blind was less than half that of all Canadians, even though the former statistic related only to individuals between the ages of 20 and 64, whereas the latter referred to all Canadians over the age of 14.

TABLE 8.14

Percentage of Registered Blind and of Total Population Employed: Canada and the Provinces, September 1975

Location	Percentage of Blind Employed[a]			Percentage of All Individuals Over 14 Employed[b]
	Full-Time	Part-Time	Total	
Newfoundland	11.1	6.1	17.2	45.3
New Brunswick and Nova Scotia	13.1	3.5	16.6	51.8
Quebec	10.6	3.2	13.8	54.4
Ontario	25.4	5.4	30.9	60.4
Manitoba	33.0	3.3	36.3	59.7
Saskatchewan	19.4	6.2	25.6	58.1
Alberta	39.3	9.7	48.9	63.5
British Columbia[c]	22.0	6.9	29.2	55.2
Canada	20.0	5.0	25.0	57.4

Source: C. Greenland, *Vision Canada*, Vol. 1 (Toronto: CNIB, 1976), at 97; and calculated from figures supplied in Canada. Statistics Canada, *Historical Labour Force Statistics*, Cat. No. 71-201 (Ottawa: Statistics Canada, 1977).

[a] Percentage of registered blind individuals between the ages of 20 and 64.

[b] Percentage of total population over 14 years of age.

[c] Greenland's figures are for B.C. and the Yukon. The Statistics Canada figures are for B.C. only.

The Greenhalgh study surveyed all individuals registered as blind in the United Kingdom in 1973. Of the 25,125 respondents, 22.4 percent were employed in the competitive labour market, 8.8 percent were employed in sheltered workshops, 1.6 percent were in training, 7.0

percent were unemployed but seeking employment,[5] and 60.2 percent were neither working, seeking work, nor training.

It is not without interest to note that the employment rates of the blind, as found in the Canadian and British studies cited in this Section, are not only very similar to one another but also similar to those found by Greenblum for the United States. (See Table 8.7, at p. 165.) These studies all indicate that the average employment rate among the blind is in the range of 20-30 percent. However, as the detailed statistics presented by Greenblum — see Table 8.8, at p. 166 — and Statistics Canada indicate, these average figures must be applied with caution, as employment rates among those under 35 years of age are higher than among those over 35, and as employment rates among males are higher than those among females.

The study conducted by Jeppsson-Grassman on visual impairment in Sweden was slightly more optimistic. Even though only 34 percent of the visually impaired population between the ages of 18 and 65 were employed, of those who became visually impaired between the ages of 25 and 45, and had jobs previous to the onset of impairment, 75 percent were employed in 1985. Jeppsson-Grassman attributes these high numbers to Swedish labour laws in the 1970's and early 1980's, which undoubtedly forced employers to become more cautious in dismissing their newly-impaired employees. It should also be noted that, in this study, half of those who remained employed reported losing the opportunity to control job decisions which they had before they became visually impaired.

V. HEARING IMPAIRMENTS

In addition to the Greenblum paper summarized in Section II of this Chapter, the following studies provide information concerning employment of the deaf:

Crammatte, A. B., *Meeting the Challenge: Hearing Impaired Professionals in the Workplace* (Washington, D.C.: Gallaudet University Press, 1987).

Quigley, S., *Educational and Occupational Status of Young Deaf Adults in Illinois* (Urbana, Ill.: Institute for Research on Exceptional Children, University of Illinois, 1969).

Rosenstein, J. and A. Lerman, *Vocational Status and Adjustment of Deaf Women* (New York: Lexington School for the Deaf, 1963).

Schien, J. and M. Delk, Jr., *The Deaf Population of the United States* (Silver Spring, Md.: National Association of the Deaf, 1974).

---

[5] If those in sheltered workshops and in training are not considered to be members of the labour force, the unemployment rate — as normally defined — among the blind in this study was 23.7 percent.

Crammatte's study is based on data collected on hearing impaired professionals in both the deaf and the hearing labour market sectors. Some interesting results were reported on salaries and promotions. It was found that 43.3 percent of the hearing impaired in the deaf labour market earned between $10,000 and $19,999, 41.5 percent earned beween $20,000 and $29,999, and only 9.2 percent earned between $30,000 and $39,999. For the hearing impaired employed in the hearing sector of the labour market, 25.8 percent earned between $10,000 and $19,999, 35.8 percent earned between $20,000 and $29,999, and 25.1 percent earned between $30,000 and $39,999.

Median salaries were found to be $20,814 in the deaf sector, and $26,408 in the hearing sector. Combining the two groups, the median salary was $21,957, compared to the national median income of $23,663. In addition to the hearing sector being more monetarily rewarding than the deaf sector for the hearing impaired, Crammatte also points out that promotions occur more frequently in the hearing labour market sector. As many as 51.8 percent of the hearing impaired in the deaf sector reported that they had never had a promotion, compared to 20.2 percent in the hearing sector reporting the same.

It may be of interest to note that more than 75 percent of all respondents were employed in the deaf sector, and for women this percentage was as high as 87 percent. Of those working in the deaf sector, 80.5 percent were teachers.

The second and third studies were surveys of the graduates of schools for the deaf. Quigley's survey, conducted in 1965, questioned those who had left Illinois programs for the deaf between 1957 and 1967. Among both males and females in this group, he found employment rates which were slightly lower than the population average and unemployment rates which were slightly higher than average. (Quigley, at Table 17, p. 38.) The Rosenstein and Lerman survey, conducted in 1962, interviewed 235 women who had left the Lexington School for the Deaf between 1935 and 1957. They found employment rates which were significantly lower than those among the general population. (Rosenstein and Lerman, at Table XX, p. 46.)

The most reliable study of the deaf is that by Schein and Delk. They were able to develop a list of 291,248 Americans who were presumed to be deaf. In response to questionnaires sent to each of these individuals in 1972, 168,844 responses were received. Of these, approximately 40 percent represented individuals who had become unable to hear and understand speech (Schein and Delk's definition of deafness) before the age of 19. Out of this group, 83.9 percent of white males and 49.6 percent of white females were members of the labour force, compared to 79.6 and 43.2 percent, respectively, of the general population; while 2.2 percent of white males and 9.5 percent of white females were unemployed compared to the population percentages of 4.5 and

5.9, respectively. (Schein and Delk, at Table V.1, p. 75.) Furthermore, this tendency for deaf males to have lower unemployment than males in general, and for deaf females to have higher unemployment rates than females in general, was shown to apply to virtually all age groups of the deaf.

On the other hand, among the deaf, both males and females were shown to have lower annual earnings than were their counterparts in the general population. In particular, deaf white males were found to have an average annual income of $7,738, in comparison with a $9,902 average for all white males; and deaf white females were found to have an average annual income of $4,405, in comparison with a $5,767 average for all white females. (Schein and Delk, at Table V1.2, p. 102.) However, this differential was found to be slightly narrower, the later in life had the onset of deafness been. Whereas, among both males and females, average annual income was found to be $5,663 for those who had been born deaf, the comparable income for those who had become deaf between the ages of 6 and 18 was $6,871.

In summary, it appears that among males, hearing impairment has little effect, if any, upon the ability to obtain employment. It does, however, result in earnings which are approximately 1/3 lower than average, through the restriction of employment prospects. Among women, on the other hand, deafness reduces both employment and earnings, although the latter effect appears to be more significant than the former.

VI. BRAIN DAMAGE

I have been able to locate eight studies which cast some light on the employability of those who have suffered from a restriction of their brain function. These are:

Brooks, N., et al., "Return to Work Within the First Seven Years of Severe Head Injury" (1987), 1 (1) *Brain Injury* 5-19.
Johnson, R., "Return to Work After Severe Head Injury" (1987), 9 (2) *International Disability Studies* 49-54.
McMordie, W. R., S. L. Baker and T. M. Paolo, "Return to Work After Head Injury" (1990), 4 (1) *Brain Injury* 57-69.
Olshansky, S. and D. Beach, "A Five-Year Follow-Up of Mentally Retarded Clients" (1974), 35 *Rehabilitation Literature* 45-9.
Rao, N., et al., "Return to Work After Rehabilitation Following Traumatic Brain Injury" (1990), 4 (1) *Brain Injury* 49-56.
Roberts, A. H., *Severe Accidental Head Injury: An Assessment of Long-Term Prognosis* (London: Macmillan, 1979).

Stambrook, M., et al., "Effects of Mild, Moderate and Severe Closed Head Injury on Long-Term Vocational Status" (1990), 4 (2) *Brain Injury* 183-90.

Wehman, P. H., et al., "Return to Work for Persons With Traumatic Brain Injury: A Supported Employment Approach" (1990), 71 *Archives of Physical and Medical Rehabilitation* 1047-52.

The study by Brooks et al. examined 98 patients with severe head injuries to determine the rate and predictability of returning to work within seven years of the injury. It was found that physical, cognitive, and emotional changes as a result of the injury contributed to a decline in employment from 86 percent pre-injury to 29 percent post-injury.

The study found that the effect of previous occupational level was positively related to returning to work. More specifically, ". . . 50 percent of those working before injury at a managerial or similar level returned to work, compared with 33 percent in a skilled manual job, and only 21 percent in an unskilled job."[6] Age was found to have a significant effect on return to work, the critical age being 45. Even though no differential age effect is observed before this, the chances of returning to work for those over the age of 45 drop from 39 percent to 12 percent.

Lastly, the most significant predictors of returning to work in this study were the ability to carry on a conversation — 11 percent with the deficiency, and 46 percent without the deficiency were working — and the ability to understand a conversation, with similar results. The authors did point out that a deficiency in the ability either to carry on or to understand a conversation was a very good predictor of failure to return to work, yet the absence of such a deficiency did not ensure return to work.

Johnson studied 47 individuals who had suffered severe head injuries, and experienced post-traumatic amnesia for over one week, but who remained in a disoriented state for less than one year. Similar to the Brooks study, it was found that those in non-manual jobs had a greater chance of success in returning to work (48 percent) than those in manual jobs (31 percent). Also, of the 10 women who were included in the study, six attempted to work again, but only two (33 percent) returned to their previous job. In comparison, 80 percent, or 20 of 25 men who sought employment after their injury returned to the same job. Of the 47 individuals, 16 did not make any attempt to work post-injury, mostly because they were severely handicapped or they had poor memories.

---

[6] Brooks, N., et al., "Return to Work Within the First Seven Years of Severe Head Injury" (1987), 1 (1) *Brain Injury* 5-19, at p. 16.

The study by McMordie et al. explored return to work factors for 177 head-injured patients age 19 and up. At the time of injury, 69 percent of the sample were employed, and 27 percent were attending school. It was found that 45 percent of the sample returned to work, but only 19 percent found competitive employment. The study also suggested that age was not an important determinant of return to work among younger people. Those over 40 were less likely to return to work than those under 40, however.

Olshansky and Beach followed up 192 mentally retarded clients of the Community Workshops in Boston, Massachusetts after they had left the Workshops. According to the authors these individuals had been selected to attend the workshops because, although they constituted ". . . that part of the population of retardates who cannot make it by their own efforts or those of their families and friends . . . they . . . were considered to be in the so-called 'educable' group . . ."[7] Of the 192 clients from whom Olshansky and Beach obtained information, 41.7 percent (80) were employed, 29.7 percent (57) were unemployed, 18.8 percent (36) had never worked and were considered unemployable, and 9.9 percent (19) were either in institutions or were employed in sheltered workshops.

Rao et al. studied 79 patients who had suffered from closed-head injuries. Ninety-seven percent of the subjects experienced severe to extremely severe post-traumatic amnesia, ranging anywhere from one day to 74 weeks. None of the patients were unemployed previous to their injury, 90 percent of the patients were employed and 10 percent were attending school. All 79 subjects received inpatient rehabilitation services. The authors found that 66 percent of the subjects returned to work or school, and of that group 65 percent returned to a job at the same skill level as their previous one. The return to work or school subjects ". . . were younger, more likely to have a normal CT scan or one indicative of unilateral damage, had shorter duration of coma, and were in patient rehabilitation for a shorter length of time."[8]

The study by Roberts considered those who had suffered severe, non-missile head injuries. Of the total population of 7,000 patients who had been admitted after head injury to the Accident Service of the Radcliffe Infirmary, between 1948 and 1961, a random sample was drawn. To this sample was added a smaller, select series of ". . . the most severely head injured, drawn from other sources, who had remained unconscious for longer than a month after injury."[9] The main findings of this

[7] Olshanksy, S. and D. Beach, "A Five-Year-Follow-Up of Mentally Retarded Clients" (1974), 35 *Rehabilitation Literature* 45-9, at p. 48.
[8] Rao, N., et al., "Return to Work After Rehabilitation Following Traumatic Brain Injury" (1990), 4 (1) *Brain Injury* 49-56, at p. 51.
[9] Roberts, A.H., *Severe Accidental Head Injury: An Assessment of Long-Term Prognosis* (London: Macmillan, 1979) at p. 3.

survey, as they relate to employability, are summarized in Table 8.15. Among 16 to 35-year-old patients, it is only those who suffered more than five weeks post-traumatic amnesia and who were decerebrate at the time of admission who later encountered long-lasting difficulty in returning to work or school. Among those older than 35, on the other hand, the duration of post-traumatic amnesia appears to have been a much more significant determinant of the individual's return to school or work than was the state of brain function at the time of admission.

Stambrook et al. conducted a follow-up study of 131 male head-injury patients who were divided into three categories with respect to

TABLE 8.15

Percentage of Individuals Who Failed to Return to Work or School Following Severe Accidental Head Injury: Oxford,[a] 1948-1961

Age and Number of Weeks of Post-Traumatic Amnesia[b]	Severity of Brain Damage		
	Confused	Semi-Purposive or Purposive	Decerebrate
16-35 years old			
1-3 weeks	5.3%	0.0%	20.0%
3-5 weeks	0.0	4.3	14.3
5-13 weeks	0.0[c]	12.5	36.0
over 13 weeks	— [c]	100.0[c]	92.0
36 years old and over			
1-3 weeks	7.4	30.8	0.0[c]
3-5 weeks	28.6	27.3	100.0[c]
5-13 weeks	71.4	11.1	33.3[c]
over 13 weeks	— [c]	100.0[c]	90.9
Total	22.0	29.7	75.0

Source: A. H. Roberts, *Severe Accidental Head Injury: An Assessment of Long-Term Prognosis* (London: Macmillan, 1979). p. 175, Table 13.10. Reprinted by permission of Macmillan, London and Basingstoke.

[a] The Table is based upon a random sample of 331 patients drawn from the 7,000 patients admitted after head injury to the Accident Service of the Radcliffe Infirmary, Oxford, between 1948 and 1961.

[b] The sample was restricted to those who suffered at least one week of post-traumatic amnesia.

[c] Fewer than 5 patients in the sampling cell.

the severity of the injury: mild (n = 26), moderate (n = 55), and severe (n = 50). Of 31 subjects in the severe category who had full-time jobs prior to their injury, only 55 percent returned to full-time employment. In comparison, 80 percent of the moderately injured, previously employed subjects returned to full-time employment. It should also be noted that subjects who returned to work in the moderate and severe group experienced a reduced level of occupational status; whereas eighty-eight percent of the mildly injured patients who returned to work experienced the same status level as before. Finally, of the 25 patients who were unemployed prior to their injury, 100 percent remained so post-injury, regardless of the severity of their injury.

The last study, by Wehman et al., is a follow-up of 41 persons who had experienced severe head injuries, most of whom were unable to live on their own as a result of their injury. An average of seven years had transpired since the injury, and each patient had received support employment in order to be placed into the competitive job market. Previous to the study, 36 percent of the subjects had obtained a competitive position on their own after the injury. Ninety-one percent of that group had been competitively employed pre-injury. It was found that of the 41 patients who were placed in competitive jobs, 29 of them, or 71 percent, were still employed. They worked an average of 31.2 hours a week and typically held positions in clerical, warehouse, and service-related positions. In addition, the authors found that the subjects required an average of 291 hours of coaching in order to be placed and maintained in supported employment. Before supported employment was implemented, ". . . clients worked 15 percent of the total month during which they could have worked after the injury."[10] This figure rose sharply to 75 percent after supported employment.

VII. BACK INJURY

Statistics Canada's Health and Activity Survey collected information concerning the effects of back injury on earnings and employment. Some data, obtained from a special tabulation of this information, concerning the relative earnings of back injury sufferers and non-disabled individuals is summarized in Table 8.16. There it is seen that back injuries appear to reduce the earnings potential of women more than men and that back injuries have a much less pronounced effect on earnings as education increases.

---

[10] Wehman, P.H., et al., "Return to Work for Persons with Traumatic Brain Injury: A Supported Employment Approach" (1990), 71 *Archives of Physical and Medical Rehabilitation* 1047-52, at p. 1051.

TABLE 8.16

Earnings of Back Injury Sufferers As a Percentage of the Earnings of the Non-Disabled: Canada, 1985

Age and Sex	Level of Education	
	Grade 9-12	University Degree
Female		
15-24 years	49.6%	n.a.
25-34 years	34.2	70.7
35-64 years	27.8	110.0
Male		
15-24 years	42.2%	n.a.
25-34 years	59.2	91.0
35-64 years	58.4	87.2

n.a. : sample size too small.

Source: Canada. Statistics Canada, *The Health and Activity Limitation Survey*, (Ottawa, Statistics Canada, 1986) Special Tabulation.

I have also been able to identify four academic studies which provide information on the effect which back injury has on prospects for employment. These are:

Deyo, R. A., and A. K. Diehl, "Psychosocial Predictors of Disability in Patients with Low Back Pain" (1988), 15 (10) *The Journal of Rheumatology* 1557-64.

Gallagher, R. M., et al., "Determinants of Return-to-Work Among Low Back Pain Patients" (1989) 39, *Pain* 55-67.

Taylor, M. E., "Return to Work Following Back Surgery: A Review" (1989), 16 *American Journal of Industrial Medicine* 79-88.

Wigley, R. D., N. Carter, J. Woods, M. Ahuja, and K. G. Couchman, "Rehabilitation in Chronic Back Pain: Employment Status After Four Years" (1990) January, *New Zealand Medical Journal* 9-10.

The employment outcomes of 179 patients with low back pain were studied by Deyo et al. All patients had undergone bed rest and x-ray treatment. The only variable that was found to be significantly related to employment status after treatment was employment status prior to entry into the clinic. The best predictor of *continued* employment was a negative response to the question "Do you feel sick all the time?" It may be of interest to note that a physical examination was found *not* to be a good predictor of return-to-work.

Gallagher et al. studied 150 subjects to identify the physical, behavioural, and psychological determinants of returning to work among low back pain sufferers. Eighty-seven subjects were chosen from a university low back pain clinic, and the remaining 63 were chosen because they had applied for Social Security compensation as a result of their back pain. All subjects were unemployed at the onset of the study, and had worked at least 3 months before becoming unemployed. The follow-up study was conducted 6 months later to determine return-to-work factors. The majority of the clinic sample was under the age of 44 (83 percent) compared to only 41 percent of the Social Security Sample. Sixty-nine percent of the clinic sample had been unemployed for less than six months. In the Social Security sample 64 percent had been unemployed for more than one year. Gallagher et al. found that 41.4 percent of the clinic sample, and only 15.9 percent of the Social Security sample had successfully returned to work after 6 months. After controlling for age and duration of unemployment, physical examination and biomechanical measures did not have any predictive power to determine whether an individual would return to work. It was further stated that length of time out of work had a negative impact on vocational outcome, probably due to the weakened job identity as time passed, making it more difficult to return to work. Finally, Gallagher et al. found that perceived ease of changing occupations had an effect on returning to work, making it 3 times more likely for an optimistic person, as opposed to someone who perceives a job change to be difficult, to return to work. This effect was found to be stronger in younger patients.

A review of 19 studies from 1980 to 1986 on return-to-work following back surgery was conducted by Marvin Taylor. All studies were follow-ups ranging from one to over 20 years following back surgery for low back pain. Fifty-nine percent of all patients were male, and the average age of the subjects was 40. Taylor summarized that those patients who underwent only one operation had an 82 percent chance of returning to work, whereas this probability was only 59 percent among patients requiring multiple surgery. Seventy-seven percent of all patients returning to work returned to an occupation similar to that which in which they had worked before the operation. Some of the important factors that were found to determine return-to-work were: "history of back pain, a history of previous back surgery, the level of work activity, the length of unemployment, . . . (and) . . . the extensiveness of the surgical procedure."[11] Eleven percent of all subjects required further back surgery.

Finally, the New Zealand study was based on 102 responses (21 female) to a questionaire in order to determine employment prospects for those suffering from chronic back pain. The study was conducted 4-5 years after the patients had been treated and received rehabilitation. It was found that the employment rate for men between the ages

---

[11] Taylor, M.E., "Return to Work Following Back Surgery: A Review" (1989), 16 *American Journal of Industrial Medicine* 79-88, at p. 86.

of 45 and 64 was much lower (31 percent) than the rate for men below the age of 45 (70 percent). Forty-five percent of the 11 women under the age of 45, and 11 percent of the nine women between the ages of 45 and 64 were employed. However, due to the small number of female respondents, this figure may not be reliable. In total, 51 of the 102 respondents were employed, of whom 39 percent had different jobs with a new employer, and 16 percent were in their previous jobs. Only 21 percent of those employed were earning the same salary after the injury as before. Twenty-six percent were actually earning more, but the majority (54 percent) were earning less than before their injury. Seventeen of 81 men responded that they had retired, but only 3 of them were over the age of 60.

VIII. EPILEPSY

Statistics Canada's Health and Activity Survey collected information concerning the effects of epilepsy on earnings and employment. Some data, obtained from a special tabulation of this information, concerning the relative earnings of epileptics and non-disabled individuals are summarized in Table 8.17. There it is seen that, although all groups appeared to suffer a reduction in earnings relative to non-disabled workers, no clear cut pattern among groups is discernible.

I was also able to find two academic articles that shed some light on the effects of epilepsy on the prospects for employment. These were:

Hasegawa, S., et al., "The Ability to Work and Employment Situation for People with Epilepsy" (1988), 42 (3) *The Japanese Journal of Psychiatry and Neurology* 578-79.
Thompson, P. J., and J. Oxley, "Socioeconomic Accompaniments of Severe Epilepsy" (1988), 29 *Epilepsia* S9-18.

Hasegawa et al. initially selected 215 epileptic patients who had received more than one year of treatment at Teradomari Hospital in Niigata. After classifying the patients into different groups, according to their capability to perform work, it was found that 116 patients were capable of doing normal work, 46 patients were able to do simple tasks, and 53 patients were unable to do any work. Of the 116 patients capable of performing normal work, 66 percent had seizures of varying frequencies, and 34 percent had not experienced a seizure for over a year. Of these 116 patients, 64 percent (74) had steady occupations, 12 percent (14) were engaged in irregular jobs, 5 percent (6) were unemployed, and 19 percent (22) were housewives and students. The frequency of seizures for the 74 patients who had steady occupations was slightly lower. Fifty-nine percent had experienced some seizures, and 41 percent had

TABLE 8.17

Earnings of Epileptics As a Percentage of the Earnings of the Non-Disabled: Canada, 1985

Age and Sex	Grade 9-12	Some Post-Secondary, Certificate/Diploma
Female		
Total, all ages	78.6%	55.9%
15-24 years	n.a.	79.0
25-34 years	n.a.	54.2
35-64 years	n.a.	n.a.
Male		
Total, all ages	54.4%	78.2%
15-24 years	47.1	n.a.
25-34 years	43.0	n.a.
35-64 years	n.a.	64.9

Source: Canada. Statistics Canada, *The Health and Activity Limitation Survey* (Ottawa: Statistics Canada, 1986) Special Tabulation.

been seizure free for over one year. Hasegawa et al. also found that, among a sample of 39 male patients capable of working, the average income was 80 percent of that of normal males in the same age brackets. The female income ratio for 23 epileptic females was found to be 79 percent of that of non-disabled female salary earners.

Thompson and Oxley studied 92 patients and 23 outpatients at an epilepsy centre in the U.K. in order to determine socioeconomic consequences for those suffering from uncontrolled seizures. At the time of admission, 89 percent of the inpatient sample experienced seizures at least once a week. The average duration of stay for the inpatients at the centre was 3 months. Only 11 percent of the 92 patients were in open employment, and unskilled work was most commonly reported to be the form of employment. Of the remaining subjects not in paid employment, 47 percent had been employed in the past, and of those 91 percent had been employed in the unskilled labour market.

Seventy-one percent of the 92 patients at the centre claimed that they had significant difficulties in the area of work, compared with 22 percent of the sample of 23 outpatients reporting the same difficulties. However, only 37 percent of the centre patients, and 22 percent of the outptients, reported having financial difficulties. Thompson and Oxley did point out that the relatively low figure for the epilepsy centre admissions could be due to the lack of financial responsibility and contribution these patients make to bill payments, as the families are most likely to be carrying the financial burden.

IX. AMPUTATION

The following two articles provide information on the employment consequences for amputees:

Millstein, S., D. Bain, and A. Hunter, "A Review of Employment Patterns of Industrial Amputees — Factors Influencing Rehabilitation" (1985), 9 *Prosthetics and Orthotics International* 69-78.
Sturup, J., et al., "Traumatic Amputation of the Upper Limb: the Use of Body-Powered Prostheses and Employment Consequences" (1988), 12 *Prosthetics and Orthotics International* 50-2.

The Millstein study followed up over 1000 amputees at the Ontario Workers' Compensation Board to determine their employment status and factors influencing successful return to work. Of the total group studied, 89 percent were employed post-operation. Broken down by level of amputation, upper limb amputees had the highest success rate (93 percent) compared with 87 percent for lower limb amputees, and 74 percent for multiple limb amputees. However, only 21 percent of the total sample returned to their previous job, and 42 percent reported that they returned to a modified job. Over half of the total sample reported negative employment effects as a result of their amputation, including a decreased opportunity for promotion and salary increase.

According to Millstein et al., the most disadvantaged in terms of returning to employment were women, their unemployment rate was 2.5 times that of men, and older subjects, 48 percent of those over 45 years of age compared to only 22 percent of those under the age of 45 reported being unemployed. In this sample, the unemployed included those not looking for work and the prematurely retired.

A more specific study was conducted by Sturup et al. to find out whether the use of prostheses affected employment among 43 one-arm amputees. Of 19 below-elbow amputees, 17 used their prostheses, and of the remaining 24 above-elbow amputees, 12 used theirs. Also, 16 of 21 patients who lost their dominant arm, and 13 of 22 patients who lost their non-dominant arm used their prostheses. It was found that non-users of prostheses experienced a higher employment rate (8 of 14) than users (11 of 29). Sturup et al. attributed these results to the probability that non-users occupied jobs prior to their amputation in which they only needed to use one hand. Users, in comparison, had to leave the job market in order to become rehabilitated, and as a result may have lost their previous jobs. In support of this claim, it was found that non-users generally held non-strenuous, skilled jobs, and users were more likely to occupy the unskilled labour market.

It should be noted, that in contrast to the Sturup study, Millstein et al. found that prosthesis users had a better chance of being employed, probably due to prosthesis users having a more positive attitude. This contrasting result may be attributed to the fact that the Millstein study included lower limb amputees, and these were the most frequent users of their prostheses. Since the Sturup study did not include lower limb amputees, a lack of correlation could be found between the two studies.

X. BURN INJURIES

I was able to locate one study that provides information concerning the return to work for those who have suffered from a burn injury:

Bowden, M. L., P. D. Thomson, and J. K. Prasad, "Factors Influencing Return to Employment After a Burn Injury" (1989), 70 *Archives of Physical and Medical Rehabilitation* 772-74.

This study concentrates on 155 previously employed burn patients admitted to a burn centre during a two year period, and discusses some factors that may determine return to work, and length of time until returning to work. On average it took 63 days for a patient to return to work following a burn injury. Bowden et al. found that extent of burn was a significant factor in determining length of time from burn to return to work. Among those patients for whom 0-10 percent of the total body area was burned, it took an average of 47 days to return to work. This figure increased consistently as the percent of body area burned increased. Among those patients with burns to as much as 51-80 percent of their total body area, the average time to return to work was 170 days. Age also had a significant positive effect on time until returning to work, ranging from an average of 44 days for patients between the ages of 18 and 24, to 68 days for those between 35 and 44, and up to 78 days for patients between 55 and 60. Upon reviewing a number of previous studies prepared on this subject, Bowden et al. concluded that there has been a universal trend towards a reduction in the time it takes to return to work following a burn injury.

XI. ARTHRITIS

I was able to find one study which provided useful information on the subject of arthritis and employment:

Mitchell, J. M., R. V. Burkhauser, and T. Pincus, "The Importance of Age, Education, and Comorbity in the Substantial Earnings Losses of Individuals With Symmetric Polyarthritis" (1988), 31 (3) *Arthritis and Rheumatism*, 348-57.

Mitchell et al. reported on data collected in "The 1978 Social Security Survey of Disability and Work". The section of the survey used in this study, on the topic of arthritis, focussed on answers provided by 5,652 subjects considered to be representative of the U.S. civilian, non-institutionalized population between the ages of 18 and 64.

Fifty-eight percent of all women and 87 percent of all men were working at the time of the survey. Thirty-nine percent of women and 71 percent of men with Arthritis Diagnosis (answering 'yes' to having Arthritis or Rheumatism) reported being employed. Of those reporting having Arthritis Symptoms ("Subjects who reported pain in the hip, knee, ankle, foot, shoulder, elbow, or hand, or swelling in one of these joints . . ."[12]), on the other hand, 43 percent of women and 70 percent of men were working. And among those who suffered from both Arthritis Diagnosis and Arthritis Symptoms, only 34 percent of women and 63 percent of men were employed. The worst employment prospects were for individuals suffering from Symmetric Polyarthritis, which in this study was defined as ". . . symmetric pain or swelling in 2 or more specific joints, i.e., at least 4 joints (i.e., both hands and both knees)".[13] Only 31 percent of women and 56 percent of men in that category were working.

XII. CONCLUDING COMMENTS

There are three comments which I believe it useful to make in concluding this Chapter. First, with respect to most of the disabilities considered, I have identified fewer studies than I would have liked. In part, this is because I found very few statistical studies of the employability of disabled individuals. In part, however, it is because many of the studies which I was able to locate used data gathering and reporting techniques which were sufficiently questionable, statistically, that they could not be relied upon. Indeed, I rejected as unhelpful as many studies as I included. I would caution all of those involved in the trial of a personal injury action that they should not accept the testimony of the opposing expert without questioning closely the statistical validity of his sources.

---

[12] Mitchell, J.M., R.V. Burkhauser, and T. Pincus, "The Importance of Age, Education, and Comorbity in the Substantial Earnings Losses of Individuals With Symmetric Polyarthritis" (1988), 31 (3) *Arthritis and Rheumatism*, 348-57, at p. 349.

[13] *Ibid.*, at p. 350.

Second, because the severity and nature of injuries within classifications can vary significantly among patients, even the most reliable of the statistics reported in this Chapter cannot be used as more than indicators of the individual plaintiff's employment prospects. These statistics must be supplemented with the informed opinion of a medical or vocational rehabilitation expert. On the other hand, as a doctor's experiences may be based upon an unrepresentative sample and as his or her statistical information may be based upon reliable sources, it is important that the cross-examiner be careful to identify the source and validity of the expert's opinion in such matters.

Finally, over the lifespan of this book, I anticipate that a considerable amount of information will be made available from Statistics Canada's Health and Activity Survey. Although the source of this information is impeccable, a great deal of caution will have to be exercised in the manner in which it is applied. The primary source of problems is that the Statistics Canada data, virtually by necessity, average together large groups of dissimilar individuals. This means that two groups which appear to be comparable will not be. For example, assume that Statistics Canada has reported that the average income among 15 to 64-year-old males with some particular disability is $30,000 per year whereas among similar, non-disabled males it is $35,000. It would be tempting to argue that this implies that individuals with that disability earn 85.7 percent as much as comparable, non-disabled individuals. However, it does not. The reason is that the distribution of other socio-economic characteristics among these two populations may be very different. It could be, for example, that the disabled group contains a higher concentration of young males than does the non-disabled, thereby creating a lower average income for that reason alone. Similarly, it may be that the disabled population contains a relatively high percentage of individuals with low educational levels, something which would not be unexpected given the higher accident rates within manual occupations than within non-manual, again creating an earnings differential which was not caused by the disability. As I do not anticipate that Statistics Canada will provide information which will allow these factors to be disentangled, their data will have to be used with extreme caution. The more reliable sources will be those studies, usually academic in nature, which employ sophisticated statistical techniques, such as multiple regression analysis, to control for all the multitude of interactive factors involved in determining income and employment.[14]

---

[14] At the time of writing of this book, August 1991, I was aware of a Ph.D. thesis being written in the Economics Department of the University of Toronto which was attempting to perform the relevant statistical tests of the Health and Activity Limitation Survey data. The author, however, requested that I not release her name as, at the time of writing, her research was in its preliminary stages.

9

RETIREMENT

The purpose of Chapters 4 to 8 was to identify the plaintiff's current and potential earnings streams in each of the years following the accident. For most individuals, this stream comes to an end at the age of *retirement*. The purpose of this Chapter will be to review the studies which identify: the average age of retirement; and variations among retirement ages with respect to factors such as pension availability, health, occupation, and sex.

In the first edition of this book, I listed a large number of such studies and attempted to summarize the main findings of all of them. In this edition, I will not do this, for two reasons. First, two Canadian books have recently been published which do an excellent job of surveying the literature. Those readers who wish a more detailed analysis than I will provide here are recommended to:

Bruce, Christopher J., *Economics of Employment and Earnings* (Toronto: Nelson Canada, 1990), Chapter 10.
McDonald, P. Lynn, and Richard A. Wanner, *Retirement in Canada* (Toronto: Butterworths, 1990) Chapters 4 and 6.

Second, the literature on retirement is now so large that it simply would not be possible to review all of the relevant research in a book of this type. The bibliography to McDonald and Wanner's book, for example, contains over 400 references to retirement-related research publications.

I have divided this Chapter into two Sections. In the first, I report some data concerning retirement ages in Canada. In the second, I review the literature which has attempted to identify the determinants of variations in retirement ages among individuals.

I. RETIREMENT AGES IN CANADA

Table 9.1 presents the most recent data available concerning average retirement ages, by sex, for Canada. These data are taken from the fourth "cycle" of the General Social Survey — an annual survey of approximately 10,000 Canadians undertaken by Statistics Canada. Of the respondents to this survey in 1989, 584 males and 435 females indicated that they were "retired" and provided information concerning the ages at which they had retired. As it seems likely that many of the individuals who responded that they had "retired" before the age of 55 had left the labour force for reasons which we do not normally associate with retirement — for example, they may have suffered a major disabling injury or disease which prevented them from working — and which would already have been accounted for by the factors discussed under the heading of "negative contingencies" in Chapter 7 of this book, I have presented two sets of figures in Table 9.1. The first set provides information concerning the percentage of all respondents who retired at each of a number of ages; while the second set provides comparable information only for those individuals who had indicated that they had

TABLE 9.1

Ages of Retirement: Canada, 1989

Age of Retirement	Percentage of All Retirements		Percentage of Retirements in Age Group 55-75	
	Male	Female	Male	Female
Under 55	13.3%	26.3%	—	—
55-56	5.0	7.4	5.8%	10.1%
57	4.9	8.5	5.7	11.6
58	5.5	4.6	6.4	6.3
59	5.5	5.1	6.4	7.0
60	7.6	5.9	8.8	8.0
61	6.3	3.3	7.3	4.4
62	4.7	3.6	5.5	4.9
63	7.2	6.4	8.3	6.7
64	18.9	11.9	22.0	16.3
65	6.9	6.2	8.0	8.5
66	3.9	2.9	4.6	3.9
67-68	4.2	2.2	4.9	4.2
69-70	3.7	2.7	4.2	3.7
71-75	1.9	1.8	2.2	2.4
Over 75	0.5	0.3	—	—
Average Age of Retirement	60.7	57.4	62.4	61.7

Source: Statistics Canada, *General Social Survey* (Ottawa: Statistics Canada, 1990). Special Tabulation.

retired between the ages of 55 and 75. This Table shows that the average retirement age overall is 60.7 for males and 57.4 for females; but that these figures rise to 62.4 and 61.7, respectively, when the analysis is restricted to those who retired between the ages of 55 and 75.

For the purpose of calculating future losses of income, it is the latter figures which provide, I believe, the more reliable estimates of the average retirement age. However, these figures are biased downward slightly by the fact that they were obtained by averaging the retirement ages of only those individuals who answered that they had already retired. But the individuals who were most likely not to have retired at the time of the survey were those whose planned retirement ages were the highest. That is, a survey such as this identifies a higher percentage of "early" retirees than it does "late" retirees and, hence, underestimates the average age of retirement. What this suggests is that the average retirement age, for those who retired after age 55, was probably approximately 63 for males and 62.5 for females.

Table 9.1 also indicates that these averages hide a considerable amount of diversity among the retirement ages of Canadians. Even among those who retired between ages 55 and 75, 24.3 percent of males and 35 percent of females had retired before their 60th birthdays. And approximately 25 percent of both sexes retired after their 65th birthdays. One possible source of this diversity is differences in average retirement ages among occupations or industries. The General Social Survey referred to in Table 9.1 asked respondents to identify the industry in which they had worked immediately before their retirement. The average retirement ages for individuals from each of seven major industrial classifications for all workers, i.e., for the set of workers identified in the first two columns of Table 9.1, are presented in Table 9.2. There is a slight, but not pronounced tendency for workers in administration, finance, and durable manufacturing to retire earlier than the average and for workers in the service sector to retire later.

Finally, Table 9.3 reproduces the main findings of a 1977 study of retirement among Canadian males. Three of the most consistent findings of all analyses of retirement are observed in this Table. First, particularly among those males who do not own their own businesses (the first two columns of Table 9.3) there is a strong preference for retirement at age 64.[1] Second, there is a slight tendency for government employees to retire earlier than private sector employees.[2] And, third,

---

[1] In 1988, 89.9 percent of individuals covered by pension plans belonged to plans whose "normal" retirement age was 65. (See Canada. Statistics Canada, *Pension Plans in Canada*, 1988 Cat. No. 74-401 (Ottawa: Statistics Canada, 1988.)

[2] In 1988, 67.3 percent of government employees covered by pension plans belonged to plans which provided full (28.9 percent) or partial (38.4 percent) indexing with respect to the consumer price index. The comparable figures with respect to private employees were 7.5 percent, 0.5 percent, and 7 percent, respectively. (See Statistics Canada, *supra*, note 1.)

there is a clear tendency for self-employed males, including farmers, to retire later than other workers.

TABLE 9.2

Average Age of Retirement by Industry and Sex: Canada, 1989

Industry	Male	Female
Agriculture/Primary	60.9	58.5
Manufacturing: Non-Durable	61.2	56.8
Manufacturing: Durable	60.9	50.6
Construction/Transportation	59.9	[a]
Wholesale/Retail Trade	61.5	57.7
Services	62.9	59.1
Administration/Finance	59.7	55.2

[a] Insufficient observations.

Source: Statistics Canada, *General Social Survey* (Ottawa: Statistics Canada, 1990) Special Tabulation.

TABLE 9.3

Probability of Being Retired by Age and Employment Sector:
Canadian Males, 1977

Age	Public Sector	Private Sector	Percentage of Individuals Retired[a]	
			Own Farm	Own Business
55	12	10	8	16
60	15	13	10	17
62	21	19	18	22
63	27	24	22	27
64	38	32	29	32
65	66	56	44	40
66	78	70	60	50
67	83	77	67	58
68	88	82	72	66
70	91	88	79	76
75	94	92	87	86

Source: Ciffin, S., and J. Martin, *Retirement in Canada: Volume I, When and Why People Retire*, Cat. No. SWP-7704 (Ottawa: Health and Welfare Canada, May 1977) Figure 7.

II. STUDIES OF THE DETERMINANTS OF RETIREMENT AGE

A defect of the data reported in Section I is that it does not indicate why retirement rates vary as they do. There is no indication, for example, of why it is that (in the survey reported in Table 9.3) whereas 13 percent of private sector workers had retired by age 60, 12 percent had still not retired by age 70. Nor is very much known about the (apparent) differences in retirement behaviour among the various industries reported in Table 9.2. If these differences arose from differences in pension plan benefits, for example, and if the pension plan of the plaintiff's employer was known to differ significantly from those of other employers in the same occupation, that information could be used to predict a retirement age which differed from the average. In order to provide some information concerning these issues, I have reviewed a large selection of statistical studies which have attempted to identify the primary determinants of retirement age. These studies find there to be seven categories of factors which are significantly correlated with actual and expected age of retirement. These factors are:

Pension income

The availability of a pension has been found to affect retirement decisions in two ways. First, it is clear that, as the annual value of the individual's pension rises relative to his or her employment income, the probability that the individual will retire also increases. There is some debate among economists as to whether this phenomenon arises because individuals who plan to retire early choose to work for employers with generous pension plans or whether it arises because individuals who work for employers with generous pension plans find it to their advantage to retire early. But the resolution to this debate is not of interest for the purposes to which we wish to put the information here. All that the court needs to know is that the more generous is the pension plan, the earlier is the expected retirement age, *ceteris paribus*.

Second, most pension plans are set up in such a way that the present, or commuted, value of the future stream of pension benefits peaks at some age and then declines. As the individual works longer (i.e., delays retirement) two counteractive forces work on the present value of the pension stream. Under most pension plans, the annual value of the individual's pension increases with each extra year worked — both because the individual has made additional contributions to the plan and because most pensions are based upon the value of the individual's salary in the last year(s) of employment. Offsetting this is the simple fact, that when the individual works an additional year, he or she is necessarily taking one less year of retirement. If the annual value of the pension increases sufficiently with an additional year of employment, the first of these effects will offset the second and the present value of the pension stream will increase. If, however, the annual value of the pension increases by only a small amount when an extra year is worked, the present value of the pension stream will decrease. What empirical research has found is that workers are more likely to retire, the lesser is the increase (or the greater is the decrease) in the present value of the pension stream associated with an additional year of employment.

Mandatory retirement

The findings with respect to the effect of mandatory retirement provisions on retirement age have been mixed. In the General Social Survey, referred to in Tables 9.1 and 9.2, it was found that approximately 29 percent of workers had retired because of the mandatory retirement age at their places of employment. However, in the Health and Welfare study referred to in Table 9.3, it was found that over 60 percent of those who had retired because of compulsory retirement and other reasons, retired at the ages they preferred. Most formal statistical studies that have investigated this question have found that mandatory retirement provisions do result in slightly reduced ages of retirement, on average.[3] But there have been some which find *later* retirement in firms with mandatory retirement.[4]

Employment income

Most studies find that the age at which individuals retire increases as their incomes increase, even after differences in pension entitlement are allowed for. Some studies also find that individuals are more likely to delay their retirement the greater is the expected increase in their annual earnings between their current age and age 65.

---

[3] See especially A. Hall and T. Johnson, "The Determinants of Planned Retirement Age" (1980), 33 *Industrial and Labor Relations Review*, 241-54; G. Hanoch and M. Honig, "Retirement, Wages, and Labor Supply of the Elderly" (1983) 2 *Journal of Labor Economics*, 131-51; Mark Hayward, et al., "Occupational Influences on Retirement, Disability, and Death" (1989), 26 *Demography* 393-409; and E. Palmore, L . George, and G. Fillenbaum, "Predictors of Retirement" (1982), 37 *Journal of Gerontology* 733-42.

[4] Hall and Johnson, *ibid.*, reported that women who faced mandatory retirement were more likely to retire *after* age 65 than those who did not face such a requirement.

Other financial considerations

One study has found that individuals tend to retire earlier, the greater is the value of their assets.[5] Others have found that those who had paid off the mortgages on their homes tended to retire earlier than those who had not.[6] And one found that those with non-labour market sources of income tended to work fewer hours between the ages of 58 and 69 than did those who did not have this source.[7]

Ability to work

One of the most consistent findings in the retirement literature is that those individuals with the poorest health are the most likely to retire early. There is also some evidence that those who dislike their jobs expect to retire earlier than those who like their jobs and that individuals who find their jobs to be difficult are more likely to retire before age 65 than those who do not.

Occupation

Most studies find that self-employed workers (and farmers) tend to retire later than do other workers. Also, professional and managerial workers, those with relatively high occupational status, and those in the private (as opposed to government) sector have all been found to retire later than individuals in other occupations.

Education

Most studies find that individuals are likely to retire later, the greater are their educational levels.

Summary

Of all of the factors that researchers have considered as potential determinants of retirement age, two stand out — pension income relative

---

[5]   R. Burkhauser, "The Pension Acceptance Decision of Older Workers" (1979), 14 *Journal of Human Resources* 63-75.

[6]   R. Barfield and J. Morgan, "Trends in Planned Early Retirement" (1978), 18 *Gerontologist* 13-18; and Hall and Johnson, *supra*, note 3.

[7]   Hanoch and Honig, *supra* note 3.

to potential earnings and health. Researchers find consistently that, as the individual's pension income increases relative to the income which could be earned if he or she continued to work, and as the individual's health worsens, the probability that the individual will retire "early" increases. It is important to note that both of these factors may have offsetting effects on the plaintiff's decision to retire after an accident. First, it may result in later retirement because the interruption of work which is associated with a major personal injury often results in a significant reduction in pension benefits, particularly if the individual is forced to enter a new occupation and particularly if this reorientation takes place when the individual is over 40. Second, many personal injuries leave the plaintiff in "poor health." Thus, even if the individual has not suffered a significant annual reduction in earning capacity, it is possible that there could be a substantial future loss, simply because the plaintiff can be expected to retire earlier with the injury than if the injury had not occurred.

10

HOUSEHOLD SERVICES

It is not only those who participate in the labour market who make productive contributions to society — the woman who looks after her own children, for example, is performing a function which is (at least) as valuable as that performed by a daycare centre or a nanny; and the man who builds his own fence is producing something which is as valuable as that which would have been produced by a carpenter. Thus, if an injury or fatality prevents the individual from performing these household services, the plaintiff has suffered a loss as surely as if the ability to earn pecuniary income had been curtailed.

However, although it may be clear that a loss has been incurred, it is generally much less certain what the value of that loss might be. The purpose of this Chapter will be to review recent attempts to perform this valuation. This review will be conducted in two parts. In Section I of the Chapter I will discuss three theoretical approaches to the valuation of household services. I shall conclude from this discussion that it may be desirable that the valuation of these services be obtained by employing a method which requires that one identify the number of hours which would have been devoted to various household activities. Accordingly, Section II will deal with the estimation of these numbers of hours.

I. THREE THEORETICAL APPROACHES

Three approaches to the valuation of household services have been suggested. They are generally referred to as: the opportunity cost, market value, and housekeeper approaches. The advantages and disadvantages of each will be discussed individually, and a summary section will contrast the relative merits of the three.

1. Opportunity Cost

Assume that an individual is faced with a choice between two courses of action, A and B. Action A will produce for the individual a monetary return of $10 while B will result in the production of a less tangible benefit, such as a home-cooked meal or a washed car. In economic terms, the choice of one of these courses in preference to the other is said to create an opportunity cost. In particular, if selection of B requires that the opportunity to engage in A be foregone, the opportunity cost of B is said to be the $10 which would have been produced by A. And, similarly, the opportunity cost of A is the value of the services which could have been produced by B. If it is assumed that the individual is rational and it is observed that she selects B in preference to A, an economist would conclude that the goods and services produced by activity B must be valued at least as highly as their opportunity cost, here $10. Thus, even though it may not be possible to assign a precise value to the self-produced goods arising from activity B, it can be said that those goods must be worth at least $10 — if they had been worth less than $10, a rational individual would have chosen activity A.

The implication of the concept of opportunity cost for the valuation of household services should be clear. If an individual has given up the opportunity to work in the labour market in order to devote herself full-time to such household activities as cooking, cleaning, and child rearing, then the labour market earnings foregone can form the basis of a valuation of those household services. Assume, for example, that the plaintiff has suffered an injury which prevents her from engaging in household work. Assume also: that before her injury she had chosen to remain at home rather than enter the labour market; that her earnings in the labour market would have been $20,000 per year; and that she would have spent $5,000 per year on daycare services for her children had she been in the labour market. In this case, the opportunity cost approach would find that she (and her husband) had valued her household services at $15,000 ($20,000 − $5,000) or more. Thus, the injury would be said to have resulted in a loss of at least $15,000 (per year).

There are two major advantages to the use of the opportunity cost approach. First, as very few calculations are required — one needs only to estimate the wages which the plaintiff would have earned had she chosen to work — it is inexpensive to apply. Second, one of the reasons why individuals may choose to work in the home is that they may be able to obtain a greater amount of leisure when at home than when they enter the labour market. As a result, the foregone earnings (net of daycare costs) identified by the opportunity cost approach will measure the value of the sum of the increased production of household services and the increased enjoyment of leisure which are obtained when the individual chooses to forego entry into the labour market. If the plaintiff's injury has prevented her both from producing household services and from enjoying leisure pursuits, the opportunity cost approach will provide a measure of the sum of these losses.

On the other hand, the opportunity cost approach suffers from a number of drawbacks. First, if the court wishes to compensate the plaintiff only for her loss of household services, or if her injury has left her unable to work but able to enjoy leisure pursuits, the foregone earnings measure will overcompensate the plaintiff as it values the sum of household production and leisure.

Second, if the plaintiff had been working "full-time" in the labour market at the time of her injury, the opportunity cost approach implies that the hours she had devoted to household production should be valued at the wage which the plaintiff would have received had she spent those hours in the labour market. That is, the assumption is made that the hours of household production in which the plaintiff engaged were chosen in preference to hours of labour market activity. But this assumption cannot be supported if the plaintiff is employed in an occupation with a "standard work week" whose length cannot be varied by the individual. In such a situation, once the individual decides to work, her work hours are chosen for her and her hours of household production and leisure are simply the residual which remains. Also, recent empirical work by James Morgan[1] suggests that the values which individuals place on their own household services are unrelated to the wage rates they earn in the labour market. Thus, his work would seem to indicate that the opportunity cost approach is not an accurate measure of the value (as perceived by the individual) of "spare time" household activities.

Third, if the individual whose services are to be valued has been killed, the relevant measure of those services would appear to be their value to her dependants, and not the value which she placed upon them. It may be, for example, that she had left a 40-hour per week job, paying $20,000 per year, in order to increase her household production by 10 hours per week and her leisure by 30 hours. This choice may well have been worth $20,000 to her, but, to the extent that her dependants did not obtain the full benefits of her additional hours of leisure, there is no reason to believe that they valued the reallocation of her time as highly as she did (that is, at $20,000). Use of the opportunity cost approach in this situation would appear to lead to overcompensation of the plaintiffs.

2. Market Value

Under the market value approach, an estimate is made of the number

---

[1] James Morgan, "Trends in Non-Money Income Through Do-It-Yourself Activities, 1971 to 1978", in Martha S. Hill et al., eds., *Five Thousand American Families, Volume X* (Ann Arbor, Mich: Survey Research Center, Institute for Social Research, University of Michigan, 1981) Chapter 10, 317-55.

of hours which were devoted to the production of various household services. These hours are then valued by associating with them the wage rates paid to individuals who provide such services on the competitive market. For example, assume that a husband was found to have spent 3 hours per week repairing and maintaining the family's automobiles and 4 hours per week caring for the family's garden. Those services might be valued at ($15 x 3) + ($7 x 4) = $73 per week if automobile mechanics earned $15 per hour and gardeners $7 per hour.

There are a number of theoretical and practical drawbacks to the use of this approach. The primary theoretical drawback derives from the difficulty of disentangling certain types of leisure pursuits from their associated household services. Whereas most individuals might consider cooking, sewing, gardening, automobile maintenance, and household repairs to be "work," it is also the case that there are many who treat these activities as hobbies, or leisure. The importance of this distinction is that whereas it can normally be assumed that an individual who considers an activity to be work can be expected to engage in it only if it produces an "output," an individual who considers an activity to be leisure may engage in it even if it produces no output of value. Furthermore, even though time devoted to leisure may possess intrinsic value, there is no reason to believe that that value will be correlated with the wage rate which would have to be paid to third persons in order to induce them to devote a similar amount of time to the activity in question.

In short, it would be inappropriate to apply the market value approach to the number of hours actually devoted to household activities if there was reason to believe that some of those hours represented leisure. When the individual who pursued those activities has been killed, his or her family cannot claim that curtailment of the deceased's leisure activities has imposed a pecuniary loss upon them because those activities had provided them with no benefit. And when the individual's ability to pursue leisure activities has been curtailed by injury, there is no reason to believe that the market value approach will attach an appropriate value to the loss of those hours. In order to avoid these problems, I would suggest either (i) that counsel employ estimates of hours spent in household activities drawn from surveys of large numbers of individuals; or (ii) that some effort be made to distinguish between household work and household leisure when evaluating the activities of the specific individual in question.

A further drawback to the use of the market value approach is that it assumes that the individual valued his or her services at the market rate. For example, if the hourly wage for a gardener is $10, the market value approach assumes that all individuals who do their own gardening value their time (spent gardening) at $10 per hour. But there is no reason to believe this. Indeed, as the individual who did her own gardening had the opportunity to purchase the services of a gardener for $10 per hour, but did not, it is difficult to argue that she placed a value as high as $10 per hour on those services. Rather, the most that can be said is that $10 represents an upper limit on the value which the individual placed on an hour of gardening (unless she obtained leisure value from it).

On the other hand, if the individual has been killed, one cannot be certain whether her dependants valued her services at the market rate or not. It may be that they would not have been willing to pay market wages for those services; but it is also possible that they may have been willing to pay more. In the latter case, however, payment of the market rate would not undercompensate the dependants as they would be able to obtain a replacement for the services of the deceased at that rate. For this reason, the market value approach would appear to be of greater relevance to fatal accident than to personal injury cases.

Third, a practical problem which arises in the use of the market value approach is that the wage rates which are paid to various service workers may differ significantly from the costs of employing those workers. For example, the hourly rate charged by a garage for repairs to an automobile may be two to three times as great as the wages paid to automobile mechanics. Thus, the use of the latter to measure the value of home repairs may lead to an underestimate of that value. This problem will apply to all situations in which the standard practice is that service workers are employed by firms which organize and "sell" the services of those workers to households. (Plumbing firms might be another example.) In these situations, it may be necessary to replace the market wage by the commercial hourly rate when evaluating household services.

Finally, the market approach will overestimate the value of the individual's services in those cases in which professionals can work more quickly, or provide a higher quality of services, than can the average householder. This argument might apply, for example, to household repairs or to gardening. On the other hand, there are situations in which most individuals would argue that third parties provide services which are inherently inferior to those provided by the average individual. Child care and home cooking might be included in this category, for example. An *ad hoc* approach may be necessary to adjust for the over- or under-compensation which would arise from these factors.

3. Housekeeper

A third approach which has been suggested is to value the services of the individual at the cost of hiring a housekeeper. Although this suggestion possesses some superficial attractiveness, upon closer inspection it proves to be no more than a variant of the market value approach. For example, assume that the individual whose services are to be replaced was working full-time in the home: cooking, cleaning, washing laundry, caring for children, etc. As each of these activities could be performed by a live-in housekeeper, their market value might reasonably be obtained by identifying the salary (inclusive of room and board) of such a housekeeper. In this situation, the market value and housekeeper approaches prove to be identical.

In all other situations, however, the housekeeper approach would appear to be inappropriate. If the individual whose services are to be replaced was performing services which a housekeeper might not be expected to undertake — such as maintaining automobiles, gardening, or repairing household appliances — the value of those services could not be related to the cost of a housekeeper. Also, if the individual had been devoting less than, say, 30 hours per week to household activities, it might be inappropriate to employ a live-in or full-time housekeeper to perform those activities. Rather, a more appropriate approach would be to enquire as to the cost of hiring individuals on an hourly basis to perform each of the activities in which the injured party had formerly engaged. That is, the market value approach is the appropriate one to be used in this circumstance.

4. Summary

In my view, the selection of the appropriate technique for valuing household services depends upon two factors: whether the individual who performed those services has been injured or killed; and whether that individual had previously been working in the household "full time" or "part time." Combining these two factors produces four possible categories. I will consider each of these categories in turn.

(a) Fatal accident — full time housework

In subsection 1, above, I argued that it might be inappropriate, when an individual who worked full time in the household had been killed, to compensate the dependants on the basis of the opportunity cost approach. The reason for this is that that approach implicitly values the deceased's leisure time as well as his or her household services. Thus, if it is only the loss of the latter for which the dependants can claim, the opportunity cost approach will overcompensate the plaintiffs.

The housekeeper and market value approaches, on the other hand, would appear to be consistent with the doctrine of *restitutio in integrum* in most cases. To the extent that a housekeeper can provide all of the household services which would otherwise have been provided by the deceased, employment of a housekeeper will leave the plaintiffs in the same position, with respect to household services, that they were in before the tortious act. Only if the deceased had been providing services which a housekeeper could not now provide — for example, counselling of children, gardening, or hanging of wallpaper — will the housekeeper approach produce an inaccurate measure of loss. In such a circumstance, it may be desirable to supplement the allowance for a housekeeper's salary with a market value-based allowance for non-housekeeper services.

(b) Fatal accident — part time housework

When the individual who has been killed had been engaged in household production on a part-time basis, the opportunity cost approach becomes unsatisfactory, primarily because there is no evidence that the value which individuals place on that production is correlated with their labour market earnings. And the housekeeper approach is only relevant if (i) the household activities in which the deceased engaged can be performed by a housekeeper and (ii) it proves possible to hire a housekeeper on a part-time basis.

As the latter conditions generally cannot be met, it will often be necessary to employ the market value approach in this type of case. As I noted above, use of this approach leaves open the question of whether it is the wage rates paid to service workers which should be employed to value hours of household service production, or whether it is the prices which are charged for various services which should be employed for that purpose. The latter valuation process has the advantage that it will allow the plaintiffs to purchase the relevant services on the competitive market. It has the disadvantage, on the other hand, that it will overcompensate the plaintiffs if they place a value on those services which is less than the replacement costs.

The primary advantage of using wage rates to value household services is that a large number of reliable statistical sources are available which will provide information concerting wages.[2] It also has the advantage that a lower bound will be placed on the cost of purchasing replacement services in the competitive market. That is, if service workers can be approached directly, rather than through firms which provide services, the lowest price at which it will be possible to hire them will be the prevailing wage rate. On the other hand, to the extent that it is not possible to hire service workers directly (at the prevailing hourly wage) use of market wages to value household services may lead to the

---

[2] See Chapter 4.1, for an extensive bibliography of Canadian wage statistics.

undercompensation of the plaintiffs. In short, no measure of household services is ideal in this situation. Thus, no definitive resolution of this matter will be reached until the appeal courts have made their rulings.

(c) Personal injury — full time housework

If the court is willing to compensate the plaintiff for lost leisure time as well as for lost household services, the most appropriate of the three approaches discussed above is the opportunity cost approach. Otherwise, the selection of an appropriate approach proceeds, *mutatis mutandis*, as it did for the "fatal accident — full time housework" category, above.

(d) Personal injury — part time housework

As Morgan[3] found no correlation between individuals' valuations of their household services and their labour market wage rates, it would be inappropriate to employ the opportunity cost approach to value the services of those who had worked in the home only part time. Rather, the appropriate approach would, once again, appear to be the market value technique.

II. TIME DEVOTED TO HOUSEHOLD SERVICES

If the market value approach is to be used to evaluate household services, it will be necessary to estimate the numbers of hours which were devoted to household production. In this Section I will discuss four techniques for obtaining this estimate.

1. Analysis of Current Expenditures

A method which is commonly used, is to identify the number of hours of services which the plaintiff has purchased annually since the accident. Although this method has the advantage of simplicity, in most cases it significantly underestimates the plaintiff's loss. The reason for this is that the plaintiff normally does not have sufficient funds to replace all of the services which he or she was previously able to perform or which were formerly performed by the deceased.

---

[3] *Supra*, note 1.

2. Recall

Another method of identifying the number of hours which were devoted to household production is to ask the plaintiff(s) to recall that number. In my experience, however, this technique proves to be extremely unreliable — particularly in fatal accident cases. Although reasonable estimates can usually be made of the time devoted to such recurring activities as cooking, child-minding, and grocery shopping, most individuals experience great difficulty estimating the numbers of hours which were devoted to such irregular activities as home repairs, snowshovelling, and automobile maintenance. For this reason, I would recommend that the plaintiffs' recall be supplemented with a technique which I will term the "time diary."

3. Time Diary

I would recommend that at the first meeting between plaintiff and counsel, counsel request that the plaintiff begin to keep a time diary. The purpose of this diary would be to record every (irregular) circumstance, as it arose, in which the injured party or deceased would have provided a household service (but cannot do so now). For example, assume that the plaintiff is a widow whose husband would have maintained the family automobiles, cared for the garden, and made minor repairs to the house. Every time that the sidewalk needed shovelling, the lawn needed mowing, the car needed repairs, the toilet needed unclogging, etc., she would be instructed to make a note of that fact and to record the number of hours she might have expected her husband to have devoted to that activity. As personal injury and fatal accident cases rarely take less than a year (from the time of first contact between lawyer and the client) to reach the courts, by the date of trial the plaintiff should have been able to obtain a reliable estimate of hours lost. Furthermore, as this estimate will be based upon documented occurrences, it is to be expected that the court will attach greater credence to it than to an estimate based solely on memory.

4. Survey Data

For two reasons, it may be desirable to supplement the plaintiff's testimony with information drawn from statistical surveys of time use. First, until the courts obtain experience with testimony concerning household services, it may be useful to show that the plaintiff's estimate of hours devoted to household production does not differ appreciably from the average numbers of hours obtained from large samples of individuals. Second, the testimony of the plaintiff can relate only to experiences in the past. It may be, however, that these experiences will not provide an accurate prediction of the future. For example, it is not to be expected that the number of hours which were devoted to household services when a family's children were young would provide an accurate prediction of hours devoted to that activity in later life.

Tables 10.1 to 10.5 summarize the main findings of six surveys (Table 10.4 summarizes two studies) of time devoted to household activities. Of these, the most important is Table 10.1 as it reports data which was collected from a very broad, representative sample of Canadians. For each sub-group in this Table, two sets of data are presented. The first row reported for each group, "average," summarizes the average

TABLE 10.1

TIME SPENT PER DAY ON HOUSEHOLD SERVICES: CANADA, NOVEMBER 1986

Work Status[a]		Average Minutes per Day in:				Average Hours Per Week in Total
		Domestic Work	Child Care	Shopping	Total	
Employed						
Men	— average	53	15	39	107	12.5
	— reporting	104	86	132		
Women	— average	113	27	54	194	22.6
	— reporting	136	94	128		
Keeping House						
Women	— average	224	63	75	362	42.2
	— reporting	232	151	157		
Retired						
Men	— average	88	3	78	169	19.7
	— reporting	140	74	167		
Women	— average	150	8	68	226	26.4
	— reporting	171	150	164		

[a] The "average" figures represent average minutes per day among all members of the category. The "reporting" figures represent average minutes per day among only those members of the category who replied that they had spent some time in the activity.

Source: Canada. Statistics Canada, *Preliminary Data, Cycle 2: Time Use and Social Mobility Modules* (Ottawa: Statistics Canada, undated) General Social Survey.

TABLE 10.2

Weekly Hours Devoted to Household Activities by Sex, Employment of Wife, and Presence of Young Children: Greater Vancouver, 1971

	Wife Employed				Wife Not Employed			
	Child[a]		No Child[b]		Child[a]		No Child[b]	
Activities	M	F	M	F	M	F	M	F
Cooking and wash-up[c]	1.7	9.5	1.2	7.0	1.2	13.0	1.2	12.9
House cleaning	0.7	6.9	1.3	5.1	1.1	8.6	1.1	9.1
Shopping	1.6	3.0	1.6	2.8	0.9	5.1	0.7	4.9
Laundry[c]	0.1	2.9	0.1	2.1	0.1	5.1	0.0	5.9
Child care	1.6	4.2	0.0	0.2	1.5	8.7	0.2	0.7
Repair, maintenance, etc.	5.2	1.5	4.2	0.7	3.4	1.6	2.8	3.3
Total[d]	11.2	28.2	8.4	18.6	9.2	42.9	6.7	37.5

Source: Calculated from: Martin Meissner, et al., "No Exit for Wives: Sexual Division of Labour and the Cumulation of Household Demands" (1975) 12 *Canadian Review of Sociology and Anthropology* 424-39, Tables IV and V.

[a] At least one child under the age of 10.
[b] No children under the age of 10.
[c] Includes half of the hours identified as "irregular food, clothes."
[d] Columns do not add to "totals" due to rounding (by Meissner, et al.).

TABLE 10.3

Weekly Hours Devoted to Household Activities by Sex and Employment: Halifax, 1971

	Males		Females	
Activities	Employed	Not Employed	Employed	Not Employed
Housework	2.8	4.2	14.0	30.1
Child care	1.4	1.4	2.8	9.1
Maintenance	2.8	4.9	0.7	1.4
Gardening, animal care	0.7	0.0	0.7	0.7
Total[a]	7.0	10.5	17.5	41.3

Source: Andrew S. Harvey and Susan Clark, *Descriptive Analysis of Halifax Time-Budget Data* (Halifax: Institute of Public Affairs, Dalhousie University, 1975) Table 5.

[a] Columns may not add to "totals" due to rounding (by Harvey and Clark).

TABLE 10.4

Weekly Hours Devoted to Household Activities[a] by Sex and Employment: Jackson, Michigan, and 44 U.S. Cities, 1965-66

	"Forty-Four" Cities[b]			Jackson, Michigan		
	Males:	Females		Males:	Females	
Activities	Employed	Employed	Housewives	Employed	Employed	Housewives
Cooking	0.8	6.0	11.1	0.8	5.8	12.5
Home chores	1.2	8.1	14.8	1.9	7.4	14.8
Laundry	0.2	3.3	7.7	0.1	3.5	7.2
Shopping[c]	3.0	4.0	4.7	2.6	4.9	5.3
Gardening, animal care	0.2	0.4	0.9	0.4	0.4	0.8
Other house	2.5	2.8	4.2	3.5	2.8	3.0
Child care	2.6	4.4	13.2	2.5	4.7	13.8
Total[d]	10.5	28.8	56.4	11.7	29.4	57.4

Source: Alexander Szalai, ed., *The Use of Time* (The Hague: Mouton, 1972) Tables 4-2.11 and 4-2.12.

[a] Figures reported represent the sum of "primary" and "secondary" activities.

[b] A national probability cross-section drawn from 44 American metropolitan areas in which the central city had a population of at least 50,000.

[c] The sum of "marketing" and "errands, shopping."

[d] Columns may not add to "totals" due to rounding.

numbers of minutes spent per day by the average individual within the group. For example, the average employed male reported that he spent 53 minutes per day in "domestic work" (meal preparation, meal clean-up, indoor cleaning, outdoor cleaning, laundry, ironing, mending, home repairs, maintenance, gardening, pet care, etc.) 15 minutes in child care, and 39 minutes in shopping, for an average of 107 minutes per day, or 12.5 hours per week. The second row reported for each group, "reporting," summarizes the average numbers of minutes per day only for those who reported that they spent any time in that activity. Thus, for example, although the average employed male spent 15 minutes per day in child care, among those who reported that they spent *some* time in child care, the average was 86 minutes. The figures in the "reporting" row are presented in order to offer some indication of the adjustment which might reasonably be made if it was known that the individual in question would be better represented by the "reporting" category than by the "average" category. For example, Table 10.1 suggests that if the deceased had been an employed male who had helped with the care of his children, it might be reasonable to increase the estimate of his daily child care services to 86 minutes from 15, and, therefore, raise the estimate of his weekly hours of household services to 20.75 from 12.5. (The figures in the "reporting" rows have not been added up to obtain total minutes per day, or hours per week, as there is no suggestion that those reporting participation in one category of activity would also report participation in the other two.)

TABLE 10.5

Weekly Hours Devoted to Household Activities by Sex and Employment of Wife: Syracuse, N.Y., 1967-68

Activities	Males		Females	
	Wife Employed[a]	Not Employed	Wife Employed[a]	Not Employed
Meal preparation	1.4	0.7	10.5	16.1
House care	4.2	4.2	7.7	11.2
Clothing care	0.7	0.7	5.6	9.1
Family care	2.1	2.8	4.2	13.3
Marketing and management	2.8	2.8	5.6	7.0
Total	11.2	11.2	33.6	56.7

Source: Kathryn E. Walker and Margaret E. Woods, *Time Use* (Washington: American Home Economics Association, 1976) Table 3.12.

[a] These figures were taken from the rows which indicated that the wife worked 30 hours or more per week. Walker and Woods also present information concerning wives who worked 1-14 hours per week and 15-29 hours per week. This information has not been included in Table 12.4.

Of the remaining Tables, two report American surveys and two Canadian. As one would expect, all of the surveys indicate that more time is devoted to household activities: by women than men; by women who do not work in the labour market than by those who do; and by individuals who have young children than by those who do not. Although there are some notable differences among the various studies — particularly between the American and Canadian findings with respect to "housewives" — it would appear that the following conclusions are justified:

(i) Men whose wives are not working and who have no young children spend approximately 7-10 hours per week on housework, while men with young children can spend as little as 9 hours on housework but as much as 20 (if they actively assist in child care).

(ii) Among all males, approximately 40-50 percent of housework involves repair and maintenance activities.

(iii) Employed women average approximately 18-20 hours per week on housework if they have no young children, and approximately 30-35 hours in that activity if they do have young children.

(iv) Women who do not work in the labour market spend appreciably more hours on housework than do those who have entered the labour market: approximately 35-40 hours if they do not have young children and 40-50 hours if they do have.

(v) Finally, the Statistics Canada data in Table 10.1 indicates that retired men and women spend approximately 4-6 more hours per week on housework than do working men and women.

Some additional information is also available concerning the effects of age, education, and numbers and ages of children.

Age

Gauger and Walker[4] found, in the survey summarized in Table 10.5, that women who were employed in the labour market devoted approximately 5 more hours per week to housework after age 40 than before age 40. At the same time, their husbands reduced their household activities by approximately 2 hours per week. In households in which the wife did not work in the labour market, Gauger and Walker found that the wife's household production was not significantly correlated with her age. Her husband's production, however, increased significantly as she grew older, more than doubling between the (wife's) age groups "under 25" and "55 and over". The Halifax study reported in Table 10.3 provided some support for the American study. It found that both men and women increased their hours of housework as they grew older. However, although this tended to be a monotonic increase among men, among women there was a peak in the 31 to 40-year-old group with a slight decrease between that age group and 41 to 64-year-olds.

Education

In an American study, Hill and Stafford[5] found that college-educated women spent more time on both housework and child care, when they had young children, than did women with high school education. And

---

[4]   William H. Gauger and Kathryn E. Walker, *The Dollar Value of Household Work* (Ithaca, N.Y.: New York State College of Human Ecology, Cornell University, 1980); and "Time and its Dollar Value in Household Work" (Fall 1973) *Family Economics Review* 8-13.

[5]   C.R. Hill and F. P. Stafford, "Parental Care of Children: Time Diary Estimates of Quantity, Predictability, and Variety" (1980) 15 *Journal of Human Resources* 219-39.

the latter devoted more time to these activities than did women with less than high school education. The authors of the Halifax study, using less sophisticated statistical techniques, were unable to confirm the American findings.

Age and number of children

Gauger and Walker[6] found that women, whether employed in the labour market or not, devoted more time to housework the greater was the number of their children and the younger were those children. No clear pattern in the relationship between husband's hours and either numbers or ages of children could be found, however.

Further Reading

Cooper-Stephenson, K. D. and I. B. Saunders, *Personal Injury Damages in Canada* (Toronto: Carswell, 1981) at pp. 213-27.

Ferber, Marianne, and Bonnie Birnbaum, "One Job or Two Jobs: The Implications for Young Wives," (1980) 7 *Journal of Consumer Research* 263-71.

Fischer, Charles, "Forensic Economics and the Wrongful Death of a Household Producer" (1987) 46 *American Journal of Economics and Sociology* 219-28.

Gage, M. Geraldine, "Economic Roles of Wives and Spouse Economic Development," (1975) 37 *Journal of Marriage and the Family* 121-28

Hauserman, Nancy R., "Homemakers and Divorce: Problems of the Invisible Occupation," (1983) 17 Fam. L. Q. 41-63.

Hawrylyshyn, O., "Towards a Definition of Non-Market Activities" (1977) 23 *Review of Income and Wealth* 79-96.

Hawrylyshyn, O., *Estimating the Value of Household Work in Canada, 1971*, Cat. No. 13-566 (Ottawa: Statistics Canada, June 1978).

Hersch, Joni, "Effect of Housework on Earnings of Husbands and Wives: Evidence from Full-Time Piece Rate Workers," (1985) 66 *Social Science Quarterly* 210-17.

Minton, M., with J. Libman Block, *What is a Wife Worth?* (New York: William Morrow, 1983).

Pottick, F. J., "Tort Damages for the Injured Homemaker: Opportunity Cost or Replacement Cost?" (1978) 50 U. Colo. L. Rev. 59-74.

Proulx, M., *Five Million Women* (Ottawa: Advisory Council on the Status of Women, June 1978).

Segalla, T. F., "The Unemployed Housewife-Mother: Fair Appraisal of Economic Loss in a Wrongful Death Action" (1971-72) 21 Buffalo L. Rev. 205-16.

---

[6] *Supra*, note 4.

11

DEPENDENCY RATES

In fatal accident litigation, the plaintiffs cannot claim compensation for the full value of the deceased's after-tax income.[1] Rather, their claim is restricted to that fraction of the deceased's income which would have benefitted them directly, and which they now will have to replace from alternative sources. Although this fraction, which is usually called the "dependency rate," plays a crucial role in the determination of damages in fatal accident cases, most testimony concerning this factor is based upon "rules of thumb" rather than upon any meaningful analysis of the expenditure pattern of either Canadian families in general or of the plaintiffs in particular. The purpose of this Chapter will be to propose a methodology for determining both a dependency rate which is specific to the plaintiffs in a particular action and a general dependency rate, applicable in cases where detailed information concerning the plaintiffs' expenditure patterns is unavailable.

The argument will be developed in two major sections. In the first of these I will summarize the research which provides information concerning the manner in which families spend their incomes and show how this information can be used to estimate the dependency rates for specific families. In the second section, I will then report upon a number of experiments which I have conducted to determine the *average* dependency rates for Canadian families of various sizes and incomes.

Finally, because children normally require fewer resources than do adults, it is necessary to calculate separate dependency rates for the cases in which both of a child's parents have been killed. Some evidence will be presented in Section III with respect to this question.

---

[1] For an excellent summary of the legal principles, see K.D. Cooper-Stephenson and I. B. Saunders, *Personal Injury Damages in Canada*, (Toronto: Carswell, 1981) Ch. 9. See also Chapter 3 of this book.

I. FAMILY-SPECIFIC DEPENDENCY RATES

1. Dependencies by Category of Expenditure

There are two sources of information concerning the plaintiffs' dependency on family income. The first of these is information drawn from the family's records and from the testimony of the plaintiffs themselves. This source often proves to be inadequate, primarily because the family's records and memories are not sufficiently precise to allow for division of expenditures among family members or among categories of expenditure. Most individuals, for example, would have difficulty identifying the percentage of the family food budget which could be attributed to the husband, or the average annual family expenditures on such capital goods as cars, furniture, and appliances.

Accordingly, it will often prove useful, as a check on the validity of the plaintiffs' testimony, to introduce statistical evidence drawn from surveys of large numbers of families. The most reliable source of such data in Canada is Statistics Canada's Family Expenditure Survey, in which approximately 10,000 families are interviewed once every two to four years. The most recent such Survey was conducted in 1986 (although a 1990 "round" of interviews has been conducted and information should be available by late 1992). The primary source of information concerning the 1986 Survey is

Canada. Statistics Canada, *Family Expenditures in Canada*, Cat. No. 62-555 (Ottawa: Statistics Canada, March 1989).

This report breaks down family expenditures into thirteen major consumption categories plus income taxes, security, and charitable donations. Also, each table provides summary information concerning: number of families in the sample, average family size, number of adults and children, age of head, and income before taxes, all of which may be of importance when presenting evidence in court.

Table 11.1 is offered as an example of the type of information which can be drawn from *Family Expenditures in Canada*. This Table has been constructed by removing "personal taxes" from the expenditures listed in Table 8 of that publication, and then recalculating the distribution of the remaining expenditures as percentages of after-tax income. The problem facing the court when employing information such as that presented in Table 11.1 is to identify the allocation of each of the fifteen categories of expenditures among the members of the plaintiff family. In the analysis which follows, information and argument will be provided to assist the court in this allocation process. As an example of how this analysis might be applied, dependencies will be calculated for each of the two "typical" families described in Table 11.

Table 11.1

Distribution of Family Expenditures, After Taxes, by Family Type: Canada, 1986

| | Family Type | | | |
| | Two Adults | | Two Adults, Two Children[a] | |
Expenditure Category	Percentage Distribution	Dollar Expenditure	Percentage Distribution	Dollar Expenditure
(i) Food	16.6%	$ 4,460.0	17.8%	$ 6,618.0
(ii) Shelter	19.9	5,328.0	18.3	6,809.0
(iii) Household Operation	4.6	1,244.0	5.6	2,089.0
(iv) Household Furnishing	4.7	1,273.0	4.7	1,763.0
(v) Clothing	7.0	1,867.0	8.3	3,097.0
(vi) Personal Care	2.2	579.0	2.5	917.0
(vii) Medical and Health Care	2.5	666.0	2.2	809.0
(viii) Transportation	17.8	4,786.0	16.8	6,273.0
(ix) Recreation	6.0	1,623.0	6.6	2,444.0
(x) Reading	0.8	210.0	0.7	243.0
(xi) Education	0.3	92.0	1.4	518.0
(xii) Tobacco and Alcohol	4.0	1,084.0	3.5	1,285.0
(xiii) Miscellaneous	2.9	781.0	3.1	1,147.0
Current Consumption	89.3%	$23,993.0	91.5%	$34,012.0
(xiv) Security	5.1	1,366.0	6.1	2,287.0
(xv) Gifts and Contributions	5.5	1,468.0	2.5	940.0
Total Expenditures	100.0%	$26,827.0	100.0%	$37,239.0

[a] These data represent all families composed (only) of a married couple and their single children (living at home). The average such family has 1.98 children.

Source: Statistics Canada, *Family Expenditures in Canada, 1986,* Cat. No. 62-555, (Ottawa: Statistics Canada, March 1989) Table 8

(a) Food

Two steps must be taken in order to determine the dependency with respect to expenditures on food. First, it is necessary to identify the rela-

tive consumption levels among family members of different ages and
sex. Second, allowance must be made for the fact that economies of
scale from bulk buying are lost when one member is removed from the
family.

Formal statistical information with respect to the former question
is difficult to obtain, primarily because families are unable to identify
for researchers the precise percentages of the food budget which are
allocated to different family members. What is available, however, are
food budgets based upon nutritional requirements. Two such budgets
are summarized in Table 12.2. The first two columns of that Table have
been taken from a U.S. Department of Agriculture publication[2] and
are stated in terms of expenditures by age and sex relative to the recommended expenditures for adult males. Thus, for example, the consumption level recommended for 12 to 13-year-old girls is seen to cost 80
percent of that recommended for adult males. The third and fourth
columns summarize similar recommendations prepared by a team of
nutritionists for the Social Planning Council of Toronto.[3] However,
whereas the U.S. figures relate to all families, the Toronto figures are
intended to represent a minimum, nutritionally balanced basket of food.

Comparison of the U.S. and Toronto data in Table 11.2 indicates
a remarkable degree of uniformity in the estimates. This uniformity
is such that I would suggest that the relativities in Table 11.3 could
be employed with some confidence in the determination of the dependency rate.

As an example of the use of these figures, assume that the family
unit is initially composed of husband, wife, and two children between
the ages of 2 and 5.[4] The family expenditure on food may be described
as being equivalent to (.5 + .5 + .8 + 1.0 =) 2.8 units of adult male
expenditure. That is, food expenditures on the wife and children com-
pose (1.8/2.8 =) 64 percent of family expenditures. This does not mean,
however, that if the husband were to die the widow and children would
be able to maintain their pre-accident food consumption by spending
an amount equal to 64 percent of the family's pre-accident food budget.
With the loss of the husband, expenditures per family member can be
expected to rise because of the reduced ability to buy in bulk (what
economists call loss of "economies of scale").

Two Canadian agencies, while developing minimum budgets
required for poor families, have suggested percentage adjustments which

---

[2] U.S. Department of Agriculture "Cost of Food at Home," (Spring 1980), *Family Economics Review.*
[3] Social Planning Council of Metropolitan Toronto, "The Cost of Raising a Child in
the Toronto Area in 1986," (November 1987) 6, no. 5 *Social Infopac.*
[4] This age-sex assumption will be made for all families of two adults and two children throughout the Chapter (unless otherwise indicated).

TABLE 11.2

Cost of Food at Home, by Age and Sex, Relative to Adult Males

Age	U.S. 1979 Average Income[a]		Toronto 1986 Single-Parent Family[b]	
	Male	Female	Male	Female
0-1	.36	.36	.47	.47
1-2	.43	.43	.47	.47
2-3	.43	.43	.47	.47
3-4	.53	.53	.55	.55
4-5	.53	.53	.55	.55
5-6	.53	.53	.55	.55
6-7	.68	.68	.65	.65
7-8	.68	.68	.65	.65
8-9	.68	.68	.65	.65
9-10	.85	.85	.76	.76
10-11	.85	.85	.76	.76
11-12	.85	.85	.76	.76
12-13	.90	.80	.89	.79
13-14	.90	.80	.89	.79
14-15	.90	.80	.89	.79
15-16	1.00	.80	1.00	.74
16-17	1.00	.80	1.00	.74
17-18	1.00	.80	1.00	.74
Adult	1.00	.80	1.00[c]	.74[c]

[a] U.S. Department of Agriculture "Cost of Food at Home," (Spring 1980), *Family Economics Review* at p. 42.
[b] Social Planning Council of Metropolitan Toronto, "The Cost of Raising a Child in the Toronto Area in 1986," (November 1987) 6, no. 5 *Social Infopac.*
[c] Assumed to equal expenditures for 17 to 18-year-olds.

can be made when family size is reduced.[5] The Toronto Social Planning Council has recommended that this adjustment be 10 percent when family size is reduced by one member except when size is reduced from two to one member, when they have suggested an adjustment of approximately 15 percent. The Montreal Diet Dispensary, on the other hand, has recommended an adjustment of approximately 10 percent for all

[5] The source of the following information is *Determining the "Basic Needs" of Canadians* (Internal Working Document) by B. Phyllis Will (Ottawa: Social and Economic Studies Division, Statistics Canada, July 1987).

family sizes. In both cases, therefore, the post-accident expenditures of a widow and two children will not be equivalent to 1.8 adult male "units," as was calculated above, but to (1.8 x 1.10 =) 1.98 units; and their "food" dependency will not be 64 percent but (1.98/2.80 =) 71 percent. Furthermore, if the Toronto guidelines are followed, an even more significant adjustment is required if the pre-accident family unit consisted of only a husband and wife. In that case, the pre-accident expenditure is 1.8 male units and the post-accident expenditure becomes (.8 x 1.15 =) 0.92 units. Thus, the widow's dependency increases from (.8/1.8 =) 44 percent to (.92/1.8 =) 51 percent when economies of scale are taken into account.

The data in Table 11.3 and the assumption that removal of one person from the family will increase the food costs of the remaining family members by 10 percent have been used in the construction of row (i) of Table 11.6, which lists the dependency rates with respect to food for two-person and four-person families, by husband deceased and wife deceased, respectively. For this purpose, the four-person family is, again, assumed to consist of husband, wife, boy between the ages of 2 and 5, and girl between the ages of 2 and 5.

TABLE 11.3

Relative Dependencies With Respect to Expenditures on Food

Sex	Age	Expenditures on Food Relative to Adult Males
Male	0-6	0.5
	6-9	0.7
	9-12	0.8
	12-15	0.9
	15+	1.0
Female	0-6	0.5
	6-9	0.7
	9+	0.8

(b) Shelter

This category consists primarily of payments for rent, mortgage, repairs, maintenance, and utilities, none of which could be expected to be reduced appreciably following the death of a spouse. For this reason, I recommend that the dependency be set at 96 percent. This is the figure I have entered in row (ii) of Table 11.6.

(c) Household operation

This category consists, principally, of expenses for telephone, child care, domestic services, laundry, pet care, household cleaning supplies, paper supplies (e.g., toilet paper and garbage bags), and gardening supplies. Of these, only expenses on laundry and paper products can be expected to vary appreciably with family size. These expenses make up approximately 30 percent of the household operation budget. As a very conservative estimate would suggest that one spouse would be responsible for 50 percent of these expenses in a two-adult family and 33 percent in a two-adult, two-child family, it would seem appropriate to set the dependencies in those two cases at approximately 85 percent and 90 percent, respectively.

A complication arises, however, when the deceased had been providing child care. With the death of this individual, the surviving spouse may have to purchase day care or nanny services which would not otherwise have entered into the family's budget. The Family Expenditure Survey can provide some indication of the impact of this alteration in the family's circumstances. For example, data provided in that Survey suggests that, among families composed of two adults and two children, those who purchase at least some child care services spend approximately 80 percent more on household operation than do those who purchase no child care services.[6] When combined with the assumptions made above with respect to purchases of laundry and paper products, this suggests that, when the caregiver dies, the survivors' dependency on household services is approximately 170 percent[7] — the survivors need to spend more on household services after the death of the caregiver than they had before that death.

(d) Household furnishings and equipment

As there is no element of this category on which expenditures would be reduced by the death of a spouse, the dependency is 100 percent.

---

[6] The average family of two adults and two children spent $2,409 per year on household operation according to the 1986 Family Expenditure Survey. Of this, $794 was the average expenditure on child care. Hence, as an approximation, it can be said that a family which did not spend anything on child care spent ($2,409 - $794 =) $1,615 on household operation. As only 59.8 percent of two-adult, two-child families purchased child care, the average family which did purchase those services spent ($794/0.598 =) $1,328. That is, those families spent approximately ($1,615 + $1,328 =) $2,943 on household operation, or ($2,943/$1,615 =) 1.82 times as much as families which spent nothing on child care.

[7] These figures refer only to the average family. Where specific information concerning the child care expenses of the plaintiffs is available, that information should be used to supplant the averages employed here.

(e) Clothing

A number of sources are available which identify average annual expenditures on clothing by age and sex. The most reliable of these is the 1986 Family Expenditure Survey. Table 11.4 summarizes the main findings of that Survey for three different income groups. As with Table 11.2, each figure in this Table represents the average annual expenditure on clothing by individuals in a particular age-sex group as a fraction of the average annual expenditure by an adult male.

Table 11.4 shows there is a fair amount of consistency between the two upper-income groups. Relying upon that data, I have assumed that a family of two adults and two children under six would require approximately 0.4 adult male units for the boy's clothing, 0.5 for the girl's clothing, 1.65 for the wife's clothing, and 1.00 for the husband's. Thus, the dependency would be approximately (2.55/3.55 =) 72 percent if the husband should die and (1.90/3.55 =) 54 percent if the wife should die. In a family of two adults, the equivalent dependencies would be 62 and 38 percent, respectively.

TABLE 11.4

Cost of Clothing, by Family Income, Age, and Sex,
Relative to Adult Males

Age	Under $15,000		$25,000-34,999		$45,000-59,999	
	Male	Female	Male	Female	Male	Female
0-4	.58	.55	.38	.49	.40	.47
5-9	.79	.99	.61	.68	.61	.79
10-14	.95	1.14	.76	1.07	.80	1.03
15-19	1.46	1.98	1.00	1.48	1.04	1.52
Adult	1.00	1.43	1.00	1.61	1.00	1.74

Source: Statistics Canada, *Family Expenditures in Canada, 1986,* Cat. No. 62-555 (Ottawa: Statistics Canada, March 1989) Text Table VIII.

(f) Personal care

This category includes expenditures on such items as haircuts, hair and makeup preparations, soaps, deodorants, and shaving preparations. The recommended budget developed by the Social Planning Council of Toronto shows the relative expenditure pattern summarized in Table 11.5. In this Table the family of four described above has personal care expenditures equivalent to those of approximately (.40 + .40 + 1.60

+ 1.00 =) 3.40 male "units." Should the husband die, the remaining family members would need expenditures equivalent to 2.40 male "units" to maintain their pre-accident standard of living. Thus, their dependency proves to be 71 percent. Similar calculations produce the remaining figures in row (vi) of Table 11.6.

TABLE 11.5

Personal Care Expenditures Per Family Member, Relative to Adult Male

Age	Male	Female
0-2	0.21	0.21
2-5	0.43	0.43
6-11	0.47	0.47
12-15	0.61	1.33
16 +	1.00	1.63

Source: Derived from: Social Planning Council of Metropolitan Toronto, "The Cost of Raising a Child in the Toronto Area in 1986," (November 1987) 6, no. 5 *Social Infopac* at p. 6.

(g) Medical and health care

Approximately 35 percent of this expenditure was devoted to health insurance premiums in 1986. Thus, the responsiveness of this element of the medical budget to the death of a spouse will depend upon the structure of insurance premiums. However, as premiums are generally no higher for four-member families than three-member and as premiums generally do not double when family size is increased from one to two, I shall assume for purposes of illustration that the dependency with respect to health insurance premiums is 100 percent for a four-person family and 60 percent for a two-person family.

The remaining 65 percent of the average family's medical budget is devoted primarily to eye care, dental care, and drug purchases. Lacking any firm data on the distribution of these expenses within the family I shall, again for purposes of illustration, assume that they are divided equally. Thus, the dependency in a four-person family is estimated to be $((.35 \times 1.00) + (.65 \times .75) =)$ 84 percent. The comparable dependency for a two-person family is $((.35 \times 6) + (.65 \times 5) =)$ 54 percent.

(h) Transportation

Approximately 90 percent of this budget item is devoted to the purchase, maintenance, and operation of cars and trucks. Thus, the most important determinant of the dependency in this respect will be the number of vehicles owned by the family. If both adults drive but own only one car, the death of one of them can be expected to have little effect on vehicle costs; that is, the dependency would be relatively high. However, if the family owned more than one vehicle, including one which was used primarily by the deceased, the dependency may be as low as 50 or 60 percent. For the purposes of illustration, I have assumed in the construction of Table 11.6 that the family had two cars, giving it a dependency with respect to vehicles of approximately 60 percent.

The remaining 10 percent of the transportation budget is devoted to public transportation (including air fares). Assuming that these expenditures are divided evenly among family members, the total dependency with respect to transportation is $((.9 \times .6) + (.1 \times .75) =)$ 62 percent for a four-person family and $((.9 \times .6) + (.1 \times .5) =)$ 59 percent for a two-person family.

(i) Recreation

Approximately 50 percent of the average family's recreation budget is devoted to expenditures which may not vary with the size of the family, such as purchases of recreational vehicles and home entertainment equipment. The remaining 50 percent is devoted to admissions to events, purchases of home recreational equipment (such as games and crafts), and purchases of sport and athletic equipment. Assuming that the latter expenses are shared equally among family members, the dependency with respect to recreation proves to be $((.5 \times 1.0) + (.5 \times .75) =)$ 88 percent for a four-person family and $((.5 \times 1.0) + (.5 \times .5) =)$ 75 percent for a two-person family.

(j) Reading

The approximate division of this expenditure is: 45 percent on newspapers, 25 percent on magazines, and 40 percent on books. Assuming that newspaper expenses do not vary by size of family and that one third of book and magazine purchases are specific to one of the adult members of the family, the dependency with respect to reading proves to be approximately $((.45 \times 1.0) + (.55 \times .67) =)$ 82 percent for all families.

(k) Education

In the absence of any information concerning the plaintiff family, and recognizing that less than 3 percent of the education expenses listed by Statistics Canada are devoted specifically to young children, the only assumption which can be made with respect to this category is that expenses are divided equally between the two adults if there are no older children in the family. That is, for purposes of Table 11.6 the dependency is 50 percent.

(l) Tobacco and alcohol

As with education, in the absence of specific information about the family and assuming that there are no older children in the family, the dependency for these items must be set at 50 percent. (For those who do have specific information concerning the family, it may be of interest to note, that, among those families who reported purchases of these items, approximately 3 percent of after-tax income was devoted to tobacco products and approximately 2.5 percent to alcoholic beverages.)

(m) Miscellaneous

Of the expenses listed under "miscellaneous" in the family expenditure survey, approximately 70 percent were items such as interest on personal loans, purchases of lottery tickets, bank charges, lawyers' fees, and funeral expenses, none of which would vary significantly with family size. Assuming that the dependency with respect to these items is 90 percent and with respect to the remaining items is 50 percent, the total dependency with respect to the miscellaneous category is $((.7 \times .9) + (.3 \times .5) =)$ 78 percent.

(n) Security

Approximately 50 percent of the expenditures in this category are for pension fund payments, 20 percent for life insurance premiums, and 30 percent for unemployment insurance premiums. Thus, the value of the dependency will be determined primarily by the labour force attachments of the adult members of the family and by the number and age of children.

Consider, first, the life insurance premiums. In a two-adult family, life insurance is normally taken out on the life of the main income earner, with the second family member being the beneficiary. If either family member dies, the need for such insurance is reduced significantly. That is, the dependency is (approximately) zero. In a family with children, however, it is the children who will often be made the beneficiaries. Therefore, regardless of which parent has died, the remaining parent can be expected to continue his or her payments to a life insurance scheme. Indeed, that parent may even increase life insurance coverage to take account of the fact that a further death would leave the children with no parents. In such a case, a 100 percent dependency would appear reasonable.

The value of the dependency with respect to unemployment insurance contributions will be determined by the employment status of the adult members of the family. If the deceased was employed and the survivor is not, no contributions will now have to be made to unemployment insurance; therefore, the dependency is zero. On the other hand, if the deceased was not employed and the survivor is, contributions will be unaffected. That is, the dependency is 100 percent. And if both adults were fully employed, the dependency will be 50 percent.

Finally, there are two conceptual approaches to the incorporation of pension contributions. To the extent that (post-retirement) pension income is derived solely from the investment of the (pre-retirement) contributions of the employee and the employer, the present value of the individual's pension can be obtained either by discounting the expected future stream of pension income or by discounting the future stream of employer-employee contributions (see Chapter 1). Under each of these approaches, the resulting figure is then weighted by the dependency rate which would apply at the time of retirement. As there will be no children living at home at that time, and as most retired couples will not have expenses for "security," this dependency rate can be approximated by the rate for two-adult families with respect to current consumption.

If the first approach discussed above is employed, it is the future stream of lost pension income which is incorporated in the plaintiff's claim. Thus, when calculating the dependency on employment income, pension contributions are ignored. That is, the dependency rate with respect to those contributions is treated as though it were zero. When this approach is taken (and if it is assumed that both spouses worked if there were no children but that the wife looked after the children if there were children) the dependency rate with respect to security expenditures in total becomes .15 (the dependency on unemployment insurance) if there are no children. If there are children, on the other hand, the dependency rate becomes $((.20 \times 1.0) + (.30 \times 1.0) + (.5 \times 0.0) =)$ 50 percent when the wife dies and $((.20 \times 1.0) + (.30 \times 0.0) + (.50 \times 0.0) =)$ 20 per cent when the husband dies. These figures have been reported in row (xiv) of Table 11.6, under the heading "Security — pension," to indicate that pension benefits form part of the claim for damages.

Alternatively, the loss of future pension income may be incorporated by including the employer's (foregone) contributions to the pension plan when calculating the value of lost fringe benefits. The dependency rate with respect to this expenditure, as I suggested above, may be approximated by the dependency rate with respect to current consumption in a two-adult (retired) family. As this figure has not been calculated as yet, I leave the determination of the dependency on "security," when pension contributions are being considered to be an element in fringe benefits, to the end of this Section.

(o) Gifts and contributions

This category consists of gifts to individuals outside of the family spending unit, for example to parents and children living in separate households, and of charitable donations. I believe it can be argued that if the well-being of the survivors is to be maintained at the pre-accident level, these contributions must also be maintained at the pre-accident level. For example, assume that a husband and wife together had been contributing $500 per year to charity. I suggest that the satisfaction that the husband obtained from that donation was not reduced in any way by the fact that his wife was a co-donor. Therefore, if he is to obtain the same level of satisfaction from his activities as a (charitable) donor following his wife's death as before her death, his donations must continue at the same $500 level. That is, the dependency with respect to this category is 100 percent.

2. The Total Dependency

Table 11.6 summarizes the assumptions which were made with respect to each dependency rate in Section 1, above. The figures from the relevant column in this Table can be combined with those in Table 11.1 to obtain the family's "total dependency rate"; that is, the percentage of pre-accident family income which the remaining family members will have to receive in order to allow them to purchase the same consumption goods after the accident as they did before. This is done simply by multiplying the percentage of family income devoted to each expenditure category, from Table 11.1, by the dependency associated with that category, from Table 11.6, and then adding the resulting figures across all categories.

A detailed example of this calculation is shown in Table 11.7 for a two-adult family in which the wife had been working in the labour market and the husband has died. The first column in this Table is taken from Table 11.1 and displays the percentages of pre-accident income spent on each of the fifteen categories of goods and services.

TABLE 11.6

Sample Dependencies by Expenditure Categories:
Two- and Four-Person Families, Canada, 1986

| | Family Type | | | |
| | Two Adults | | Two Adults, Two Children | |
Expenditure Category	Wife Deceased	Husband Deceased	Wife Deceased	Husband Deceased
(i) Food	61%	51%	79%	71%
(ii) Shelter	96	96	96	96
(iii) Household Operation				
— deceased was caregiver	N/A	N/A	170	170
— both spouses worked	90	90	85	85
(iv) Household Furnishing	100	100	100	100
(v) Clothing	38	62	54	72
(vi) Personal Care	38	62	53	71
(vii) Medical and Health Care	54	54	84	84
(viii) Transportation	59	59	62	62
(ix) Recreation	75	75	88	88
(x) Reading	82	82	82	82
(xi) Education	50	50	50	50
(xii) Tobacco and Alcohol	50	50	50	50
(xiii) Miscellaneous	78	78	78	78
(xiv) Security				
— pension	15	15	50	20
— no pension	50	50	85	55
(xv) Gifts and Contributions	100	100	100	100

The second column, taken from Table 11.6, indicates the value of the dependency for each expenditure category. That is, it is the percentage of each pre-accident outlay which would have to be expended in order to uphold the widow's pre-accident living standard. The third column, which is the multiple of the figures in the first two columns, represents the amounts of money, expressed as percentages of pre-accident family income, necessary to maintain the pre-accident standard of living. For example, row (i) indicates that 16.6 percent of the pre-accident family budget of a two-adult family is devoted to expenditures on food, and that the dependency figure with respect to food is 51 percent (when it is the husband who has died). Therefore, if the widow is to eat the same "basket" of food after the accident as before, the amount of money made available for food must equal (16.6 x .51 =) 8.5 percent of pre-accident income.

TABLE 11.7

Total Dependency: Two-Adult Family, Wife Worked In Labour Market, Husband Deceased

Expenditure Category	Pre-Accident Expenditure as a Percentage of Pre-Accident Income	Dependency by Expenditure Category	Post-Accident Expenditure as a Percentage of Pre-Accident Income
(i) Food	16.6%	51%	8.5%
(ii) Shelter	19.9	96	19.1
(iii) Household Operation	4.6	90	4.1
(iv) Household Furnishing	4.7	100	4.7
(v) Clothing	7.0	62	4.3
(vi) Personal Care	2.2	62	1.4
(vii) Medical and Health Care	2.5	54	1.4
(viii) Transportation	17.8	59	10.5
(ix) Recreation	6.0	75	4.5
(x) Reading	0.8	82	0.7
(xi) Education	0.3	50	0.2
(xii) Tobacco and Alcohol	4.0	50	2.0
(xiii) Miscellaneous	2.9	78	2.3
Current Consumption	89.3%		63.7%
(xiv) Security			
— pension	5.1	15	0.8
— no pension	5.1	50	2.6
(xv) Gifts and Contributions	5.5	100	5.5
dependency			
— pension			70.0%
— no pension			71.8

Continuing this process in Table 11.7 it is found that the widow can maintain her level of "current consumption" if she spends 63.7 percent of pre-accident income on those activities; whereas, before the accident, she and her husband together devoted 89.3 percent of income to them. That is, the dependency with respect to this set of activities is approximately (63.7/89.3 =) 71 percent. This figure can now be used to determine the dependency with respect to "security" when compensation is made for lost contributions to a pension fund (rather than for

lost pension income). Assuming that the dependency from retirement
benefits is 71 percent — the dependency with respect to current consumption — the dependency with respect to security becomes $((.20$ x
$0.0) + (.30$ x $.50) + (.50$ x $.71) =)$ 50 percent for a two-person family
when either spouse has died. When the couple has young children (and
the wife stayed home to care for them), the dependency with respect
to security becomes $((.20$ x $1.0) + (.30$ x $1.0) + (.50$ x $.71) =)$ 85 percent if it is the wife who has died and $((.20$ x $1.0) + (.30$ x $0.0) +$
$(.50$ x $.71) =)$ 55 percent if it is the husband who has died. Row (xiv)
"- no pension" of Tables 12.6 and 12.7 have been completed accordingly. Returning to Table 11.7, it is now possible to determine that the
widow's dependency in a two-adult family is 70 percent if no compensation is made for current contributions to pension, and 71.8 per cent
if such compensation is made.

3. Application of the Methodology to Specific Cases

The purpose of the preceding analysis was to outline a general method
for determining dependency rates on family income. In that analysis,
general information drawn from the Consumer Expenditure Survey was
used in order to develop a number of examples. If no information at
all is available concerning the expenditure patterns of the plaintiff family,
it may be necessary to use these general data to obtain an estimate of
the plaintiffs' claim. Section II of this Chapter has been provided in
order to deal with such cases. My experience has been, however, that
most plaintiffs are able to provide at least *some* information concerning their family-specific spending patterns. For example, most plaintiffs are able to identify quite readily the percentage of family income
which they had spent on food and shelter (before the death in question). In such a case, I recommend that the average distribution of expenditures, as presented in Table 11.1, for example, be adjusted to take
this information into account. For example, if it is learned that a two-
adult family had been spending 20 percent of its income on food, instead
of the average 16.6 percent, I would recommmend that 20 percent be
used instead of 16.6 percent in that category and that the percentages
in all other categories be adjusted downward accordingly. (The relevant adjustment in this case would require that each of the other percentages be multiplied by $((1.00 - .20)/(1.00 - .166) =)$ .959.) Other
types of information specific to the family may indicate that the dependency rates by category should be altered. For example, it may be learned
that one of the family members required special, unusually expensive
clothing for work or that the family was spending an unusually large
percentage of its "household operation" category on child care. In each

case, the survivors' dependency rates with respect to those categories would have to be adjusted.

II. GENERAL DEPENDENCY RATES

Often, very little is known about the family's expenditure pattern, or the litigants wish to make a preliminary estimate of the survivors' dependency loss without having to undertake detailed calculations of the dependency rate. In these cases, it might prove useful to have available "rule of thumb" dependency rates which can be applied quickly and easily. The purpose of this Section will be to develop a set of such rates for various classes of families, distinguished primarily by family income and by number of family members.

I begin this analysis by identifying the dependency rates for a married couple with no children and for a married couple with two children between the ages of 2 and 5, using the division of expenditures among categories summarized in Table 11.1 (i.e., the average division for all Canadian families of these types) and the dependency rates by category set out in Table 11.6. In the case of the couple without children, I assume that both spouses have been working in the labour market. I present estimates of the dependency rates both for the case in which it is assumed that the dependent is to be compensated for the loss of the pension income stream, the "pension" case, and for the case in which it is assumed that the dependent is to be compensated for the loss of the employer's contributions to the pension fund, the "no pension" case. In the case of the couple with two young children, I do not calculate the dependency for the "pension" scenario, but I do calculate the dependency for both the case in which the wife had been working in the labour market and for that in which she had remained home to look after her children. The dependency rates for these various scenarios are reported in the first sections of Table 11.8. In the column headed "Wife Dies" the husband's dependency on family income varies from 69.8 percent, in the case of a two-adult family in which the husband is to be compensated for his wife's potential stream of pension benefits, to 77.7 percent, in the case of a two-adult, two-child family in which the wife worked and the husband is to be compensated for the loss of the employer's contributions to the pension fund.

Table 11.8 also presents information concerning three additional sources of variation in dependency rates. Section 3 in that Table reports the dependency rates for a two-adult, two-child family at four different levels of family income. These dependency rates have been based upon the dependency rates by category which are contained in Table 11.6 for a two-child family with mother acting as caregiver; but the distributions of expenditure by category for families of income levels

$10,000-$14,999, $25,000-$30,999, $45,000-$49,999, and $60,000 or over have been substituted for the distribution of expenditures summarized in Table 11.1. Section 4 provides dependency rates for families with two children between the ages of 12 and 15 (instead of between 2 and 5, as in Section 1). And Section 5 provides information concerning dependency rates for families with four children — aged 4, 8, 12, and 16, respectively.

The figures in Table 11.8 suggest the following conclusions:

[1] In the case of a couple without children, each spouse's consumption equals approximately 70 percent of family income; that is, each spouse's dependency upon the other is approximately 70 percent.

[2] Each child adds approximately 4 percent to the dependency of the family upon the deceased. For example, Table 11.8 shows that if a wife who was in the labour market dies, the dependency of the survivors is approximately 71 percent when there are no children, 75-79 percent when there are two children, and 86 percent when there are four children.

[3] Dependency rates are not significantly affected by family income levels — except at extreme income levels. For example, in Section 3 of Table 11.8 the dependency rates for a family with two young children are remarkably constant across all income levels when it is the husband who has died and are also consistent across all but the very lowest income level when it is the wife who has died. Similarly, in calculations which I have not reported in Table 11.8, I found that dependency rates for a family of two adults were consistent at all income levels except at the very highest incomes in the case in which the wife had died.

[4] The dependency rate is approximately 2 percent higher when the children are teenagers than when they are of pre-school age. (Compare Section 4 in Table 11.8 with the first row in Section 2.)

III. DEPENDENCY OF CHILDREN UPON PARENTAL INCOME

When both parents have died, the relevant dependency becomes the percentage of family, after-tax income which had been spent on the surviving children. The primary source of information concerning this issue is a series of studies which have been conducted in the last decade in an attempt to establish child support guidelines in divorce cases. Five such studies will be reviewed here, two Canadian and three American:

Atkins, Frank J., Cara L. Brown, and Christopher J. Bruce, *Child Rearing Expenditure Estimates for Canada* (Report prepared for the Department of Justice, Canada, 1991) (unpublished).

TABLE 11.8

**Variations in Average Dependency Rates Across
Families of Differing Numbers, Ages, and Incomes**

Family Type	Wife Dies	Husband Dies
1. No Children (Wife Works)		
— pension	69.25%	69.80%
— no pension	71.04	71.58
2. Two Children Between Ages of 2 and 5 (No Pension)		
— wife in labour market	77.18	77.70
— wife is caregiver	82.86	76.79
3. Two Children Between Ages of 2 and 5 (Wife is Caregiver — No Pension)		
Family Income		
— $10,000-$14,999	79.03	80.41
— $25,000-$29,999	76.53	79.23
— $40,000-$44,999	76.20	79.17
— $60,000 and over	75.52	79.10
4. Two Children Between Ages of 12 and 15 (Wife Works — No Pension)		
	80.15	79.79
5. Four Children (Wife Caregiver — No Pension)		
	85.55	85.24

Douthitt, Robin A., and Joanne M. Fedyk, *The Cost of Raising Children in Canada* (Toronto: Butterworths, 1990).

Espenshade, Thomas, *Investing in Children* (Washington, D.C.: The Urban Institute Press, 1984).

Olson, Lawrence, *Costs of Children* (Toronto: Lexington Books, 1983).

Terrell, William T., *Child Expenditure Estimates: First Run of an Equal Share Poverty Adjusted Model (ESPAM)* (Wichita, Kans.: October 1986) (unpublished).

Atkins, Brown, and Bruce calculated their child expenditure figures as a percentage of *after-tax* income. On this basis, their "best" estimates of the costs of raising one child were: 27 percent of family income for lower income families, 20 percent for middle income families, and 18 percent for upper income families. The comparable figures for raising two children were: 43 percent, 33 percent, and 30 percent. Also, their estimates suggested that parents spend slightly more than twice as much (per year) on children aged 7-18 than they do on children aged 0-6.

Douthitt and Fedyk estimated the percentage of *gross* income devoted to children to be between 9 and 16 percent for the first child, depending on province and income group, with an average of approximately 12 percent. Second, whereas the other researchers found that families spent more on older children than younger, Douthitt and Fedyk generally found the reverse. Also, whereas other researchers found no correlation, or a negative correlation, between socio-economic class and percentage of family income spent on children, Douthitt and Fedyk found a very significant positive relationship between these variables. Finally, Douthitt and Fedyk found that two children cost approximately 65 percent more than one, and that three children cost approximately 35 percent more than two.

Espenshade estimated that families spent approximately 30 percent of their *after-tax income* on expenditures on children if they had one child, 40-45 percent if they had two children, and 50 percent if they had three children. Furthermore, he found that children from birth to age 6 cost approximately 75 percent as much (per year) as did children aged 6-18 and that the percentage of family income devoted to children did not vary significantly among socio-economic groups.

Olson found that expenditures on children were approximately 21 percent of *gross* income for families with one child, 37 percent for families with two children; and 52 percent, 60 percent, and 65 percent for families of 3, 4, and 5 children, respectively.

Terrell also calculated expenditures on children as a percentage of *gross* family income. Within a one-child family, he estimated this expenditure to be 16 percent of family income for pre-school children and 20 percent for teenage children. He also estimated that families spent approximately 75 percent as much on the second child as on the first, and 85 percent as much on the third as on the second. Like Espenshade, he found very little difference in expenditure patterns among socio-economic groups — although he did observe a slight decline in the percentage of income spent on children as family income increased.

Some of the most important findings of these five studies have been summarized in Table 11.9. The first figure in each element of this Table represents the expenditure on children as a percentage of after-tax income, while the second represents expenditures as a percentage of gross income. The bracketed terms are estimates, based on the assumption that income taxes represent approximately 20 percent of gross income for the average family. It is seen from Table 11.9 that "reasonable" estimates of the percentage of *after-tax* income spent on children would be approximately 25 percent for a one-child family, 40 percent for a two-child family, and 50 percent for a three-child family. The comparable percentages from *gross* income are approximately 20 percent, 32 percent, and 40 percent, respectively. Finally, the information provided above would also seem to support the contention that children 0-6 cost approximately 75 percent as much, per year, as did children 7-18.

TABLE 11.9

Costs of Raising Children, as a Percentage of Family Income

Number of Children	Income Base	Atkins Brown & Bruce	Douthitt & Fedyk	Espenshade	Olson	Terrell	Approximate Average
One	After-tax	18-27	(11-20)[a]	30	(26)[a]	(20-25)[a]	25
	Gross	(14-22)	9-16	(24)	21	16-20	20
Two	After-tax	30-43	(19-33)	40-45	(46)	(35-44)	40
	Gross	(24-34)	15-26	(32-36)	37	28-35	32
Three	After-tax	N/A	(26-43)	50	(65)	(48-60)	50
	Gross	N/A	21-34	(40)	52	38-48	40

[a] Terms in brackets are estimates — obtained by assuming that after-tax income is 80 percent of gross income.

12

REMARRIAGE AND DIVORCE

Two factors constrain the duration of time over which the plaintiff can claim a pecuniary loss following the death of a spouse. First, had the deceased lived, it is possible that the couple would have become divorced, thereby ending or reducing[1] the dependency of the plaintiff on the deceased. Second, if the plaintiff should remarry and receive the same level of support (both financial and emotional) from the new spouse as would have been received from the deceased, the Court has held, in many instances,[2] that the plaintiff's loss has come to an end. Thus, the period of loss, according to this view, is held to extend only to the point at which the remarriage occurs. Because the latter factor proves to be of far greater significance for the valuation of damages than does the former, it is remarriage which I will consider first.

I. REMARRIAGE

Statistics Canada periodically publishes very detailed figures concerning remarriage and divorce. The most recent of these publications is:

Adams, O.B., and D.N. Nagnur, *Marriage, Divorce and Mortality: A Life Table Analysis for Canada and Regions*, Cat. No. 84-536 (Ottawa: Statistics Canada, September 1988).

Table 12.1 reproduces some of the most important figures concerning the remarriage of widows and widowers from the latter publication. There it is seen, first, that the probability that males will remarry if their spouses die is very much higher than is the probability that females will remarry; and, second, that the probability of remarriage declines significantly for both sexes as they become older. The Table indicates, for example, that approximately 12.5 percent of 30-year-old widowers will remarry during the following year but that this probability falls

---

[1] Of course, even had the marriage ended in divorce, one partner might have been required to make matrimonial support payments to the other.

[2] See, for example, *Sharp-Barker and Barker v. Fehr* (1982), 39 B.C.L.R. 19 (S.C.).

to 7.7 percent for 45-year-old widowers and to 4.3 percent for 60-year-olds. It also indicates that the comparable probabilities for widows are, approximately, 8.4 percent for 30-year-olds, 2.6 percent for 45-year-olds, and 0.7 percent for 60-year-olds. These figures suggest that the period of dependency loss will be much shorter for males than for females and much longer for older plaintiffs than for younger.

TABLE 12.1

Selected Remarriage Statistics for Widows and Widowers:
Canada, 1984-1986

Age	Probability of Remarriage in Next Year		Number of Years Expected to Remain Unmarried	
	Male	Female	Male	Female
20	0.02554	0.02177	11.70	19.30
25	0.13355	0.08893	8.54	19.13
30	0.12484	0.08434	9.31	23.94
35	0.10285	0.04966	11.71	27.72
40	0.09907	0.03410	13.54	28.91
45	0.07664	0.02648	15.19	28.18
50	0.05413	0.01733	16.00	26.24
55	0.04987	0.00988	15.86	23.06
60	0.04341	0.00691	14.64	19.03
65	0.03945	0.00632	12.34	14.59

Source: Canada. Statistics Canada, *Marriage, Divorce and Mortality: A Life Table Analysis for Canada and the Regions, 1984-1986*. Cat. No. 84-536E (Ottawa: Statistics Canada, 1988) Tables 13 and 14.

Additional information concerning the determinants of the probability of remarriage is available from academic research. I have been able to locate nine such studies. These are:

Bahr, S. J., "The Effects of Welfare on Marital Stability and Remarriage" (1979), August, *Journal of Marriage and the Family* 553-60.
Bulcroft, K., R. Bulcroft, L. Hatch, and E. F. Borgatta, "Antecedents and Consequences of Remarriage in Later Life" (1989), 11 (1) *Research on Aging* 82-106.
Glick, P. C., and S. L. Lin, "Recent Changes in Divorce and Remarriage" (1986), 48 *Journal of Marriage and the Family* 737-47.
Gurak, D. T., and G. Dean, "The Remarriage Market: Factors Influencing the Selection of Second Husbands" (1979), 3 (2) *Journal of Divorce* 161-73.

Mott, F. L., and S. F. Moore, "The Tempo of Remarriage Among Young American Women" (1983), May, *Journal of Marriage and the Family* 427-35.

Northcott, H. C., "Widowhood and Remarriage Trends in Canada: 1956 to 1981" (1984) *Canadian Journal of Aging* 63-77.

Oh, Sunjoo, "Remarried Men and Remarried Women: How Are They Different?" (1986), 9 (4) *Journal of Divorce* 107-13.

Smock, P. J., "Remarriage Patterns of Black and White Women: Reassessing the Role of Educational Attainment" (1990), 27 (3) *Demography* 467-73.

Spanier, G. B., and P. C. Glick, "Paths to Remarriage" (1980), 3 (3) *Journal of Divorce* 283-98.

These studies found the following factors to be important in determining the likelihood and timing of remarriage:

Education:

Seven of the nine studies found level of education to be linked to the probability of remarriage. The most consistent findings were those for white women. Five of the six articles that studied white women and found a link between education and remarriage stated that the higher her level of education, the less likely was a white woman to remarry. Contrasting results were found for men. Oh (at p. 110) found an unexpected negative relationship between level of education and the probability of remarriage, whereas Bulcroft et al. (at p. 92) reported higher education to be linked to a higher likelihood of remarriage.

Age at First Marriage:

Although information is only available for women in this area, two studies are informative. Smock (at p. 472) found that, for white women, the younger the woman was at first marriage, the more likely she was to remarry. White women who first married at age 24 or older were 56 percent less likely to remarry than those who married under the age of 19. Spanier and Glick (at p. 290) found similar effects, showing an inverse relationship for white women between age at first marriage and likelihood of remarriage.

Age at Separation:

Spanier and Glick (at p. 290), Gurak and Dean (at p. 166), and Glick and Lin (at p. 743) all found a consistent inverse relationship between age at separation and likelihood and timing of remarriage. Spanier and Glick (at p. 294) found the same relationship to hold for widowhood.

Children:

Glick and Lin (at p. 741), Gurak and Dean (at p. 165), Smock (at p. 472), and Spanier and Glick (at p. 291) all found that, for women, children served as a deterrent to remarriage. All four studies found that, as the number of children a woman had increased, so did the likelihood of her remaining unmarried once divorced or widowed. According to Smock, the effect of children on remarriage for black women was significantly larger than for white women. Bulcroft et al. (at pp. 90-91) found similar results for men. Although number of living children did not have a significant effect on remarriage for men (presumably because the children may be living with the mother), number in the household was found to be negatively related to remarriage.

Work Status:

Mott and Moore (at p. 431), and Oh (at p. 111) both found that women who were working were less likely to remarry. Specifically, Oh stated that women who were in the labour force were 22 percent less likely to be remarried than those women who were not working. Oh found that remarriage rates for men were not significantly affected by their work status.

Welfare:

Bahr (at p. 558) and Mott and Moore (at p. 431) both found that remarriage rates for women receiving welfare were lower than remarriage rates for women not receiving welfare. Bahr found that white women who did not receive any welfare were approximately three times more likely to remarry than female welfare recipients. However, black welfare recipients' remarriage rates were not significantly different from rates for black women not receiving welfare.

Health:

Studies by Bulcroft et al. (at p. 92) and Mott and Moore (at p. 432) both indicated that poor health is a deterrent to remarriage. Whereas Bulcroft et al., observing males only, found poor health to be negatively related to remarriage, Mott and Moore found that, for women, there was an increasingly negative relationship between health and remarriage as time since divorce increased.

Income:

Oh (at p. 111-12) found that remarriage was an increasing function of income for males, and a decreasing function for females. Specifically, a $10,000 increase in income for men elevated the probability of remarriage by 7 percent. In contrast, a $10,000 increase in earnings decreased the likelihood of remarriage for women by as much as 15 percent.

Other Factors:

Spanier and Glick (at p. 288) found length of first marriage to be inversely related to likelihood of remarriage. Seventy-three percent of white women and 52 percent of black women whose first marriage lasted less than five years were remarried within five years of their divorce. In comparison, only 34 percent of white women and 17 percent of black women remarried within five years after a marriage that lasted 10 or more years. Finally, the study by Bulcroft et al. (at p. 91) reported an inverse relationship between length of time widowed or divorced and likelihood of remarriage.

II. DIVORCE

The available Canadian data are summarized in Table 12.2. This Table indicates, first, that the divorce rate is not high, in absolute terms. In no age group do as many as 2 percent of the individuals obtain divorces in any given year. Second, the expected duration of marriage is such that every group can expect (in the statistical sense) to remain married until at least age 63. (Twenty-year-old married males and females can expect, on average, to remain married for slightly more than 43 years.) Finally, the highest incidence of divorce by age is in the 25 to 45-year-old group.

The following studies also provide useful information:

Bahr, S. J., "The Effects of Welfare on Marital Stability and Remarriage" (1979), August, *Journal of Marriage and the Family* 553-60.
Bahr, S. J. and R. J. Galligan, "Teenage Marriage and Marriage Dissolution" (1984), 15 (4) *Youth and Society* 387-400.
Balakrishnan, T. R., K. Vaninadha Rao. E. Lapierre-Adamcyk, and K. J. Krotki, "A Hazard Model Analysis of the Covariates of Marriage Dissolution in Canada" (1987), 24 (3) *Demography* 395-406.
Becker, G. S., E. M. Landes, and R. T. Michael, "An Economic Analysis of Marital Instability" (1977), *Journal of Political Economy* 1141-87.

TABLE 12.2

Selected Divorce Statistics: Canada, 1984-1986

Age	Probability of Divorce in Next Year		Number of Years Expected to Remain Married	
	Male	Female	Male	Female
20	0.00326	0.00630	43.16	43.21
25	0.01297	0.01646	39.65	40.44
30	0.01828	0.01790	37.70	39.03
35	0.01715	0.01554	36.10	37.34
40	0.01546	0.01354	33.98	34.98
45	0.01230	0.01047	31.27	32.08
50	0.00933	0.00692	27.93	28.45
55	0.00603	0.00448	23.96	24.24
60	0.00386	0.00274	19.54	19.66
65	0.00245	0.00186	14.81	14.86

Source: Canada. Statistics Canada, *Marriage, Divorce and Mortality: A Life Table Analysis for Canada and the Regions, 1984-1986.* Cat. No. 84-536E (Ottawa: Statistics Canada, 1988) Tables 17 and 18.

Bumpass, L. J. and J. A. Sweet, "Differentials in Marital Instability: 1970" (1972), 37 *American Sociological Review* 754-66.

Glick, P. C. and S. L. Lin, "Recent Changes in Divorce and Remarriage" (1986), 48 *Journal of Marriage and the Family* 737-47.

Kienan, K. E., "Teenage Marriage and Marital Breakdown: A Longitudinal Study" (1986), 40 *Population Studies* 35-54.

Koo, H. P. and B. K. Janowitz, "Interrelationships Between Fertility and Marital Dissolution" (1983), 20 *Demography* 129-45.

Lehrer, E. L., "Determinants of Marital Instability: A Cox-Regression Model" (1988), 20 *Applied Economics* 195-210. [1]

Lehrer, E. L., *The Stability of First and Higher Order Marriages: A Comparative Analysis* (University of Illinois at Chicago, 1990). [2]

McCarthy, J., "A Comparison of the Probability of the Dissolution of First and Second Marriages" (1978), 15 *Demography* 345-59.

Moore, K. A. and L. J. Waite, "Marital Dissolution, Early Motherhood and Early Marriage" (1981), 60 *Social Forces* 20-40.

U.S. Department of Commerce, Bureau of the Census, *Social and Economic Variations in Marriage, Divorce, and Remarriage: 1967,* Series P-20, No. 223, October 7, 1971.

These studies found the following factors to be of significance in the prediction of divorce rates.

Age at Marriage:

Bahr and Galligan (at p. 395), Becker et al. (1160), Bumpass and Sweet (756), Lehrer [1](206), McCarthy (352), Moore and Waite (32) and U.S. (22, 24, and 25) all found that marital stability was an increasing function of age at marriage, at least until the latter was 30. Balakrishnan et al. (at p. 402) found that those who marry before the age of 20 are three times more likely to become divorced than those who marry after the age of 25. Lehrer, [2](19), found similar results to those of Balakrishnan in her study of women only. Becker et al. and U.S. Department of Commerce, however, found that men who marry after the age of 30 are more likely to divorce than those who marry between the ages of 25 and 30.

Education:

Bahr and Galligan (at p. 396), Bumpass and Sweet (756), McCarthy (353) and Moore and Waite (32) all found that those who had completed high school were less likely to become divorced than those who had not matriculated. Lehrer [1](at p. 205), however, found only education of women at the time of her interview, and not at the time of marriage, to have a significant negative impact on divorce. In a later study, Lehrer [2](at p. 21) found that as the husband's schooling rose from 12 to over 16 years, the likelihood of the marriage being dissolved by the fifth year dropped by about 50 percent.

Earnings and Income:

Becker et al. (at p. 1160) and U.S. Department of Commerce (22) both found that divorce rates among males declined as their incomes rose — although Becker et al. (at p. 1160) also found a slight increase in divorce rates among the wealthiest group of males. Moore and Waite (at p. 29) found no strong correlation between income and divorce but did find that a slight increase in marital assets was correlated with a reduction in the probability of divorce. Finally, Becker et al. (at p. 1169) noted that divorce rates rose as the wife's income increased relative to that of her husband.

Number of Children:

Becker et al. (at pp. 1165-66) and Moore and Waite (at p. 37) both found that the presence of young children significantly reduced the probability of divorce; while Koo and Janowitz (at p. 137) found that childless couples were more likely to separate than were couples with children.

Length of Marriage:

Becker et al. (at p. 1162) and U.S. Department of Commerce (at pp. 22-25) both found that the probability of divorce fell significantly as the duration of the marriage increased. The U.S. Department of Commerce study, for example, found that divorce rates in the first 5 years of marriage were 2 to 3 times as high as they were in the 16th year and later.

Religion:

Becker et al. (at pp. 1166-67) found that couples with different religious backgrounds were 10-20 percent more likely to divorce in the first four years of marriage than were couples who shared a common religion. Lehrer [2](at p. 23), and Lehrer [1](at p. 205) found a difference in the religion of the two spouses to almost double the probability of marital dissolution by the fifth year of marriage. Bumpass and Sweet (at p. 756) also found that Jewish women were 7 percent less likely than the average woman to divorce, while Episcopalian women were 8 percent — and Fundamentalist and Baptist women were 3 percent — more likely than the average to divorce. Lehrer [1](at p. 207) found that if either one or both of the partners were affiliated with the Catholic church, the probability of marital dissolution decreased. Finally, Lehrer [1](at p. 207) also found that more frequent attendance of religious services decreased the risk of separation.

Parents' Marital Status:

Bumpass and Sweet (at p. 756), Lehrer [1](at p. 207), and Lehrer]2](at p. 27) all found that parents' marital breakdown has a positive effect on subsequent dissolution of the children's marriage. Bumpass and Sweet found that women whose parents had suffered divorce or separation had a divorce rate 6 percentage points higher than the average.

Time of Conception:

Balakrishnan et al. (at p. 399) and Lehrer [1](at p. 207) both found premarital birth and premarital conception to have a positive impact on marital dissolution. Specifically, Balakrishnan showed that couples experiencing premarital birth were four times more likely to be divorced after five years of marriage than those couples who did not conceive before marriage. Premarital conception more than doubled the probability of marital breakdown after five years of marriage. Kiernan (at p. 44) found that the risk of marital dissolution decreased as the interval between marriage and the birth of the first child increased.

Other Factors:

McCarthy (at pp. 352-53) showed that the probability that second marriages would end in divorce within the first 10 years was almost 60 percent higher than the comparable probability among first marriages. Bahr (at p. 556) found that white welfare recipients were three times more likely to get divorced than whites not on welfare. This same study found the effect of welfare on black marital breakdown to be insignificant. Lehrer [1](at p. 206) found that if the wife is older than the husband, the probability of marital dissolution increases for whites but not blacks; however, if the wife is substantially younger than the husband, the likelihood of separation is positively affected for blacks but not whites. Finally, Balakrishnan (at p. 402) reported that women who cohabitate before marriage are 50 percent more likely to experience marital breakdown than women who did not engage in premarital cohabitation.

13

THE DISCOUNT RATE

Once the value of the plaintiff's stream of future losses has been determined, it is necessary to identify the value of the lump-sum amount which will have to be invested today in order to replace that stream. Two factors which have not yet been discussed will be of importance to the determination of the lump-sum award. These are the interest rate at which the award is to be invested and the value of any management fees which will be charged by financial experts to assist the plaintiff with the investment of the award. These factors will be discussed in separate sections in this Chapter.

I. THE REAL RATE OF INTEREST

1. Definition

Typically, the value of a loss in a future time period is estimated by calculating the value in the current year and inflating that value to the year in which the loss is expected to be incurred. For example, it might be determined that a loss which is expected to occur one year from now would have a value of $10,000 if it had been incurred today. Thus, if the rate of inflation is expected to be 5 percent, the value of the loss, one year from now, would be calculated to be:

$$
\begin{aligned}
\text{Loss (1 year)} &= \$10,000 + (5\% \times \$10,000) \\
&= \$10,000 + (0.05 \times \$10,000) \\
&= \$10,000 \times 1.05 \\
&= \$10,500 \qquad\qquad\qquad (13.1)
\end{aligned}
$$

If it was known that $10,500 was to be replaced one year from now, the court's goal would be to identify the amount of money which would have to be invested today in order to generate a return of $10,500 within that year. Let us assume that the current interest rate is 8 percent. What we know is that if we invest some amount, $Z, today at 8 percent, one year from now we will receive a return of:

$$\begin{aligned}
\text{Return (1 year)} &= \$Z + (8\% \times \$Z) &&= \$Z + (\text{interest rate} \times \$Z) \\
&= \$Z + (0.08 \times \$Z) &&= \$Z + (\text{interest rate} \times \$Z) \\
&= \$Z \times 1.08 &&= \$Z \times (1 + \text{interest rate})
\end{aligned}$$
$$(13.2)$$

Alternatively, therefore, if we knew the value of the return we were seeking one year from now, we could determine what $Z was to be. For example, if it is known that the return one year from now is to be $10,500, it can be determined that:

$$\begin{aligned}
\$10,500 &= \$Z \times 1.08 &&= \$Z \times (1 + \text{interest rate}) \\
\$Z &= \$10,500/1.08 &&= \text{Return}/(1 + \text{interest rate}) \\
&= \$9,722.22
\end{aligned}$$
$$(13.3)$$

That is, the amount which has to be invested today in order to generate some predetermined amount one year from now is found by dividing the desired amount by (1 + the interest rate). [Note: if $9,722.22 is invested at 8 percent, the amount which will be available one year from now will be $9,722.22 x 1.08 = $10,500.]

Finally, notice that the amount which was to be replaced one year from now was obtained by multiplying some current value (in this case, $10,000) by (1 + the rate of inflation). Thus, (13.3) could have been rewritten:

$$\begin{aligned}
\$Z &= (\$10,000 \times 1.05)/1.08 = (\$10,000 \times (1 + \text{inflation}))/(1 + \text{interest}) \\
&= \$10,000 \times \frac{1.05}{1.08} \qquad = \$10,000 \times \frac{(1 + \text{inflation})}{(1 + \text{interest})}
\end{aligned}$$
$$(13.4)$$

But the term (1 + interest) divided by (1 + inflation) — the inverse of the term on the right-hand side of (13.4) — is defined by economists to be (1 + *the real rate of interest*). That is, the real rate of interest is just the observed rate after the rate of inflation has been "netted" out. Thus, we now see that the value of the lump-sum award can be determined by replacing the term on the right-hand side of (13.4) with

$$\$Z = \frac{\$10,000}{1.02857} = \frac{\$10,000}{(1 + \text{real rate of interest})}$$
$$(13.5)$$

As most calculations of lump-sum awards contain an inflationary term in the numerator (to inflate the value of the loss) and an interest rate term in the denominator (to discount the future loss to the present), it is generally possible to simplify those calculations by replacing the inflation and interest terms with a real interest rate term, as in (13.5).

Although this substitution can be justified in terms of the simplification which it offers, its major significance derives from a second source. Whereas both the rate of interest and the rate of price inflation have fluctuated widely in the past and can be expected to do so again in the future, those fluctuations have tended to be in concert with one another. As a result, the real rate of interest, which is a ratio of these two values, has been much less variable than either of its components. For example, whereas the Canadian rate of inflation varied between 1.79 and 12.49 percent — a spread of 10.7 percent — between the years 1964 and 1990; the real rate of interest, as calculated in the last column of Table 13.1, varied between − 0.46 and + 6.49 percent — a spread of 6.98 percent — in the same time period. As this lower variation imparts a greater certainty to forecasts of real rates of interest than to forecasts of either the nominal (that is, the observed) rate of interest or the rate of inflation, economists and actuaries generally choose to employ the real rate of interest as the rate at which future losses are to be "discounted" to the present, that is, as the *discount rate*.

Finally, if forecasts of the real rate of interest are used in preference to forecasts of the inflation and nominal interest rates, one avoids the problem that the latter two forecasts may be based upon inconsistent assumptions. For example, assume that agency A has publicly forecast an inflation rate of 4 percent while agency B has forecast a nominal interest rate of 10 per cent. One might conclude from these forecasts that the two agencies believed that the real rate of interest would be

$$(1 \ + \ \text{real interest rate}) \ = \ \frac{(1 \ + \ \text{rate of interest})}{(1 \ + \ \text{rate of inflation})}$$

$$= \ \frac{(1.10)}{(1.04)}$$

$$= \ 1.0577$$

or 5.77 percent. But this would not be the case if agency B had based its interest rate forecast on a non-public forecast of inflation of 6 per cent. (Similarly, had Agency A been asked to make a forecast of the nominal interest rate, it might have suggested 8 percent.) Use of the composite, real rate of interest allows one to avoid this inconsistency.

2. Selection[1]

Six provinces have set specific values for the discount rate by regula-

---

[1] Just as this book was going to press, November 1991, the Government of Canada issued 30-year-bonds with guaranteed 'real rates of interest' of 4.25 percent. If the government continues to issue such bonds and a market develops, it seems likely that the prevailing rate on such bonds will define the appropriate discount rate in personal injury and fatal accident actions. In that case, the discussion in Sections 2, 3, and 4, *infra*, will prove superfluous.

tion. At the time of the writing of this book (August 1991), these mandated values were:

British Columbia: for calculations of loss of income: 2.5 percent
                  for calculations of costs of care: 3.5 percent
Ontario, New Brunswick, and Nova Scotia: 2.5 percent
Saskatchewan and Manitoba: 3.0 percent

In the remaining four provinces, no mandated rate exists. The discount rate is set by the court following the evidence of experts. In these provinces, the first task is to identify the investment whose interest rate is to be used to calculate the discount rate. There is a wide variety of investment vehicles open to the plaintiff. The award could be used to purchase real estate or a business, it could be invested in stocks, bonds, mortgages, or mutual funds, it could be deposited in a savings account, or it could be used to purchase a certificate of deposit. Each of these vehicles will exhibit different characteristics and offer different rates of return. Therefore, before selecting a real rate of interest to be employed by the court, it is necessary to specify the assumptions which have led to that selection. In this subsection I will consider three characteristics of investments which will influence their suitability for use by plaintiffs. These characteristics are: security, liquidity, and duration.

The award for damages in a personal injury action is often intended to replace the plaintiff's entire lifetime stream of earnings, or to provide the plaintiff with sufficient funds to obtain medical care for the rest of his or her life. It is crucial, therefore, that the investment which is selected offer a secure rate of return. This means more than that the plaintiff should not be expected to purchase risky stocks or to speculate in the real estate market. It also implies that the plaintiff's portfolio of investments should be chosen in such a way as to reduce the variation in rates of return over time.

For example, assume that the rate of return on a particular investment could be expected to average 8 percent per year but that the standard deviation of that rate was expected to be as high as 17 per cent.[2] Two or three years of rates of return at the low end of this range could reduce the value of the plaintiff's investments so dramatically that he

---

[2] This is the actual real rate of return on an index of Canadian common stocks, 1953-1980 (see James Pesando, "Valuing Pensions (Annuities) With Different Types of Inflation Protection in Total Compensation Comparisons" (1984) 17 *Canadian Journal of Economics* 569, at p. 574). That the standard deviation was 17 percent implies that approximately 2/3 of the observed real rates of return were within 17 percent (plus or minus) of 8 percent. Conversely, over 30 percent of these rates deviated by more than 17 percent from the mean. (The range reported by Pesando is from -34.76 to +38.46.)

would be unable to recover. Indeed, assume that an investment with an average rate of return of 10 percent proved to have an 8 percent return for the first 5 years, followed by a 12 percent return for the next 5 years. The amount left to the plaintiff at the end of 10 years could be as little as 92 percent of the amount which would have been left if the interest rate had been 10 percent in each of those years. Accordingly, the variance of the real rate of return must be considered when choosing among alternative investments.

The "liquidity" of an investment refers to the ease with which it can be converted to money. Liquid assets, such as land holdings, are acceptable as long-term investments. But it must be remembered that the plaintiff is going to need a steady source of income in the short-run too. So at least some of his investments will have to be in financial instruments which can be converted into money quickly and easily.

Furthermore, it would be unwise to rely on assets with fluctuating values as a source of day-to-day income. The prices of even the most secure stocks, for example, are subject to significant swings in value. It would be unfortunate if the plaintiff were to find that, to meet living expenses, he had to sell a stock at a time when its value had declined temporarily.

Finally, it would be unwise for the plaintiff to place a significant portion of the award in long-term investments with fixed rates of interest.[3] The reason for this is that the interest rates offered by these assets are determined, in large part, by current forecasts of the future rate of inflation. If those forecasts proved to have underestimated the actual rate of inflation, the plaintiff would find that the real rate of return had fallen below the rate which had been anticipated. Furthermore, that loss could not be recovered by selling long-term assets and buying others because the value of the assets would also have fallen as their real rate of return fell.

To summarize, it will be important to ensure that the plaintiff's investments are secure and liquid, that their real rates of return have as little variance as possible, and that the values of their nominal rates of return are not fixed over long periods. Pesando suggests that all of these goals could be met if the plaintiff was to invest in short-term government bonds.[4] As well as being secure and liquid, these bonds offer the real rate of return with the lowest variance of all financial instruments and, of course, they do not tie the investor to a single nominal rate of return for long periods. On the other hand, the plaintiff will also wish to obtain the highest real rate of return possible and short-term government bonds are known to offer a relatively low rate.

---

[3] The following argument might not apply if interest rates were at an unusually high level at the time of investment.

[4] *Supra*, note 1.

For this reason, the plaintiff could be expected to select a compromise position. If he has a large award, I would suggest that this position would be to invest in a diversified portfolio of secure financial instruments, such as "blue chip" stocks and highly rated bonds (of varying maturities). As trust companies purchase this type of portfolio with the funds obtained from their guaranteed investment certificates, the rate of return on those certificates provides an excellent indicator of the rate available to the plaintiff-investor. Furthermore, trust company certificates are representative of the types of secure instruments whose purchase is open to the plaintiff who has only a limited amount of funds to invest. For these reasons, I recommend use of the rate of return on trust company certificates as the discount rate in most personal injury and fatal accident actions. Data concerning the rates of return on these certificates are discussed in the following section.

3. Historical Data

Since 1964, the Bank of Canada has published monthly figures for the average rate of return offered by 5-year trust company guaranteed investment certificates. The annual averages of these monthly statistics from 1964 to 1990 are reproduced in column (3) of Table 13.1. In columns (4) and (5), I present two estimates of the (expected) real rates of return which are implied by the nominal rates in column (3). To obtain the figures in columns (4) and (5), I have deflated the nominal rates (from column (3)) by the rate of inflation expected in each of the years 1964 to 1990. Two measures of the latter rate have been employed. The figures in column (1) approximate it by the rate of inflation experienced in the previous year (the lagged rate of inflation). Using this measure, the real rates displayed in column (4) are obtained. The figures in column (2) approximate the expected rate of inflation by assuming that that rate is a function of the actual rates of inflation experienced in the preceding three years. Using this measure, the real rates displayed in column (5) are obtained.

Table 13.1 shows that over the 1964-1990 period the real rate of return on trust company certificates generally fluctuated between 2 and 6 percent, with an average of approximately 3.4 percent. However, a significant deviation from this experience occurred in the years immediately following the formation of OPEC. The disruption to the world economy caused by the sudden increase in oil prices led both to a reduction in expectations concerning the growth rate of Western economies and to an unanticipated increase in inflation. As a result, real rates of interest fell well below their historical averages, even becoming negative in some years. If it is assumed that the period 1974-1978 was atypical, it would be appropriate to exclude the real rates of return observed during those years from the long-run average. For this reason I have included the average for the combined periods 1964-1973 and 1979-1990 at the foot of Table 13.1. These averages indicate that the long-run real rate of return may have been as high as 4 percent. On the other hand, interest rates in the 1980s were also unusually high, in large part because the Bank of Canada chose to use a "tight" money policy to combat inflation. If it can be argued that this policy will not be maintained in the long-run, then perhaps the underlying long-run average implied by the figures in Table 13.1 are lower than the average for the full period, 1964-1990.

One of the problems with the data in Table 13.1 is that they cover only a relatively short period of time. In order to provide additional information concerning the movement of interest rates over a longer period, I have included Table 13.2. This Table provides information for the years 1951-1990 concerning Government of Canada bonds which have a maturation of 10 years or longer. Two points of interest are apparent from this Table. First, movements of the rates of return on trust company certificates were very similar to those of Government of Canada bonds, although the latter tended to be slightly lower than the former. Second, interest rates in the sub-period 1964-1990, the period for which data concerning trust company certificates are available, were slightly higher than those in the full period, 1951-1990. On this basis, it might be concluded that the long-run average rate on trust company certificates is slightly lower than the 3.42 percent figure reported at the bottom of Table 13.1. Judging from the ratio of the 1951-1990 average reported in Table 13.2 to the 1964-1990 average reported in Table 13.1, it appears that the long-run average rate on trust company certificates has been approximately 3.05 percent.

4. Forecasts

(a) Long-run

Over the long-run, the real rate of interest has tended to fluctuate around a stable mean. Although the determination of this mean is not well understood, its stability is consistent with received theory about the macroeconomy. For example, although an increase in economic growth might be expected to lead to an increase in demand for investment funds — and, hence, to an increase in real interest rates — it might also be expected to increase individuals' incomes. To the extent that higher incomes will be associated with higher savings, more funds will be supplied to the investment market, keeping the interest rate down. Conversely, if economic growth should slow down, the reduced demand for

TABLE 13.1

The Real Rate of Return on Trust Company, 5-Year Guaranteed Investment Certificates: Canada, 1964-1990

Year	Rate of Inflation Lagged One Year[a]	Expected Rate of Inflation[b]	Actual Rate of Return[c]	5-Year Trust Co. Certificates	
				Return Net of Lagged Inflation	Return Net of Expected Inflation
	(1)	(2)	(3)	(4)	(5)
1964	1.75	1.37	5.26	3.45	3.84
1965	1.79	1.93	5.53	3.67	3.53
1966	2.46	2.53	6.07	3.52	3.45
1967	3.74	2.86	6.31	2.48	3.35
1968	3.57	3.68	7.02	3.33	3.22
1969	4.09	3.98	8.03	3.79	3.89
1970	4.51	3.93	8.52	3.84	4.42
1971	3.37	3.64	7.72	4.21	3.94
1972	2.84	3.99	7.62	4.65	3.49
1973	4.77	4.58	8.21	3.28	3.47
1974	7.61	6.72	9.71	1.95	2.80
1975	10.86	8.75	9.56	− 1.19	0.75
1976	10.81	9.47	10.10	− 0.64	0.58
1977	7.51	9.45	8.95	1.34	− 0.46
1978	7.99	8.56	9.27	1.19	0.65
1979	8.96	8.23	10.42	1.34	2.02
1980	9.11	9.29	12.31	2.93	2.76
1981	10.16	10.33	15.39	4.75	4.59
1982	12.49	10.64	14.43	1.72	3.43
1983	10.80	9.57	11.46	0.60	1.72
1984	5.78	8.36	11.95	5.83	3.31
1985	4.35	5.05	10.77	6.15	5.45
1986	4.01	4.16	9.70	5.47	5.32
1987	4.09	4.18	9.59	5.28	5.19
1988	4.38	4.08	10.09	5.47	5.77
1989	4.05	4.57	10.32	6.03	5.50
1990	5.01	4.39	11.16	5.86	6.49

TABLE 13.1 (Cont'd)

Averages:		
1964-1990	3.35	3.42
1964-1973 and 1979-1990	3.99	4.01
1980-1990	4.55	4.50

[a] *Source:* Canada. Statistics Canada, *The Consumer Price Index*, Cat. No. 62-001, (Ottawa: Statistics Canada) various issues.

[b] This series was developed from a formula used in an early version of RDX2. See Equation 7.23, Bank of Canada, *The Equations of RDX2 Revised and Estimated to 4Q72*, Technical Report 5, 1976, at p. 155.

[c] *Source:* Bank of Canada, *Bank of Canada Statistical Summary*, and *Bank of Canada Review*, various issues. Each figure is the simple average of the twelve monthly figures reported by the Bank of Canada.

investment could be expected to be offset by a reduced supply of funds from income. Again, the long-run real interest rate might remain relatively unaffected.

Similarly, consider the following scenario, which was popular at the time of writing: instead of financing the public debt through increases in the money supply, the government will begin to borrow more heavily on the open market, thereby driving up the real rate of interest. This scenario is certainly plausible in the short-run, but may not be so in the long-run. Consider, if the government's action raises the rate of interest, it will discourage investment. In turn, this can be expected to slow the rate of growth of the economy and to create unemployment. But if the maintenance of a low rate of unemployment is one of the goals of government policy, the government will have to take steps to encourage growth. To the extent that this encouragement involves the lowering of the real rate of interest, the conclusion is reached, once again, that real rates will tend to return to the long-run average.

On the basis of considerations such as these, and in light of the uncertainty which exists concerning economic events which will occur twenty and thirty years in the future, most economists have concluded that historical data, such as those presented in Tables 13.1 and 13.2, must be used to establish the discount rate in personal injury and fatal accident litigation. These data suggest that it would be appropriate to employ a long-run discount rate of approximately 3 percent.

Two dissenting opinions have been expressed, however. First, a number of economists have argued that financial institutions have become more efficient in the last decade and that this has allowed them to offer higher "real" rates of interest.[5] What is not clear is what the size of this effect will be. As it appears unlikely to exceed 0.5-1 percent,

[5] See, in particular, Joel Fried and David Burgess, *The Determination of Real Interest Rates, Working Paper 90-2*, (Ottawa: Department of Finance, 1990).

TABLE 13.2

Rates of Return on Goverment of Canada Long-Term Bonds, 1951-1990

Year	Rate of Inflation	Rate of Return Nominal	Real
1951	2.93	3.24	0.30
1952	10.55	3.59	-6.30
1953	2.42	3.68	1.23
1954	-0.89	3.18	4.10
1955	0.60	3.14	2.53
1956	0.15	3.62	3.47
1957	1.48	4.11	2.59
1958	3.21	4.11	0.87
1959	2.69	5.07	2.32
1960	1.10	5.18	4.03
1961	1.23	5.05	3.78
1962	0.94	5.11	4.13
1963	1.20	5.09	3.84
1964	1.71	5.18	3.41
1965	1.81	5.21	3.34
1966	2.42	5.69	3.20
1967	3.73	5.94	2.13
1968	3.59	6.75	3.05
1969	4.05	7.58	3.40
1970	4.56	7.91	3.21
1971	3.29	6.95	3.54
1972	2.88	7.23	4.23
1973	4.80	7.56	2.63
1974	7.54	8.90	1.27
1975	10.91	9.03	-1.70
1976	10.80	9.18	-1.46
1977	7.51	8.70	1.11
1978	7.99	9.27	1.19
1979	8.96	10.21	1.15
1980	9.11	12.48	3.09
1981	10.16	15.22	4.59
1982	12.49	14.26	1.57
1983	10.80	11.79	0.89
1984	5.78	12.75	6.58
1985	4.35	11.04	6.41
1986	4.01	9.52	5.30
1987	4.09	9.95	5.63

TABLE 13.2 (Cont'd)

Year	Rate of Inflation	Rate of Return Nominal	Real
1988	4.38	10.22	5.59
1989	4.05	9.92	5.64
1990	5.01	10.85	5.56
Averages:			
1951-1960			1.51
1961-1970			3.35
1971-1980			1.50
1981-1990			4.78
1951-1990			2.79
1964-1990			3.13

this argument would seem to provide support for a discount rate of approximately 3.5-4 percent.

A second source of concern comes from two University of Western Ontario economists, Robin Carter and John Palmer.[6] Their statistical tests, which employ Canadian and American data from the 1950s to the 1980s, suggest that the real rate of interest on government bonds has, on average, equalled the economy-wide rate of growth of real wages. Thus, their findings strongly caution against the use of a long-run discount rate which differs significantly from the long-run rate of growth of wages.

The most important caveat with respect to Carter and Palmer's conclusions is that the rate of growth of real wages was considerably lower than the real rate of interest over most of the 1980s. Thus, those who believe that this represents a long-term shift in the relationship between these two variables would not be advised to follow Carter and Palmer's conclusions. If, however, Carter and Palmer's findings are confirmed by further testing and by additional experience, my suggestion would be that the rate of growth of wages be set approximately 1 percent lower than the discount rate.[7] That is, those who feel strongly that

[6] R.A.L. Carter and John Palmer, "Real Rates, Expected Rates, and Damage Awards" (1991) 20 *Journal of Legal Studies*, 439-62.

[7] Although Carter and Palmer found that interest rates approximately equalled the rates of growth of wages in the 1950s to 1980s (i) Fried and Burgess have predicted that real rates of interest will increase in the future; and (ii) Carter and Palmer's results apply to investments with relatively low rates of return. Hence, I would suggest that, even if their results were correct for the period selected, cautious investors should be able to obtain higher rates of return in the future than Carter and Palmer's results suggest.

the real rate of interest will average 3-4 percent in the long-run should, in the calculation of lump-sum damages, employ a long-run rate of growth of real wages of 2-3 percent; whereas those who feel strongly that the rate of growth of real wages will average 1-1.5 percent should employ a discount rate of 2-2.5 percent.

(b) Short-run

It is clear from Tables 13.1 and 13.2 that the real rate of interest can be expected to deviate either positively or negatively from its long-run mean for periods of up to ten years. The effect which such a deviation will have on the appropriate discount rate will depend upon the length of the time period over which discounting is to occur. Assume, for example, that the real rate of interest is expected to be 1 percent for the first two years of the discount period and then to return to normal levels (say, 3 to 3.5 percent) for the remainder of the period. If the period in question is of thirty years, the low initial values of the real interest rate will be offset by later, higher values and will reduce the discount rate only slightly. If the discount period is only five years, however, the low real rates of the first two years will reduce the average rate over the period markedly. For this reason, the greater the deviation of the current real rate from its long-run average and the shorter the discounting period, the more significant should be the effect of the current interest rate on the choice of the discount rate.[8]

II. MANAGEMENT FEES

As most plaintiffs will not have been accustomed to investing large sums of money, the courts will often allow for the possibility that the plaintiff will hire a financial advisor to assist with the investment of his or her lump-sum award. As the charge for these services is normally calculated as a percentage of the invested sum, the simplest way to calculate the costs of this *management fee* is to deduct the percentage charge from the discount rate. For example, assume that if the plaintiff invests $100,000 the interest rate will be 10 percent and the management fee will be 1 percent. The interest earned in the first year will be $10,000 (= 0.10 x $100,000) and the management fee will be $1,000 (= 0.01 x $100,000); that is, the net return to the plaintiff will be $9,000. But this is equivalent to earning 9 percent. Thus, rather than calculating the investment income and the management fee separately, it would

---

[8] For this reason, during 1990 and 1991, I recommended that the courts use a two-part discount rate — 5 percent for all calculations up to 1995 and 3 percent for all periods after that date.

have been possible to deduct the management fee from the interest rate and to have made only one calculation.

Although this approach is commonly followed, it is based upon an assumption which generally proves to be false. That assumption is that the rate of return which plaintiffs can earn if they invest their awards themselves is as high as the rate of return which professional financial advisors can obtain for them (before deduction of the management fee). In fact, the portfolio managers at a number of Canadian trust companies have assured me that, particularly on investment amounts of over $200,000, they are able to increase the rate of return sufficiently so that all but the most sophisticated investors are more than compensated for the costs of the management service. Indeed, this outcome is precisely what economic theory would predict — financial advisors would be unable to attract clients if the rate of return they offered, net of their management fees, was less than that which investors could obtain for themselves. Furthermore, it is my understanding that this conclusion applies even when the investor is a dependant adult whose funds have been deposited in a trust account. The additional costs to the trust company of meeting the conditions set by most trust accounts are so small as to leave the rate of return offered by the trust company unchanged.

The only exception to the preceding argument of which I am aware may arise in cases in which the plaintiff is a minor. In such cases, the Public Trustee will often manage the plaintiff's funds. My experience suggests that legislative constraints imposed upon the Trustee's office may be such as to reduce the plaintiff's effective rate of return below that which would have been available in the market place. Counsel may find it advisable to research this topic in the plaintiff's province of residence.

To conclude this Section, it is my recommendation that no allowance should be made for a management fee in the case of the unsophisticated plaintiff — unless there is clear evidence to the contrary, such as in the case in which legislation requires that the plaintiff's funds be invested at a low rate of return. Rather, I would recommend only that plaintiffs' counsel advise unsophisticated plaintiffs to approach a reputable trust company. With respect to plaintiffs who are sophisticated investors, on the other hand, the implication of the findings reported above are that, as these individuals can be expected to obtain higher than normal rates of return on their investments, it might be appropriate to employ a higher than normal discount rate to the calculation of the present values of their future losses.

14

EXPERTS

It is the carefully guarded prerogative of the judge or jury (hereafter referred to as the "court") to draw inferences from the facts of a case. However, on those occasions when particularly complex or technical evidence is led, the level of experience and knowledge available to the court may be such that it will encounter difficulty drawing such an inference with confidence. In these circumstances, a witness may be called who has some special knowledge or skill which can assist the court. The function of the "expert" witness, therefore, is to make available to the court those aspects of his or her (the expert's) experience and information which are relevant to the interpretation of the factual evidence.

The purpose of this Chapter will be to review various aspects of the role of the expert witness in a personal injury or fatal accident action. I begin, in Section I, by identifying the main categories of experts which are normally encountered in such an action. In Section II, I discuss a number of aspects of the employment of the expert, including establishment of the fee and preparation of the appropriate information for the expert's use. Finally, in Section III, I review the expert's testimony, particularly the examination and cross-examination of the expert witness in court.

I. THE EXPERTS

The purpose of this section is to offer a list of the experts who (often) prove useful to the assessment of damages, along with some indication of the areas in which their usefulness can be expected to be realized. I list them in rough order of their appearance at trial. (The experts virtually always follow the non-experts at trial, as it is the role of the experts to assist the court in drawing inferences from the facts as presented by the "ordinary" witnesses.)

1. Doctors

The primary role of the doctor is to identify the severity of the plaintiff's injury and to predict the future course of that injury. Also, the medical witness may identify: the types of medicines necessary, the alternative types of facilities available for care and rehabilitation of the severely injured, and the frequency of operations and other medical treatments (such as replacement of prostheses) which will be recommended. Various medical bodies have developed techniques for assessing the degrees of disability associated with different types of injury. But the figures derived in this way identify disability only in terms of physical impairment and not in terms of impairment of earning power. For this reason, evidence concerning these figures should not be employed with respect to loss of income, but should be employed only with caution.

2. Rehabilitation Nurses

In cases in which future costs of care will represent a sizeable claim, a rehabilitation nurse may be retained to identify the costs of medical supplies, wheelchairs, orderlies, and the like. There is also no reason why a nurse with the requisite information could not obtain estimates of the costs of necessities, nor the costs of converting a vehicle or house to use by an invalid.

3. Vocational and Rehabilitational Psychologists

A psychologist who is trained in vocational and rehabilitational matters has two crucial roles to play in a personal injury action. First, through the use of interviews and tests, the psychologist can identify the types of occupations for which the injured plaintiff is now suited mentally, physically, and psychologically. I have found psychologists' reports to be of particular value when the plaintiffs were minors or noncatastrophically injured.

Second, the psychologist may also be able to contribute to the prediction of the occupational course which the plaintiff would have followed if he or she had not been injured. This the psychologist can do by summarizing for the court the psychological literature concerning the prediction of occupational development and, where the plaintiff has not suffered brain damage, by testing for I.Q., aptitude, vocational preferences, etc.

Psychologists — although not necessarily vocational or rehabilitational — may also be employed in fatal accident actions to testify as to the loss sustained by children when they are deprived, through death, of their mother's care, education, and training.

Finally, neuropsychologists play a crucial role in predicting the plaintiff's employability when a brain injury has occurred. My experience has been that such injuries are among the most difficult to diagnose, individuals with brain damage can *appear* normal in court yet exhibit bizarre behaviours in the home and workplace which make it difficult to maintain personal relationships and employment. As a result, it is essential that only the most credible witnesses be called to testify concerning the prognosis for the rehabilitation of these individuals.

4. Home Economists

Those home economists who have training with respect to family budgeting may be able to assist the court, in a fatal accident action, with the determination of the dependency rate; that is, with the identification of the percentage of family income required to maintain the survivor's standard of living. Similarly, an individual with this training may also be able to assist with the determination of the future cost of care of the severely injured and with the estimation of the value of household services.

5. Accountants

Use of an accountant is important in those cases in which the plaintiff or the deceased was self-employed. In this situation, evaluation of the assets of the business operated by the individual in question and of the loss suffered by the business due to the injury to, or loss of, its owner will require expert knowledge of accounting practices. In addition, many accountants will be able to prepare the present value calculations necessary for the estimation of the lump-sum damage figure.

6. Economists/Finance Experts/Industrial Relations Experts

Three groups of experts who are largely interchangeable are economists — particularly labour economists and macroeconomists — professors of business who specialize in finance or industrial relations, and the members of schools of industrial relations — particularly those who have a background in economics. These individuals generally have formal training which will allow them to testify as to:

- wages, hours, and fringe benefits earned by different occupations, sexes, and geographic regions;

- rates of growth of wages, lifetime income patterns, and promotion possibilities;

- the incidence of such contingencies as unemployment, occupational illness, injury, and strikes;

- the plaintiff's dependency rate in a fatal accident action;
- the value of household services;
- the cost of raising children;
- the rate of price inflation (for purposes of determining the current value of the "limit" on non-pecuniary damages);
- real interest rates and net real discount rates;
- calculation of the present values of the future streams of income loss and costs of care;
- calculation of the income tax "gross up" in fatal accident cases;
- determination of the effect of pre-judgement interest on the evaluation of losses to date of trial.

7. Actuaries

The actuary has particular expertise in four aspects of personal injury and fatal accident damages:

- evaluation of employer fringe benefit packages, including pension plans;
- determination of mortality rates, particularly when the plaintiff has a less than normal life expectancy;
- calculation of the present value of pecuniary losses and future costs of care;
- calculation of the tax "gross up" in fatal accident cases.

8. Statisticians

In my view the most underutilized potential group of experts are statisticians. Whether they recognize it, or reveal it, or not, the basis of all experts' reports is an extrapolation of information concerning statistical averages to the particular plaintiff at hand. The doctor who concludes that the plaintiff's health will continue to deteriorate until institutionalization will be required within 10 years is relying upon an extrapolation either from other similar patients which that doctor has treated or from medical research with which the doctor is familiar. The accountant who predicts that the plaintiff's business would have been successful had he or she not been injured is also relying upon an extrapolation from other similar businesses which that accountant has assisted or from studies which have been conducted of similar businesses. And the economist who predicts that the plaintiff's income in a particular occupation would have averaged a certain amount per year, that it would have grown at a certain rate, and that the plaintiff would have retired at a certain age is relying almost exclusively on information concerning statistical averages of individuals "like" the plaintiff.

In each of these cases, the testimony of the expert is only as reliable as the statistics on which that testimony is based. Yet, it has been my experience that much of the information which is employed by experts is statistically very suspect. Thus, especially if the outcome of a damage assessment hinges upon a particular statistical finding, it may be useful to hire a statistician to evaluate the reliability of the finding in question.

As economists and business school professors are normally well-trained in statistical analysis, if one of them has already been retained for some other purpose, it will often be possible to have that person "double" as a statistician, at least for the purposes of an initial assessment. However, if the issue proves to be of crucial importance to the case, it may be desirable to employ a professional statistician. Also, it has been my experience that some of the most unreliable statistical evidence is that which concerns the effects of injury on employability. In such cases, the courts might be suspicious of the ability of, say, an economist to testify concerning what appears to be "medical" research, and it might be desirable to retain an individual who specialized in the interpretation of such statistics. Many medical schools in Canada employ such individuals.

II. EMPLOYING THE EXPERT

1. Identifying the Expert

Perhaps one of the most difficult aspects of employing an expert is finding one upon whom you can rely. The simplest approach is to telephone a lawyer who is experienced in either defence or plaintiff work. My experience has been that these individuals are generally most willing to assist in this way because they have an interest in seeing that poorly qualified "experts" are not employed. Alternatively, if an experienced economist or actuary has already been retained, this individual's advice might be sought. The reason I suggest these individuals is that they are generally required to read the reports of all of the other experts in the preparation of their own reports. Thus, more than any other set of non-lawyers, they tend to be familiar with the availability and quality of the expert witnesses in their regions. Finally, if the approaches identified above have not proven successful, I would suggest that the nearest university be approached.

2. The Expert's Fees

Once an expert has been identified, it will be necessary to agree to a fee schedule. To avoid misunderstanding, the cardinal rule with respect to the expert's fees is to discuss them at the first meeting. In addition, a professional expert should be able to provide counsel with a written fee schedule. The items which should be clarified at this point are: the retainer fee, the hourly rate, the expenses to be borne by counsel, and the method of payment.

(a) Retainer fee

Most experts require payment of a retainer fee. There are two reasons for this. First, the expert will generally have to make a number of disbursements before his or her report has been completed. Second, as the number of individuals offering themselves as experts is very small in Canada, it is not uncommon for an expert to be approached by both parties to an action. By committing his or her services to one party, the expert gives up the opportunity to work for the other. Thus, even though no work may be done for the party retaining him or her, the expert may have suffered a loss. The retainer fee compensates for this loss.

Finally, in a relatively straightforward case, the first few hours of work by the expert are often by far the most productive. Payment of a fixed retainer provides extra compensation for this productivity.

(b) The hourly fee

In order to maintain impartiality, the expert must not bill on a contingency basis. Rather, either a flat fee per case or an hourly fee must be charged. Because the amount of work required tends to vary widely among cases, virtually all experts bill on an hourly basis. A number of aspects of this fee should be clarified at the initial meeting: first, will the expert employ assistants and, if so, will their hourly rate differ from that of the principal? Second, how will the expert treat travel time and time spent away from home? For example, assume that the expert leaves the office for the airport at 4:00 p.m. Monday afternoon, travels to the city in which the trial is being held, and reaches home again at 6:30 p.m. Wednesday afternoon. What is the charge for the time spent travelling to and from the airport? The time in the air? The time spent having dinner with counsel in the city of the trial? And what is the charge for the Tuesday, when he or she was away from home for 24 hours?

Some experts also charge more for time spent in court than for time spent in research. An American colleague explained to me that he did this because he found the personal attacks, in cross-examination, on his competence and credibility to be very distasteful. My experience in Canada, however, has been that cross-examinations are conducted in a relatively civil manner. Accordingly, unless this practice changes there should be no reason to charge a differentiated fee for court appearances.

(c) Expenses

The expert should make clear which types of expenses will be passed on to counsel. Unless the expert travels out of town, these costs will normally prove to be nominal.

(d) Payment

The expert should indicate at what stages bills will be sent: at specified intervals, such as quarterly; after the completion of major segments of work, such as the writing of a report; or when the trial has been completed or the case otherwise settled.

Also, a clear understanding needs to be reached concerning the timing of the payment of the expert's account. Many experts have told me that the most frustrating aspect of working for lawyers is the difficulty which they experience collecting on outstanding accounts. The source of this problem appears to be the common view among lawyers — particularly plaintiffs' lawyers — that they have no responsibility to pay their accounts until they have received payment from their clients. As many lawyers are not paid until the case is settled, this can mean that the expert is asked to wait for as much as one or two years for payment. If this is the request which is being made, counsel *must* be prepared to offer the expert a substantial rate of interest on overdue accounts. It must be remembered that 60-70 percent of most experts' bills represent out-of-pocket expenses — for rent, research and secretarial assistance, quarterly payments of corporate income taxes and GST, travel, telephone and fax, etc. Thus, to ask the experts to wait for payment of their bills is, essentially, to ask them to subsidize the client's action. If this is the request which is being made, the experts can expect to be compensated through payment of a rate of interest which is at least equal to that which would be charged by a bank for such loans. This interest rate and the method of calculating interest, e.g., simple versus compound interest, should be specified in advance.

3. Information Required by the Expert

Finally, it may be useful to indicate the types of information which counsel can expect to be asked to provide to each of the experts involved in damage assessment. I begin with personal injuries involving adults, then move to injuries involving minors, and conclude with fatal accidents.

(a) Personal Injury — Adult

General information

Each expert will require:

* the name of the plaintiff;
* the plaintiff's birthdate and sex;
* the date on which the injury occurred;
* those portions of the examination for discovery which relate to the expert's area of concern.

Loss of income

Doctor: if the doctor who is providing the plaintiff's long-term prognosis has not previously been involved in the treatment of the patient, he or she will require:

* an accident report;
* records of the treatment of the plaintiff at the time of the accident and since.

Psychologist: if there is some doubt as to the effects of the injury upon the plaintiff's ability to work, it may be desirable to call a vocational and rehabilitational psychologist. This individual will require:

* a copy of the doctors' report(s);
* the educational and occupational history of the plaintiff;
* any written assessments of the plaintiff by employers, teachers, etc.;
* the results of any previous aptitude and intelligence tests.

Accountant: if the injured party was a self-employed businessperson, it will often be necessary to have an accountant disentangle the plaintiff's personal income from the earnings of the firm and from the implicit return on investment (see Chapter 4, Section IV). In this case, the accountant will require access to the firm's business records, as well as to the plaintiff's financial records and income tax returns.

Economist:

- the reports of the doctors, psychologists, and accountants. (With respect to doctors, I generally find that it is only the most recent reports which are necessary);

- the educational history of the plaintiff;

- the plaintiff's employment record, including records of positions held, promotions received, overtime worked, salary, and periods of unemployment. Records should be obtained for both the pre- and post-injury periods. Also, if another individual has replaced the plaintiff at his or her previous place of employment, it is useful to obtain that individual's record of employment from the date that he or she replaced the plaintiff;

- income tax records for 5 years prior to the injury, plus all years since the injury. (Records for more than 5 years are usually only necessary if the plaintiff's work experience has been erratic.)

- the dollar value of employer contributions to fringe benefits;

- if the plaintiff has been forced to leave employment with the employer he was with before the injury, and if he could otherwise have been expected to remain with that employer, it will be useful to find out from the employer the value of the raises the plaintiff could have expected to receive between the date of the injury and the date of trial. The former employer may also be willing to testify as to the plaintiff's anticipated prospects for promotion;

- the plaintiff's planned date of retirement;

- if the plaintiff is a woman who has not yet passed the child-bearing years, it will be necessary to obtain from her an indication of the number of children she had planned to have, before she had the accident; how long (if at all) she had planned to stay out of the labour market following the birth of each child; and whether her injury has caused her to revise these plans.

Actuary: if an actuary is to be used in addition to an economist, he or she will need to have the economist's report. On the other hand, if an actuary is to be employed in place of an economist, all of the information listed above under the heading of "Economist" will be required. Also, if the actuary is to assess the value of the plaintiff's pension and fringe benefit package, the details of that package will be required.

Household services

If the plaintiff has been prevented from performing certain household chores, it may be possible to make a claim for the lost value of these services. If so, make a copy of Table 14.1, have the plaintiff fill it out in as much detail as possible, and provide a copy to the economist or home economist. Point out to the plaintiff that weekend and weekday have been distinguished, as most people tend to follow different routines in the two time periods. Also, if the plaintiff has difficulty breaking his time down into the number of categories listed in Table 14.1, it might be recommended to combine some of the categories, say, headings (1)-(5) as well as headings (7)-(10). (For more detailed suggestions concerning the filling out of Table 14.1, see Chapter 10.)

Costs of care

Rehabilitation nurse: in order to prepare an estimate of the cost of medical care, the nurse will require the doctors' medical reports.

Home economist/economist: in order to estimate the costs of basic necessities, the economist or home economist will need the doctors' report and the report of the rehabilitation nurse.

Economist/actuary: in order to estimate the present value of future costs of care, all three of the reports listed above will be needed.

(b) Personal Injury — Minor

General information

See "personal injury — adult" above.

Loss of income

Psychologist:

• plaintiff's school records;

• results of any aptitude or intelligence tests conducted prior to the injury. (These are often available from the child's school.)

• ages, incomes, occupations, and educations of parents and siblings;

• marital stability of parents;

TABLE 14.1

Household Activities — Personal Injury Action

| Activity | Hours Per Day Devoted to Household Activities | | | |
| | Before the Injury | | After the Injury | |
	Weekdays	Weekends	Weekdays	Weekends
(1) Cooking				
(2) Cleaning				
(3) Kitchen wash-up				
(4) Shopping				
(5) Laundry				
(6) Child care				
(7) House maintenance				
(8) Car repairs/ maintenance				
(9) Gardening/ snowshovelling				
(10) Building/ do-it-yourself				
(11) Other _____				
(12) _____				

Economist: the economist will require the same data as that provided to the psychologist, plus the psychologist's report.

(c) Cost of Care

See "personal injury — adult" above.

(d) Fatal Accident

General information

Each expert will require:

- names of the plaintiffs and the deceased;
- birthdates, sexes, and relationships of plaintiffs to deceased;
- birthdate and sex of deceased;
- date of death.

Loss of income

Accountant: see "personal injury — adult" above.

Economist:

- with respect to the deceased, the economist will need the same information (other than post-injury earnings) that was suggested for the plaintiff in the section entitled "personal injury — adult" above;
- with respect to the plaintiffs, it will be necessary to provide records of their recent employment/earnings histories — including the period before the deceased's death — as well as any information available concerning their prospective employments;
- the value of the deceased's and the employer's contributions to his or her pension plan at the date of death;
- the value of pension and/or death benefits paid by the employer to the plaintiffs;
- the value of savings accumulated by the deceased.

Household services

Make a copy of Table 14.2, have the plaintiff fill it out in as much detail

TABLE 14.2

**Household Activities of the Deceased:
Fatal Accident Action**

Activity	Hours per Day Previously Devoted to Household Activities by the Deceased	
	Weekdays	Weekends
(1) Cooking		
(2) Cleaning		
(3) Kitchen wash-up		
(4) Shopping		
(5) Laundry		
(6) Child care		
(7) House maintenance		
(8) Car repairs/maintenance		
(9) Gardening/snowshovelling		
(10) Building/do-it-yourself		
(11) Other		

as possible, and provide a copy to the economist or home economist. Point out to the plaintiff that weekend and weekday have been distinguished, as most people tend to follow different routines in the two time periods. Also, if the plaintiff experiences difficulty breaking down the time of the deceased into the number of categories listed in Table 14.2, it might be recommended to him that some of the headings be combined. (For more detailed suggestions concerning the filling out of Table 14.2, see Chapter 10.)

Remarriage/divorce

If the deceased was the spouse of one of the plaintiffs it will be necessary to indicate to the economist (or actuary) whether the marriage was stable (i.e., was there a possibility of divorce?) and whether there is any reason to believe that the plaintiff is more (or less) likely to remarry than the average widow(er).

Dependency

It is desirable that the plaintiffs attempt to estimate the amount of after-tax income which they will now need in order to leave themselves as well off as they were when the deceased was alive. To assist them in this process, I have provided Table 14.3. They should be asked to estimate in that Table the manner in which the annual after-tax income of the family was distributed among the various categories listed before the deceased was killed. These estimates may be given in either dollar terms or in percentages. (Note: the bracketed terms associated with some of the categories are listed as examples of the types of goods and services incorporated in those categories.)

If the plaintiffs find it difficult to complete this Table, even an incomplete accounting will be useful as long as "after-tax annual income" is known. If even an incomplete accounting is not possible, have the plaintiffs identify whether they devoted an "unusually" high or low percentage of their incomes to any category of expenditures. For example, the deceased may have worked in a job which required greater than average expenditures on clothing, the family may have paid off their mortgage, they may have done more travelling or entertaining than the average family in their income category, or they may have devoted an unusually large percentage of their income to charity.

III. EXPERT TESTIMONY

There are five stages to the presentation of expert testimony. Before the trial there is the writing of a report. At the trial there is: the qualification of the witness, the examination-in-chief, the cross-examination, and the re-examination. Each of these stages will be discussed in turn in this section.

1. The Expert's Report

If the expert is hired early in the proceedings, it may be sufficient to ask for a report which does little more than summarize the expert's opinion. Usually, in such an opinion, the expert will be able to identify the major factors of concern in a manner which will be perfectly adequate for settlement purposes.

  As a trial approaches, however, it is important that a detailed analysis of the issues be obtained. There are three reasons for this. First, the discipline required to produce such an analysis will clarify *for the expert* many of the issues and arguments. Often, this will (i) reveal to the expert weaknesses in the approach being followed and (ii) suggest additional arguments which would strengthen the case. Second, a detailed discussion of the arguments will assist counsel in developing a strong bargaining position and in conducting the direct examination, should one be required. Finally, if the case should proceed to trial, it will often be useful to have available a detailed summary of the expert's arguments for reference by the court.

2. Qualifying the Expert

Before the expert's testimony can begin, his or her expertise must be established. This process is referred to as "qualifying." I discuss this process in two subsections. In the first, I review the procedure to be followed by counsel when presenting the expert's credentials. In the second, I discuss the standards by which I believe "expertise" should be measured.

Procedures for "qualification"

The first step to be taken by counsel who wishes to have an expert qualified is to identify the types of issues concerning which the expert is to testify. This will allow opposing counsel and the judge the opportunity to question the correspondence between these issues and the qualifications of the expert. The second step is for counsel to provide the court

TABLE 14.3

Information Required for the Calculation of Dependency Rates

	Annual Expenditures by Category Before Accident
(1) Food	
(2) Shelter (Rent, mortgage, repairs, utilities)	
(3) Household Operation (Telephone, child care, pet care, cleaning supplies, paper products, garden supplies)	
(4) Household Furnishings & Equipment	
(5) Clothing	
(6) Personal Care (Haircuts, soaps, deodorants, shaving supplies	
(7) Medical (Health insurance premiums, eye and dental care, drugs)	
(8) Transportation (Purchase, operation and maintenance of cars & trucks; bus, air, & taxi)	
(9) Recreation (Recreational equipment, home entertainment, admissions to events, sports equipment)	
(10) Reading (Newspapers, books, magazines)	
(11) Education	
(12) Tobacco and Alcohol	
(13) Miscellaneous (Interest payments, lottery tickets, lawyers' fees)	
(14) Security (Pension, life insurance, unemployment insurance)	

TABLE 14.3 (Cont'd)

---

(15) Gifts and Contributions
    (Gifts outside the spending
    unit and charitable
    contributions)
After-Tax Income (Annual)

---

opposing counsel, and the expert with copies of the expert's *curriculum vitae*. The expert should be led over the highlights of this document, with counsel obtaining a simple acknowledgement that each point is correct. The expert should *not* be asked to state his or her own education, degrees, work experience, and publications as the witness may become embarrassed by the impression that he or she is boasting and may inadvertently omit important information.

Often, before the expert's *curriculum vitae* has been entered, opposing counsel will interject that he or she is willing to accept the expert's qualifications. Usually, the purpose of such an interjection is to dissuade counsel from bringing the credentials of a particularly well-qualified expert to the attention of the court. If this is the case, it is my recommendation that counsel not succumb to the temptation to speed the trial process by accepting this offer, but rather that counsel request of the court that the normal qualification procedure be followed.

Finally, if the expert has testified for both plaintiffs and defendants in previous cases, it is useful to bring this information out as it will indicate that the legal community considers the witness to be unbiased.

Standards of qualification

The types of standards which should be met in the qualification process depend upon the nature of the evidence to be offered. My experience indicates that four categories of evidence can be distinguished. These categories, in descending order of their rigour, and the standards of expertise required of them, are:

(i) Mathematical calculations

Much of the evidence required for the assessment of damages involves the mathematical manipulation of figures. For example, in a case involving a self-employed individual whose business has been harmed by his injury or death, it may be necessary to assist the court with the interpretation of the business' accounts. And in all cases involving future losses, assistance may be required with the preparation of present value calculations.

With respect to evidence of this type, it will generally be necessary to show that the expert has passed through a formal accreditation program, such as those offered for accountants and actuaries, or that the expert has a degree in a relevant discipline from a post-secondary institution. The latter might be the case with respect to an engineer, doctor, or economist, for example.[1]

There are exceptions, however, in which extensive experience in the area might suffice. A bookkeeper who has lengthy experience with the accounts of a particular type of business might well be accepted as an expert in the interpretation of the accounts of such a business. I would suggest that exceptions such as these would become more desirable where they allowed one witness to testify as to two or more elements of a case. For example, an actuary who was to be called to perform a present value calculation in a fatal accident case might also testify as to the income taxes which would have been payable by the deceased. Such a practice would avoid the duplication of effort and expense involved in the testimony of both an actuary and a tax accountant.

(ii) Obtaining of facts from statistical publications and surveys

In the process of assessing the value of damages in a personal injury (or fatal accident) case, a great many statistics are employed. These might include, for example, the consumer price index, the levels of wages and fringe benefits in various occupations, the value of interest rates, and the rate of unemployment. With respect to most such statistics, it is necessary to possess a level of expertise which is greater than that enjoyed by the average person. There are three reasons for this. First, with the possible exception of series published by an agency as impeccable as Statistics Canada — and many provincial agencies would not fall into this category — some statistical sophistication will be required to enable the expert to report to the court concerning the reliability of the reported figures. Second, even if a reliable methodology has been employed to collect a particular set of figures, it may well be that those figures are inappropriate for the use to which they are being put. The expert must have sufficient experience with statistical reporting to be able to assist the court with this aspect of his testimony.

---

[1] I might add at this point that I believe a Master's degree or its equivalent to be the minimum requirement for most expert testimony. A Ph.D. is generally not necessary, however. The reason for this is that it is, in my experience, between the earning of the Bachelor's and Master's degrees that most students first develop their critical faculties.

Finally, with respect to most variables for which it would be desirable to collect statistics, it will be found that there is a wide variety of sources available. I have been able to identify literally dozens of studies which report on the unemployment rates of paraplegics, for example; and publications which report on occupational wage rates must number over 100 in Canada alone. In this light, a highly desirable, if not necessary, characteristic of the expert witness is a sufficient degree of experience with the field in question that the court will have some confidence that the most reliable and applicable sources have been identified.

(iii) Predictive studies

Perhaps the most useful type of knowledge which the expert can bring to the court is information concerning predictive and correlative studies. Most advances in the natural and social sciences are obtained by positing and empirically testing hypotheses. As most such hypotheses are either predictive — when A occurs B tends (not) to follow, or — correlative — A and B are (not) expected to be associated with one another — information concerning their tests can be of great use to the court. For example, if the plaintiff has suffered an injury whose severity has not fully stabilized by the time of trial, and has followed a particular course of treatment, a medical researcher may be able to report on studies of the extent of recovery which has been achieved by victims of similar injuries. Similarly, an economist may be able to summarize the findings of studies which correlate unemployment rates with characteristics which are observable in the plaintiff, such as age, sex, marital status, and education. And a vocational psychologist may be able to cite studies of the correlation between performance on various tests and subsequent success in the labour market.

In each of these cases, the tenor of the evidence is not to predict the course of development of the particular plaintiff in question, but to summarize the findings of those researchers who have investigated the correlations between certain classes of variables which appear to be relevant to this case. Thus, the first requirement of the expert is that he or she be widely read in the area which is being summarized. Second, because the statistical techniques involved in the testing of hypotheses are generally much more complicated than those employed to obtain statistics (category ii, above), the degree of statistical sophistication required of the expert is also much greater.

(iv) Experience-based evidence

Some of the medically-related testimony in a personal injury action such as that from doctors, nurses, and vocational psychologists is based upon the "experience" of the witness. For example, doctors are asked, based upon their experience, whether the severity of the plaintiff's injuries is likely to lessen over time; and the vocational psychologist may be asked whether the plaintiff has a good chance of success in a particular occupation. Evidence of this type suffers from a major difficulty; namely, that the "sample" upon which the witness is drawing his or her observations is often both (relatively) small and biased. It must be remembered that the types of injuries which are litigated to trial are generally of a "catastrophic" nature, such as paraplegia and brain damage, and that such injuries are relatively rare. As a result, even the most specialized of practitioners in the largest of cities is unlikely to have treated enough victims of a particular injury to have observed a sample large enough to be statistically reliable. Furthermore, even if the sample is large, it will have been spread over a number of years, during which time the doctor may not have kept the kinds of notes on which statistical inference can be based, and during which the types of treatments may have changed dramatically. Compounding all of these is the problem that the sample is not randomly selected. The doctor has only seen those patients directed to him or her. Unless it can be demonstrated that the plaintiff before the court is representative of those with which the expert is familiar, therefore, the expert's "experience" may be held to be of questionable value to this particular case.

This is not to say that experience is irrelevant, merely that its value must be questioned. From the discussion above, these questions would have to include:

- How many patients very similar to this one has the expert treated (or been consulted on)?
- Over how long a period?
- How are patients directed to the expert's attention?
- Can the doctor assure the court that the plaintiff is representative of the types of patients he or she has seen?

In addition to these questions, it is always useful to determine whether the expert is fully aware of the statistically-reliable studies which have been conducted with respect to the types of injuries in question. One might well be skeptical of the evidence of a witness who was not familiar with such studies.

3. The Examination-in-Chief

All the textbooks on courtroom testimony conclude that the most important condition for the successful examination of witnesses is preparation. In the case of an expert witness, this implies that counsel rehearse the examination with the witness, perhaps as much as a month in advance of the trial. This rehearsal will serve a number of purposes. First, most witnesses, particularly if they are successful, will be extremely busy people. Hence, they may inadvertently make errors or miss important points when writing their reports. Often, under close examination in the rehearsal, these problems can be identified and dealt with. Second, even if the case does not go to trial, counsel will have obtained a better understanding of the strengths and weaknesses of the argument, which will assist in the settlement negotiations. Third, if the case does go to trial, both counsel and the witness will have learned important lessons about the manner in which the examination should proceed.

At the trial, once the expert has been qualified, I believe that the judge should be given a copy of the expert report to be followed while the testimony is being given. The reason for this is that most experts' reports concern matters of some complication. If the judge has the report before him or her, the testimony can be followed much more easily. If the trial is being heard before a jury, however, it may be preferable that the jurors be provided with a simplified summary of the arguments, in order to ensure that they do not become confused.

I believe that the examination itself should consist of a detailed series of questions, each of which requires a relatively short answer. If this approach is employed successfully, it will help to keep the court apprised of the relevance of each point made by the expert. Also, if a series of short questions is being asked, it is a relatively simple matter to insert an additional question to clarify a particular matter. If counsel has asked a general question requiring a lengthy answer, on the other hand, clarification can only come at the end of the testimony, unless the examiner is willing to break into the expert's train of thought. Furthermore, if the expert is asked a question requiring a lengthy answer, one takes the risk that he or she will launch into a tedious lecture, that the expert will subconsciously begin to use overly technical language, or that the expert will overlook some important point.

The first step in the pursuit of any line of questioning is to indicate to the court the facts on which the expert's testimony is to be based. There are three techniques for revealing these facts: the expert can be asked to relate the facts as he or she understands them; counsel can put the facts to the court; or counsel's questions can be couched in terms of hypothetical questions. In choosing among these techniques, there are a number of points which should be taken into consideration. First, if the facts of the case are in dispute, it may be preferable to employ hypotheticals in order to avoid the criticism that counsel, or the expert, is usurping the court's role. Second, if the expert is asked to relate the facts of the case, the risk is run that he or she will appear to be too familiar with the plaintiff (or defendant), giving the impression that the expert is acting as an advocate rather than as an impartial observer. Third, the use of hypotheticals helps to overcome the objection that evidence concerning the behaviour of the average person is not relevant to predictions concerning a particular plaintiff or defendant. For example, whereas opposing counsel can, rightly, argue that there are many reasons for believing that a particular 40-year-old widow may have a higher probability of remarrying than the *average* 40-year-old widow, the effect of such an argument is blunted if the question-in-chief related to a hypothetical, average 40-year-old widow.

Finally, I believe that it is of vital importance that counsel offer his or her expert the opportunity to identify, "under friendly fire," the most important assumptions and weaknesses underlying the testimony. When the subject of the expert's contribution is the prediction of human events, there must be weaknesses in the analysis. Further, it is virtually certain that these weaknesses will be identified and exploited by the cross-examining counsel. It would be ostrich-like to ignore this fact during the examination-in-chief. Better that these weaknesses be discussed under friendly than hostile examination. For example, assume that the expert has testified that the average 40-year-old Canadian widow can be expected to remain unmarried for 28.91 years.[2] Compare the cross-examination of this point with the examination-in-chief which could have been conducted:

Cross-examining Counsel (CEC): You have testified that the average 40-year-old Canadian widow will remain unmarried for 28.91 years?

Expert: Yes, that is correct.

CEC: But this average is for all 40-year-old widows in Canada. Is that not correct?

Expert: Yes it is.

CEC: So it does not take into account that Mrs. X lives in Moncton as opposed to Toronto?

Expert: No.

CEC: It makes no allowance for the possibility that widows in small towns may have a different propensity to remarry than widows in large cities, or that women with university degrees may have a different propensity than women with less education?

Expert: No, it doesn't.

---

[2] Statistics Canada, *Marriage, Divorce and Mortality: A Life Table Analysis for Canada and the Regions, 1984-1986.* Cat. No. 84-536E (Ottawa: Statistics Canada, 1988) Table 14.

CEC: Nor does it distinguish between women with children and those without; between women whose husbands have left them with pensions and other assets and those who have not; nor between women of different races, religions, or cultural backgrounds?

Expert: That is correct.

This type of cross-examination cannot be prevented, but its effect can be blunted dramatically through judicious use of the examination-in-chief:

Examiner-In-Chief (EIC): The figure of 28.91 years you have given us relates strictly to the average 40-year-old widow, is that not correct?

Expert: Yes it is — to the average 40-year-old in Canada.

EIC: Thus, it does not make allowance for differences in education, income, or religion?

Expert: That is correct. It allows only for differences in age and sex, of course.

EIC: Why have you not made allowance for these other factors?

Expert: To my knowledge, there are no reliable figures which distinguish the remarriage rates of widows based on the factors you have mentioned.[3] Not having such figures available, it would merely be guesswork to attempt to adjust for them. Also, as I do not know which characteristics are associated with deviations from the average, I have no reason to assume that Mrs. X's remarriage possibilities differ from those to which I have testified.

EIC: If you were to find it desirable, in your professional work, to employ a remarriage rate, would you find the figure you have given the Court to be acceptable, given the drawbacks we have just discussed?

Expert: Yes, I would.

EIC: Can you explain why?

Expert: Yes. In the absence of any other information, this figure at least tells me that although the average 40-year-old widow remarries eventually, most do not do so within a few years. Thus, if I have some reason to believe that the subject of my inquiry

---

[3] Note: I offer this example for purposes of illustration only. In fact, as I have shown in Chapter 12, some additional information concerning remarriage is available.

is, say, less likely to remarry than most widows, I know that my estimate of the length of time she will remain unmarried should exceed 28.91 years. I am no longer simply guessing that she will be unmarried for more than, say 5 or 10 years, but am basing my estimate on fact. Also, if I have no reason to suspect that my subject is not average, I can use a 28- or 29-year figure with some justification, if not confidence.

The purpose of this exchange is to anticipate the objections of both the opposing counsel and the court and to explain that although those objections were valid, they could not contribute to the "drawing of inferences." Although the expert's information was less than perfect, at least it gave the court a basis on which to form an opinion. And that, surely, is all that any expert can hope to accomplish.

4. Cross-examination

As the two participants in the cross-examination are set in opposition to one another, it will be useful to treat them separately.

(a) Counsel

There are two major aims of the cross-examination process. The first of these is to discredit the opponent's witness in some way, in order to make the evidence of counsel's own expert preferred. The other is to cast doubt upon the usefulness of the underlying approach employed by the opponent's expert. It is important to recognize that these goals may be contradictory. If the experts being called on both sides share the same background — for example, they are both psychologists or actuaries — the probability is very high that they will employ the same techniques and assumptions as one another. Therefore, a cross-examination which impugns the assumptions of the opponent's expert will reflect equally on counsel's expert. If counsel wishes to call his or her own expert, the first approach mentioned above must be employed and the second avoided.

Unfortunately, the first approach is also the more difficult to employ as it requires a direct attack on an area about which counsel knows relatively little and about which the expert, by definition, is very well informed. There are, however, a number of potential weaknesses which can be exploited.

The first step must be to consult with your own expert. The expert can point out assumptions which are not well accepted by the discipline or which have received only tenuous support in the empirical literature. Also, there may be the occasional instance in which the opponent's expert has made a mathematical error or has inadvertently omitted a relevant fact. Another task with which an expert can be of assistance is in questioning the expertise of the witness. It might be argued, for example, that the witness' sub-discipline is inappropriate to the testimony; he or she is a child psychologist when a rehabilitational psychologist would have been more appropriate. Or the witness might be read a list of articles relevant to the testimony and be asked whether he or she is familiar with them.[4]

In a similar vein, it may be possible to lead the expert into areas which are beyond his or her expertise. If the expert willingly answers questions in these areas, he or she may subsequently be discredited when it is pointed out that the expert has no basis for offering the answers.

It may also be possible to lead witnesses into making remarks which place in question their impartiality. One method for achieving this is to draw witnesses into being defensive or argumentative. This can often be done by pointing out minor inconsistencies in their testimony, by questioning the relevance of certain facts or assumptions, or by posing hypotheticals whose assumptions deviate slightly from those employed in the examination-in-chief. The manner in which experts handle themselves under such pressure provides a good indication, I believe, of the sincerity of their declared impartiality.

Another approach to cross-examination is to attack the basis of the assumptions and methodologies employed by the expert. As I mentioned above, this approach should only be employed when counsel does not expect to call his or her own expert. An example of this type of cross-examination was presented in subsection 2, above.

Finally, there are two types of questions which I believe should be avoided. These are questions which require legal knowledge on the part of the witness and questions which assume in them a "fact" which has not been led. A commonly asked example of the former is of the form: "Is the claim you have listed under heading X not a collateral benefit?" Counsel who ask this type of question risk obtaining answers which are wrong or confusing. At best, the expert will simply point out that the issue is a legal matter, in which he or she has no expertise, something which should have been known to the cross-examiner. An example of the second type of question is: "In this period of poor economic performance, is it not true that we can expect unusually high levels of unemployment?" An answer of "no" may imply either that the expert does not expect high unemployment or that he does not consider the

---

4   Although this tactic is often used, its validity must be questioned. The *Journal of Economic Literature*, for example, lists over 8,000 articles and 1,000 books published on the subject of economics each year. Not even the most specialized of economists could read every relevant publication. And, of course, there is the danger that some of the publications included in the list would be irrelevant or too obscure to offer a valid test.

economy's performance to be poor. In a similar vein, it is not good practice to ask the expert to supply facts which counsel's own expert could supply. Do not, for example, ask an economist to tell the court what the growth rate of GNP was in 1983 unless it is certain that the expert knows the answer. Otherwise, the expert may provide a guess or estimate. If this estimate is wrong, the testimony which follows may be counter-productive.

(b) The expert

The best advice one can give to an expert about to undergo cross-examination is to avoid taking up the role of an advocate. In particular, the expert should avoid interrupting the cross-examiner — at all times the expert should be courteous and allow the examiner to complete his or her statements. The expert should answer all questions simply and truthfully and should avoid appearing argumentative. If the expert disagrees with the cross-examiner, this should be explained as simply and calmly as possible. And if the cross-examiner makes a good point, the expert should agree with it. Nothing is so disarming; and the expert will have impressed the court with his or her honesty. Finally, experts should not be afraid to say that they do not know the answers to questions or that questions are outside their areas of expertise. Very little, if anything, will be "lost" by doing this, whereas the expert's credibility will be severely strained if it can be shown that he or she has been less than frank.

An issue which has not been settled concerns the freedom of the expert witness to elaborate on answers to the cross-examination. An ordinary witness is restricted to answer exactly the question which has been asked, and no more. Some lawyers and judges to whom I have spoken agree that this rule applies to experts as well. In practice, however, I have found that cross-examing counsel and courts have generally been willing to allow experts to stray slightly beyond the specific questions asked of them, as long as they were seen to be clarifying the meaning of their answers. The practice which I have developed, after testifying more than 50 times in the Canadian courts, is as follows. If I believe that a simple answer to the question would mislead the court, I only give the simple answer if I believe that counsel who has employed me is able to recognize this; if, however, I believe that all participants in the courtroom are likely to be misled, I attempt to clarify my answer. In the latter case, if cross-examining counsel objects to my elaboration, counsel for whom I am working will have been alerted to the difficulty I perceive and will be able to return to the issue in the re-examination. And, similarly, in the former case, if counsel considers the matter to be of sufficient importance, he or she can raise it in re-examination. I should add, however, that, because I believe it to be extremely important that the expert not be seen to be argumentative or obstructive, I recommend that experts use the technique of elaborating on their testimony only very sparingly.

5. Re-Examination

Once the cross-examination has been completed, counsel is permitted to re-examine the witness. My recommendation is that this opportunity be used only to correct misperceptions which arose during the cross-examination. For these, see my discussion of the cross-examination, above.

15

STRUCTURING THE SETTLEMENT

Once the value of the plaintiff's lump-sum award has been determined, a decision has to be made concerning the manner in which that award is to be disbursed. Normally, the plaintiff has the option of (i) using the award to make capital purchases, (ii) investing in a portfolio of financial assets, and/or (iii) receiving a stream of income in the form of a structured settlement. Section I of this Chapter will describe each of these three forms of disbursement, and Section II will review the advantages and disadvantages of using each of them under various circumstances.

I. ALTERNATIVE METHODS OF DISBURSING THE AWARD

1. Capital Expenditures

Although the technique for determining the lump-sum value of the award presumes that the award will be invested at some interest rate — the discount rate — it may also be in the plaintiff's best interest to set aside some of the award for capital expenditures. A clear example of such an expenditure would be a lump-sum payment towards the mortgage on the plaintiff's family home. As long as the after-tax interest rate which the plaintiff could obtain by investing his or her award is less than the rate of interest which has to be paid on the mortgage, paying off the latter will represent a better use of the award than will an investment in the financial market. For example, assume that the rate of interest on securities is 10 percent and that the mortgage rate on a $100,000 mortgage is 12 percent. If the plaintiff uses $100,000 out of his or her award to pay off the mortgage, $10,000 per year in interest payments will be "lost," but $12,000 per year in mortgage payments will be saved. Furthermore, if the interest received from investments in the financial market would have been taxable to the plaintiff, the net return would have been less than $10,000 per year, whereas the gain from paying off the mortgage will remain at $12,000. Other similar capital expenditures might include the purchase of a specially-equipped van, purchases of medical equipment, or renovations in the plaintiff's home.

Also, if the plaintiff were to use the award to establish a business or finance further education, the implicit rate of return which could be obtained might well exceed that obtainable from investments in the financial market. For example, assume that the plaintiff had been awarded $100,000 on the assumption that it would be invested at an interest rate of 10 percent per annum in order to compensate for a loss of earning capacity of $10,000 per year. If, for the expenditure of $100,000, the plaintiff could obtain training which would increase his or her earning capacity by $15,000 per year, that expenditure would clearly be preferable to the assumed investment at 10 percent.

2. Investment in Financial Markets

If the plaintiff chooses to invest his or her award in financial markets, three broad classes of options are available: *self-directed* investments, *investment management accounts*, and *trust accounts*. In the first of these, the plaintiff makes all of his or her own decisions concerning the financial instruments — e.g., bonds, stocks, savings certificates, mutual funds, etc. — in which the award is to be invested. Normally, this form of investment would be preferred by those with small awards or by relatively sophisticated investors. The second option is to obtain the advice of a professional money manager. Trust companies, for example, offer a service known as an investment management account in which the trust company invests the plaintiff's award according to a general set of guidelines established in concert with the plaintiff. For example, if the plaintiff had indicated a preference for relatively risk-free investments, the trust company might place the funds in "blue chip" bonds. Finally, if the plaintiff wishes to have no say over the investment of his or her award, or if the plaintiff is incapable of forming preferences concerning such investment — for example, the plaintiff is a minor or is mentally incapacitated — it is also possible to establish a trust account. Under this system, guidelines are established under a trust agreement. These guidelines are then followed by the investment agency, with no ongoing input from the beneficiary.

3. Structured Settlements

Under certain circumstances which have been outlined by Revenue Canada, if the defendant purchases an annuity in the name of the plaintiff, no income taxes need be paid upon the interest generated by the investment. Such an investment is known as a *structured settlement*. There are two major sources of differences among structured settlement schemes: those which arise from the manner in which the payment period is determined, and those which arise from the manner in which the values of the individual payments are determined. Each of these characteristics will be discussed here.[1]

(a) Payment period

The structured settlement may be written in such a way that payments cease upon the death of a particular individual, usually the plaintiff. Variants of this type of *life* policy include: the joint life policy, in which payments are made to more than one individual but cease upon the first death among those individuals; and the joint and last survivor policy, in which payments continue until the last death among a number of individuals.

An important characteristic of all life-based policies is, that for a given lump-sum investment, the value of the periodic payments will be a decreasing function of the life expectancy of the covered individual(s). The longer that individual is expected to live, the longer the annuity company will have to make payments, and, therefore, the lesser its monthly (or annual) payments will be. On the other hand, the shorter the plaintiff's life expectancy, the greater will be the payments which he will be able to obtain. Thus, those counsel who represent plaintiffs whose life expectancies have been reduced below the average must take care to emphasize that fact when seeking quotes from annuity-brokers.

The second method of determining the payment period is referred to as the *guaranteed term certain*. Following this method, a term is fixed without reference to the life of the beneficiary (or any other party). Thus, for a given investment, the value of the periodic payments will be smaller the longer is the length of the guaranteed term.

Finally, a policy which is used very commonly in Canadian structured settlements is the *life plus minimum guaranteed term certain*. Essentially, this is a guaranteed term certain policy until the guaranteed term expires, after which it becomes a life policy. That is, if the covered party dies before the guaranteed term has been completed, the payments will continue (to a specified beneficiary) until the expiration of the term. If the covered party lives beyond the guaranteed term, however, the payments will continue until that individual dies. The periodic payments available under such a scheme will be greater, the shorter is the guaranteed term and the lesser is the life expectancy of the covered party.

---

[1] For a more detailed description of the various types of structured settlements which are available, see: John Weir, *Structured Settlements* (Toronto: Carswell, 1984) Chapter 3.

(b) Determination of payment values

Structured settlements are composed of two major elements: *lump-sum* payments and *periodic* payments. Lump-sum payments are amounts, determined by the beneficiary, which are paid at specified intervals during the term of the annuity. The duration of these intervals may be regular — commonly, once every five or ten years — or irregular, allowing, for example, for anticipated expenses on such items as the education of a child or renovations to house and car brought on by physical deterioration of the beneficiary. Also, as I shall note later, these payments may be used as (partial) protection against inflation. Periodic payments are normally made monthly. But there is no reason why they could not be made weekly, bi-monthly, quarterly, or annually — or according to any other schedule desired by the beneficiary.

Although it is possible that a constant payment value, such as $1,000 per month, could be employed, it is more common for the parties to specify that the value of the periodic payments should vary in accordance with a preselected formula. Most often, in Canada, this formula specifies that the periodic payment should increase on each anniversary date by a fixed percentage. For example, the payment might increase by 6 percent on each January 1. Alternatively, the payment might increase each year by a fixed dollar amount, such as $100 per month on each anniversary date.

Other possible formulae link the rate of increase of the periodic payment to a variable whose value is unknown in advance, such as the rate of consumer price inflation, the rate of interest on treasury bills, or the rate of return on mutual funds.[2] All of these schemes share the characteristic that they produce unpredictable variations in the values of payments. As these variations cannot be insured against, annuity firms have required large risk premiums to write policies including "linking" clauses. Indeed, these premiums have been so large that the resulting policies have not proven attractive to Canadian plaintiffs.

II. STRUCTURING THE SETTLEMENT

1. Capital Expenditures

Normally, if the plaintiff can make capital purchases which offer higher

---

[2] Other types of "linkages" are also possible. For example, the payments to a disabled plumber might be linked to the average annual income of plumbers. See: C. Bruce, "Four Techniques for Compensating Tort Damages" (1983) 21 U. Western Ont. L. Rev. 1-28.5.

rates of return than do other forms of investment, it is best to set aside a sufficient portion of the award to ensure that these purchases can be made. One would not wish to place the entire award into long-term bonds or into a structured settlement, for example, if the award were large enough that the plaintiff could pay off his or her mortgage and still have sufficient funds left for living expenses. Once these funds have been set aside, it must be decided whether the remaining funds are to be invested in financial markets or whether they are to be used to purchase a structured settlement.

2. Financial Markets Versus Structured Settlements

There are a number of advantages in choosing a structured settlement. First, the interest which is earned on the investment of the lump-sum will not be taxed. Depending upon the plaintiff's tax bracket, this advantage can increase the effective rate of return obtainable by the plaintiff by as much as 100 percent. For example, if the plaintiff is taxed at the top Canadian rate of approximately 50 percent, an investment of $100,000 at 10 percent will return only $5,000 per year after taxes — an effective rate of return of only 5 percent.

Second, if the plaintiff should live longer than the average person, an award invested in financial markets will run down to zero before the plaintiff's death. Structured settlements, on the other hand, are annuities guaranteed for the life of the beneficiary.

Third, if the plaintiff chooses a guaranteed term certain settlement, the annuity will continue to be paid even if the plaintiff should die before the term is over. This means that the plaintiff can ensure that there will be sufficient funds for his or her dependants.

Fourth, structured settlements provide a guaranteed income stream for individuals who might otherwise encounter difficulty managing the investment of (what is often) a sizeable amount of money. Such individuals might include minors, those who have suffered brain injury, and those who have had insufficient education to allow them to make "informed choices" concerning large investments.

Finally, from a social point of view, structured settlements might be seen as desirable to the extent that they prevent unscrupulous plaintiffs from intentionally exhausting their lump-sum awards and then falling back on the generosity of the social welfare system. For example, although the group homes provided by the government for care of paraplegics may be seen as less than ideal, it is not inconceivable that a young paraplegic in receipt of $500,000 might choose to dissipate that sum over a five- or ten-year period in reliance on the belief that he or she would be able to gain entrance to a group home at the conclusion of that period.

On the other hand, there are a number of drawbacks to structured settlements. The most important of these is that the insurers have been very reluctant to write annuities that link the values of the payments to such variable factors as the rate of inflation or the prime rate of interest, or even to offer schemes in which payments increased at a constant rate of more than 3-4 percent per annum. Accordingly, if inflation should prove to be greater than the constant rate of growth allowed for in the contract, the plaintiff will find that the purchasing power of the payments will erode quickly. For example, if the dollar value of the payment increases by 3 percent per year during a period in which price inflation averages 8 percent per year, the purchasing power of those payments will be cut to one-half within 15 years, and will be cut to one-third within 24 years. If the funds were placed in secure investments, on the other hand, the rate of interest earned on those investments would rise and fall with the rate of inflation. Thus, the plaintiff could anticipate that the available income would grow in line with the rate of inflation, regardless of how great that rate might become.

Also, once the terms of a structured settlement have been agreed, such settlements encounter the drawback that they are very inflexible. If the plaintiff discovers the necessity for some expenditure that had not been recognized at the time the agreement was reached, sufficient funds may not have been made available in the year in which that expenditure must be made. Had the plaintiff invested the award in financial markets, however, funds could have been drawn from the investment account.

3. Determination of the Plaintiff's Preferences

Given the relative advantages and disadvantages of the various uses of the lump-sum award identified above, the optimal disbursement of the award will depend in large part upon the particular circumstances of the plaintiff. Some of the more important factors influencing the plaintiff's preferences, and their implications for the type of settlement chosen, include:

(a) Children

If the plaintiff is the parent of dependant children, one way of ensuring that sufficient funds will be available to look after the children, should the plaintiff die, would be to purchase life insurance out of the annual income from the award. Alternatively, if a structured settlement has been chosen, it will be possible to select a policy based upon "life plus a minimum guaranteed term certain." The guaranteed term can be set equal to the period of time over which the youngest child can be expected to remain dependant upon the plaintiff. In this way, should the plaintiff die before the expiration of that period, funds would still be available for the support of the children.

Even if the plaintiff's children are not dependant, a "guaranteed term certain" structured settlement might be purchased in order to provide the children with an estate should the plaintiff die early. However, although this opinion has proven attractive to most plaintiffs with whom I have worked, I would suggest that it be adopted only after careful consideration. First, it must be remembered that introduction of a guaranteed term will reduce the value of the periodic payments which will be available to the plaintiff. Second, the plaintiff may have used a portion of his or her award to pay off the mortgage on a house or to purchase other major assets. If so, the plaintiff should be reminded that the sale of these items, upon death, will provide a sizeable estate. Only if the plaintiff wishes to ensure that the estate will be larger than would be produced by such a sale should a guaranteed term be adopted. And even then, it should be noted that a guaranteed term is a very poor method of creating an estate. If the plaintiff should die near the end or after the expiry of the term, this provision will have added little to the estate. On the other hand, the purchase of a life insurance policy, naming the family members as beneficiaries, would have left them with an estate whose size was determinable with precision in advance.

Finally, the plaintiff may wish to make large expenses on his or her children at irregular times in the future. The plaintiff may wish, for example, to buy cars for them on their sixteenth birthdays, to pay for their college education, or to help to set them up in businesses. Structured settlements are ideal instruments for setting aside funds for such events, as any number and value of such payments can be specified at the time the settlement is arranged.

(b) Spouse

If the plaintiff has a dependent spouse, protection of that individual's standard of living can be obtained through use of a life insurance policy on the plaintiff. But, as the amount which must be set aside for the support of the survivor changes over time, such a policy will have to be recontracted often. If a structured settlement is purchased, however, a "joint and last survivor" term can be specified in which periodic payments continue to the survivor after the first spouse has died. In this circumstance, I would recommend that the policy specify that the value of the survivor's periodic payments be 60-70 percent of that which would have been received had both spouses been alive (in recognition of the "dependency rates" calculated in Chapter 11). The most important exception to this recommendation arises when one of the spouses has been severely injured. In this case, a substantial fraction of the periodic payments may represent the cost of caring for this individual. Thus, the policy might specify that if it was the disabled individual who died first, the survivor would receive less than 60-70 percent of the joint benefits; whereas if it was the non-disabled individual who died first, the survivor would receive more than 60-70 percent of the joint benefits.

(c) Age

If the plaintiff is a minor, it may be desirable to place at least part of the award in a structured settlement whose terms include provisions requiring that lump-sums be paid at specified future dates to provide for such large expenses as investment in post-secondary education, the purchase of a house, or the establishment of a business. Also, if it is anticipated that the plaintiff will not require support after completing his or her education, it may be desirable to employ a structured settlement which has a fixed termination date — that date being the projected time of graduation or shortly thereafter.

If the plaintiff is nearing age 65, consideration should be given to the fact that he or she will become eligible for a government pension at that age. As the payments from these pensions increase with inflation, they reduce the risk of investing in structured settlements. That is, if inflation proves to be greater than was predicted when the terms of the structured settlement were established, the plaintiff will not be left entirely unprotected, because the government pension will provide at least some cushioning. For this reason, structured settlements may be more desirable for older, rather than for younger plaintiffs.

(d) Type of disability

If it is possible that the plaintiff's health might change over time, it may be preferable to invest in financial markets rather than to purchase a structured settlement, because the terms of the latter may not be sufficiently flexible to deal with such alterations. If changes in the plaintiff's health can be predicted with confidence, however, a structured settlement might become relatively more desirable. If the plaintiff's health is expected to improve, it may be desirable to purchase a structured settlement whose fixed term expires at the time the plaintiff is expected to regain his health, or to purchase a life policy with periodic payments of fixed value. The rationale for the latter is that inflation will reduce the purchasing power of the periodic payments at the same time that the plaintiff's health and earning capacity are improving. Alternatively, if the plaintiff's health is worsening, particular care will have to be taken to ensure that the payments increase in value at a rate which is at least as great as the rate of price inflation, perhaps again arguing for investment of a substantial portion of the award in financial markets.

4. Summary

Structured settlements can offer significant savings to both the plaintiff and the defendant, particularly when the plaintiff is in a high income tax bracket. They are particularly advantageous when the dollar value of ongoing or irregular expenditures can be predicted with a high degree of certainty and when the plaintiff wishes to provide a secure income stream to his or her dependants. However, they suffer the distinct disadvantage that they are inflexible in the face of uncertainty. In particular, they cannot protect the plaintiff against the effects of inflation or unexpected deteriorations in the plaintiff's health. For these reasons, it is my recommendation that the following three steps be taken when structuring the disbursement of the award:

(i) First, it must be remembered that capital expenditures on items such as education and housing often provide the greatest, and most secure, rate of return for the plaintiff. The possibilities of such expenditures should be exhausted before the plaintiff's funds are dedicated to other long-term investments.

(ii) Second, particularly if the award is relatively large or if the plaintiff is otherwise in a high tax bracket, the plaintiff's remaining funds should be divided between investments in financial markets and purchase of a structured settlement. The relative division between these two should largely be determined by the need for the plaintiff to protect his or her income against inflation and other unexpected events. The greater the need to protect against inflation — usually, the smaller are the other sources of income — the lesser will be the percentage of funds which should be "structured".

(iii) Finally, when a structured settlement is employed, it may be advantageous to call for substantial "lump-sum" payments once every five to ten years. Then, if inflation proves to be greater than anticipated, these lump-sums can be invested in the financial markets to provide some hedge against further price increases.

INDEX

S

Self-employed
  earnings of, 10-11, 103-108
Sex
  effect on earnings, 120-123
  effect on housework, 211-216
  effect on probability of disability,
    143
  effect on probability of employment,
    135-139
  effect on unemployment, 148-149
Siblings (number of)
  effect on minor's predicted earnings,
    95
Sole dependancy, 49-53
Speech impairment. *See* Disability
Statisticians
  as experts, 263-264
Structure of award, 287-295
  capital expenditures, 287-288,
    290-291
  structured settlements, 288-295
Structured settlements. *See* Structure of
  award

T

Tax credits
  rate of increase of, 41-42
Tax gross up. *See* Gross up
Time diary, 210
  See also Household services

U

Unemployment, 147-155
  definition, 15n.
Unemployment insurance, 154-155

W

Wage statistics, 67-71
Welfare
  effect on remarriage, 241
Whiplash. *See* Disability, whiplash
  See also Disability, back injury

Y

Young adults
  forecasting earnings of, 9, 98-103